Word and Image

István
Nemeskürty

Word
and Image

History
of the Hungarian
Cinema

Corvina Press

Title of the Hungarian original:
A MAGYAR FILM TÖRTÉNETE
Gondolat Kiadó, 1965
First Hungarian edition
© ISTVÁN NEMESKÜRTY, 1965

Translated by
ZSUZSANNA HORN
and FRED MACNICOL

Binding and cover by
ISTVÁN FARAGÓ

Second, enlarged edition
© ISTVÁN NEMESKÜRTY, 1974

ISBN 963 13 6707 X

Printed in Hungary, 1974
Zrínyi Printing House, Budapest
CO 1116-h-7478

Contents

In the Beginning
1896—1911

Of Budapest's many cafés the Velence was not the most splendid, but it was one of the most enterprising—and it had a good site. It was on busy Rákóczi Street, where the present Tisza Cinema stands. In this café the Hungarian cinema began its history.

The Café

The café is a remarkable institution developed by bourgeois society in the last century. It used to be—and sometimes still is—a place where merchants, businessmen, artists, clerks and even radical intellectuals could mingle. At a Budapest café you were served more than coffee; food and other drinks were available, but that was not its chief attraction. One came here for companionship, business appointments, political discussion and the exchange of ideas. To attract more patrons to come more regularly the owner was obliged to stimulate conversation and keep alive the various interests of his customers. There was always plenty of newspapers; every café subscribed to as many important European newspapers as the owner could afford—this was as vital as the quality of the coffee-beans he bought. Habitués of each café knew that their favourite paper always awaited them.

There were cafés with literary programmes, musical recitals and solo comedians; there were cafés with floor-shows and full variety programmes, music-halls reduced in scale. No extra fee was charged, either for this entertainment or for the always available newspapers. If the café-owner wanted regular patrons, he had to keep them well entertained.

No wonder that films also found their way into the café. It was the Grand Café on the Boulevard des Capucines that gave the first commercial performance of the Lumières' films. Immediately cafés in Berlin and Rome threw their doors open to the film-makers, and patrons poured through the same open doors. Now the café-owner could say: Come to us for tea, to talk business, to chat with your friends, to read the papers and every day from five to six we also show moving pictures. At first this novelty was included for the patrons without charge; only later was a special room prepared to admit visitors for a very modest entrance fee. Here people could come who were more interested in films than in coffee—and these patrons, shopkeepers, salesmen, clerks, poets, prosperous stall-keepers, people who were killing time before their suburban trains left Budapest, these were the nucleus of the film audience that was soon to swell to astonishing numbers.

That was what induced Mr Ungerleider, the owner of the Velence Café, to go in for films. Mr Bécsi, the headwaiter, let down a clean sheet in the middle of the café—the guests could enjoy the film from both sides—so nobody need change his table—brought out the projection machine, which he had learned to operate, under the table he placed a waste-paper basket where the shown reel could be caught as it came through the machine, and the performance began.

Later, when this projector was converted into a film camera, József Bécsi handled it with equal zeal; he was the first Hungarian cameraman.

In 1898 Mór Ungerleider, the café-owner, founded a firm together with his business partner József Neumann, a former stage performer. This firm, operating under the name of Projectograph, provided films for its own cinema, sold and rented projectors and cameras, and even rented the films of major foreign companies to provincial cinemas. Projectograph was the first Hungarian firm which traded in films and ran a cinema.

In the first decade of the present century Projectograph also made newsreels and educational films. These films were offered in a catalogue which may be of interest to quote:

The Races at Alag, 88 metres;
Hare Hunting in the Plain, 150 metres;
Parade in Vienna in Homage to the Emperor's Jubilee, 200 metres;
View of Budapest, 190 metres;
Arrival of the Bulgarian Ruler at Budapest, 65 metres;
Pigeon-shooting Tournament on Margaret Island, 85 metres;
Demonstrations in Budapest during the Ides of March, 100 metres;
Vine-growing at Szekszárd, 115 metres;
The Spanish King Hunting at Féltorony, 140 metres;
Fire at the Kovald Factory, 77 metres;
The Funeral of Ferenc Rákóczi II at Budapest and at Kassa, 265 metres;
Lake Balaton, the Lower Danube and the Tátra, 135 metres.

And there were also a few funny pictures among them:

Károly Baumann, 65 metres;
The Inebriated Cyclist, 120 metres;
Max and Maurice on the Turf, 120 metres.[1]

The text of a contemporary handbill gives a good idea of the dramatic composition of reconstructed (or staged) newsreels:

The Life of Vagrant Gipsies. The Robbers of Dános, a film of 136 metres, was described by the firm in the following terms: "Arrival of Strolling Gipsies in the Village. Life in the Tents. Stealing Hens and Horses. Gipsy Women Excel in Snatching Chickens, the Men in Stealing Horses. It is shown how deftly a gipsy woman can snatch a chicken from a coop and hurry with her prey to the tent where she throws it into a steaming cauldron prepared in advance by the other gipsies."[2] The farmer snores while the thieves ride off with his horse; then, complaint at the police station; "Pursuit over Hill and Dale and Water"—then the picture of the Dános murderer, Tuta Kolompár Balog, is shown at his trial.

The process of "creative work" can be now clearly seen: at that time it was easier to fool film-goers and such reconstructions were being made everywhere. Obviously, the only *real* part of this "newsreel" was what was taken at the trial of Tuta Kolompár Balog; the rest was played by actors, exactly as if a fictional film were being made.

The "exceedingly humorous, irresistibly funny film" entitled *Chess Maniac* (A sakkjáték őrültje) played by the members of the Modern Stage and directed by Endre Nagy is also worthy of notice. The film is about a passionate chess player so absorbed in the game at a café that when he leaves he judges everything in the town by the moves permitted on the chess board. That is how he walks along the street, how he contemplates the wares displayed in the market where goods and market-women suddenly change into chessmen and pawns. He boards the omnibus with a knight's move; he gets home; "when he is about to plunge his fork into the roast it vanishes and in its place he finds a knight"—and so on. We know the contents of approximately a dozen similar Projectograph films made between 1905 and 1910. Quite likely more were made, but only some of these films received any public notice. Beside the firm Projectograph, there were one or two other enterprising persons who made a few films at this time. A good many cafés were converted into cinemas, but the new cinema proprietors showed no inclination to make films themselves. They had neither capital nor experience to encourage them. For the time being Projectograph could meet the demand of the Hungarian public to complete satisfaction.

The Urania Scientific Theatre and Other Cinemas

At the time a scientific educational society was active in Hungary under the name of Urania. Founded in Germany, it maintained theatres where lantern-slide lectures were presented about scientific expeditions, about remote countries and continents, about literature, music and acting. Urania also had its own theatre.

On one occasion Gyula Pekár, a writer and politician, was to give a lecture on dancing. He asked the chief projectionist of the institute, Béla Zsitkovszky, to make a motion-picture which might be projected to illustrate his lecture. In answer to this request *Dancing* (A tánc) was made in 1901. This film was followed by a dozen similar "lecture-films" about which we know only from vague reports. These films served to illustrate the lectures of a well-organized educational society. As such, they did not belong to the category of film merchandise, produced in all parts of the world—in Hungary by the Budapest firm Projectograph—but represented a new initiative; on the other hand, this fortunate start—including *Dancing*—remained an isolated phenomenon.

There is not much to be said about the other experiments. Hungary has her own date of 1896: at the Millennial Exhibition a clever businessman, Arnold Sziklay, took pictures of Franz Joseph opening the exhibition, inspecting Mihály Munkácsy's painting *Ecce Homo* and congratulating the artist. The film has been lost; it is said to have been a failure, a failure perhaps due to the fact that the scene was taken with a camera put together largely by the cameraman himself and on an American strip of film perforated also by himself. The theatre where it was shown soon went bankrupt as did the other theatres opened at Budapest in the 'nineties, including the cinema of the Lumières in the Hotel "Royal".

At the Millennial Exhibition in 1896 there was also a cinema building, opened for Edison's kinetoscope: "The kinetoscope pavilion has the character of an open hall which has been designed in a fine style by the architect Ignác Alpár. The hall of 50 square metres has been built at a cost of nearly 6,000 forints by Ödön and Marcell Neuschlosz."[3]

However, various kinds of cinemas in tents, show-booths of itinerant cinematographers ever increased in number. In Budapest the Apollo Cinema of Ungerleider and his partners stood on the site of the present Corvin Department Store; for a long time it was the largest and the grandest of our cinemas. The tent-cinema opposite the Film Museum of our days was also famous. The excited audience thronged inside a big circus tent after listening to the enticements of a barker. Poets and authors fond of night life in the capital visited quieter small cinemas which had been converted from cafés. The well-known reporter-writer of that time, Árpád Pásztor says: "I also joined the circle of authors, painters and musicians who frequented the New York Café, went to films at a time when there were only two cinemas on the boulevard and it was 'the thing' to see both programmes on the same evening."[4]

A few years later the first film critics came from among the members of this circle: Zoltán Somlyó, Frigyes Karinthy.

According to contemporary statistics, there were 270 permanent cinemas in Hungary around 1912. In relation to the size and population of Hungary at the time, this figure may be regarded as normal by contemporary European standards. In Budapest there were 92 cinemas seating 26,332 spectators altogether. (Újpest, Kispest, Pesterzsébet, Csepel, etc. are not included. These suburbs now are parts of the capital.) Thus a cinema had approximately 300 seats. The population of the capital having been 970,000, there was a cinema for every 10,500 inhabitants.[5] Berlin with three million inhabitants at the same time had 300 cinemas. Hence the ratio was similar to that of Budapest.

As a rule provincial towns had one, sometimes two cinemas, but some had none. In the larger towns there were four or five cinemas. Kaposvár was a remarkable exception: this small town of 26,000 inhabitants had three cinemas seating 1,600 people. It was at Kaposvár that the first book on films in Hungarian appeared (a translation of the German cinematographer Paul Liesegang's book, translated by Sándor Kozma, cinematographer of Kaposvár, in the year 1911). Let us compare another big provincial town of Hungary with a German town of similar size. At Szeged there were four cinemas seating 1,250 people. The town had 125,000 inhabitants, i.e. a cinema for every 31,000 inhabitants. Mainz having a population of 110,000 had also four cinemas.[6] If a cinema is assumed to have held 300 people on the average, daily attendance may have amounted to 243,000 people in the case of three performances a day at the 270 cinemas of Hungary.

On the evidence of contemporary observers the number of cinemas tended to increase, so that a regular Hungarian motion picture industry must have seemed to have a promising and lucrative future. Lucrative even if the National Association of Hungarian Cinematographers founded at the time counted altogether sixty-seven members in 1909[7]; and lucrative even if the products of the Hungarian film industry had to share the market with those of foreign competitors. Still no regular Hungarian motion picture production industry developed in those initial years, though a weekly attendance of a million and a half could be counted on.

In fact, the early stages of development, when a film industry is taken in hand by cinema-owners themselves to produce their own products, failed to set in in Hungary. This may be ascribed to the absence of major capital concentration. Every cinema-owner thought in terms of one, namely his own cinema, and it is extremely risky to make films for one cinema. The purchase of a ready film, on the other hand, involved only the payment of the price for one copy. Moreover, the cinematographer could afford to pick and choose, and buy attractive films of a high standard. That is why no major production enterprise was launched in Hungary at this early date; a new industry of wholesale "dealing" in films began to thrive instead. On their yearly two or three trips abroad the distributors bought what they liked best from French, Italian, American, Danish, occasionally German and Austrian motion picture studios. Even a Film Exchange was founded where deals were made and prices were quoted. In the spring of 1911, when Mór Unger-leider saw the first Asta Nielsen film of Nordisk, *Avgrunden,* he quickly published a scathing review, lest somebody else should conceive the idea of purchasing this treasure; but he quickly bought his railway ticket to Copenhagen where in a few days he secured an option on all Nordisk films for years to come.[8]

The First Studio and Its Failure

The Hungarian films produced before 1910 were not made in a film studio. In fact there was no such studio in the country. The scenes of *Dancing* were shot by Béla Zsitkovszky on the roof-terrace of the Urania building in fine sunny weather; Projectograph films were taken on the spot, outdoors, in private flats, in offices.

The first Hungarian film studio, built between September 1911 and February 1912, was a 50-metre-long, 25-metre-wide glass hall, standing at the corner of Pannónia Street and Sziget Street (now Rajk László Street and Radnóti Miklós Street). Built by Hunnia, it was expected to grow into a large-scale plant.

The plans of this enterprise attracted the interest of professional circles as early as December 1910. The founder-director of Hunnia was Miklós Faludi who intended to make films with the company of the Gaiety Theatre then under his direction. This noble endeavour, however, lacked the support of professional skill. Neither the director nor the appointed producer— Sándor Góth—nor the actors and actresses knew anything about films. To make matters worse, the Frenchman who was hired as cameraman was a swindler who did not know the first thing about films either. It is a wonder that they nevertheless made about a dozen burlesques. They did not get any further, because the films failed to come into serious commercial circulation. A few cinemas tried to show them, but the copies themselves proved to be unfit for use. As a matter of fact the burlesques were sometimes based on such "brilliant" ideas as, for instance, the consequences of the beneficial effects of the aperient water Hunyadi János on bowel action (*Bitter Love or Hunyadi János*—Keserű szerelem avagy Hunyadi János).

However, even if Hunnia had produced proper motion pictures complying with the average standard of the time—which was not high—it would have been ruined by its lack of contacts with the cinemas and by the boycott of the marketing firms. It is clear that in those years film-making had to be based on an adequate number of cinemas; on a ready "market" which was sure to absorb the films produced. For lack of such cinemas in its own possession, Hunnia was at the mercy of the distributing companies, of Projectograph, in the first place, already a decade in the business. Since, in all probability, no agreement had been sought—or reached—beforehand with Projectograph, Hunnia was unable to place its films. An enterprise launched in a spirit of naive inexperience thus failed in little more than a year.

This failure had noteworthy consequences. Hungarian big capital, particularly the banks, which had been watching the film business with mistrust, shrank from supporting other film companies. Some banks had had interests at stake in the case of Hunnia, and its bankruptcy, though not a heavy loss, was certainly unpleasant. From this time Hungarian big capital declined to finance film industry.

Hunnia has left one lasting value: the film studio in Pannónia Street (now Rajk László Street).

The Industry
Takes Shape
1912—1914

In No 35, 1912, of the *Mozgófénykép Híradó* (Motion Picture News) the following advertisement was published:
THE FIRST HUNGARIAN DRAMATIC ART FILM. *Monday October 14 will be a memorable day in the history of Hungarian cinematography. The first Hungarian film drama played by Hungarian actors, in a Hungarian*

The Industry Takes Shape

setting, with a Hungarian subject will be presented on that day.

Written by Iván Siklósi and Imre Roboz, directed most likely by Mihály Kertész, the film was made by Projectograph. Its title was *Today and Tomorrow* (Ma és holnap). The leading roles were played by Artúr Somlay, Ilona Aczél, members of the National Theatre, and Mihály Kertész, of the Hungarian Theatre.

If any date can be determined to mark the birth of the Hungarian cinema, it was this year.

It is remarkable that the producing firm which had inserted the advertisement alluded to "the history of Hungarian cinematography" which was practically non-existent then.

The *intention* to produce a work of art may thus be noted. The merchandise also counted as a work of art, or so the *producer* hoped or believed. The director did not believe it to be a work of art; perhaps the producer did not consider the director an artist; in any case, his name was omitted. The writers were pointed out as having done the creative work, their names being printed in bold type.

In 1912 there appeared other triumphant advertisements of new films in several acts, possibly a thousand metres long. A well-known photographer of the central shopping district, Ödön Uher, running a race with Projectograph and actually winning the race, presented a film drama *Sisters* (Nővérek) on September 14, 1912. The script was by Andor Garvay. Under the direction of Ödön Uher himself, Erzsi Mátrai, Ida Mátrai and Emil Fenyő played the leading roles. Of these artists Emil Fenyő is still active in Hungarian pictures: lately we have seen him in *Two Half-Times in Hell* (Két félidő a pokolban).

The *Sisters* was followed by *The Diamond Collar or The Fatal Necklace* (A gyémánt nyaklánc vagy a végzetes nyakék), this film of Uher's was made at his photographic studio in Kossuth Lajos Street.

It should be borne in mind that just at that time the Hunnia film company, then only approaching the brink of ruin, still loomed in the background menacingly with its modern studio. And a new enterprise entered the field under the name of Corvinus with a single burlesque, *The Sleepwalker* (A holdkóros). The most experienced firm in Hungary, Projectograph, could not sit idly by and watch the efforts of a photographer, a filmbranch of a first-class theatre of Budapest (Hunnia), and another enterprise (Corvinus) that was threatening to conquer the market. Such keen competition was too much to endure simultaneously. The only way for Projectograph to take up the fight was to produce a film of its own. Mór Ungerleider and József Neumann were also stimulated by the fact that in 1912, they had made and presented with success a six-hundred-metre-long comedy, *The Budapest Reporter* (A pesti riporter). This film—with a scenario written by János Fröhlich, a renowned reporter of those days, directed by Aladár Fodor, correspondent of the *Pesti Napló*—is a striking example of *cinémavérité*. Aladár Fodor and his partners shot their film on the tramways of Budapest, on park benches, in cafés, recording scenes from life without any actors, apart from Berta Kornai and Károly Baumann in minor roles. Encouraged by their success Fröhlich and Fodor decided to strike out for themselves, which they soon did by founding a newsreel company under the name of Kinoriport. This inconvenienced Ungerleider and his partners who could not maintain their monopoly.

By the time regular film production got under way in Hungary the view that film-making was an art was generally accepted, at least by the small industry and an increasingly large number of writers who were interested in films. Articles and series of articles appeared, among others, in the most respectable literary journal, *Nyugat*, affirming that cinema was an art. A young journalist, Sándor Korda, went so far as to declare that the film director was a creative artist.[1] It was Korda who wrote a review of *Sisters* in 1912 in the film column established and edited by himself in the daily paper *Világ*. This was the first regular film column in a Hungarian daily paper.[2] As a matter of fact, it was this favourable atmosphere for film production that also induced Korda to give up his literary aspirations and to launch a cinema periodical with István Várnai under the title *Pesti Mozi*. This excellently edited, politically radical weekly was on sale in the cinemas. Among its contributors were Zsigmond Móricz and Zoltán Ambrus, while Marcell Vértes and Lipót Gedő were its cartoonists. Many of Karinthy's humorous sketches appeared in it for the first time. *Pesti Mozi* was launched in October 1912, when the first two "artistic feature films" were presented.

It is worth looking into the question whether this start had any peculiar Hungarian feature.

It decidedly had. One was, for instance, its definitely "literary" character: a film was considered artistic if it was related to literature. The ambitious producer wished or promised to make "literary films". Two of the three long films produced claimed to be literary (the third was a crime story). Andor Garvay and Imre Roboz were established literary figures. Neither Uher nor Ungerleider was satisfied to work along lines which were acceptable to American film producers of the period, letting the director do what he liked so long as the film was thrilling: both Uher and Ungerleider insisted on the script being written by a well-known author. Featuring popular actresses and actors was also insisted upon. Whereas the appearance of Sarah Bernhardt or Eleonore Duse on the screen in a role counted as a rare exception abroad, it is remarkable that soon after the first stumbling attempts at films, members of the National Theatre could be won over in Hungary, although fees were much lower than those paid to American, Danish, French or Italian actors.

Who were the directors? A photographer who produced and directed together with his son is a classical Hungarian example from the "primitive age" of our film industry. The photographer who became a film-maker. Then the journalist—Aladár Fodor—a typical figure everywhere. Finally the ambitious actor who was not given any leading part in his theatre: Mihály Kertész. Later, too, Hungarian film directors were recruited from this circle.

As regards the technical aspects it cannot be said that there was a film technique at this time in Hungary. There were two or three reliable cameramen—József Bécsi, Béla Zsitkovszky—a few developing and printing laboratories and several intelligent technicians who could repair and maintain cameras. However, there was no manufactured raw film or apparatus, which in France, Italy, America and everywhere else provided a firm, reassuring basis for regular production. For the time being raw film was imported from the United States, mostly from Kodak. Light conditions were poor, there was no lamp park, no one knew anything about lighting effects, therefore films could be made only in the summer. Each winter film production stopped.

In 1913 and 1914 the regular production of films increased. In 1913 ten scenarios were filmed, in 1914 eighteen, in addition to newsreels and educational films. Competition became keener. There were agents who started to advertise films before they were produced. They even financed production. Film companies sprang up like mushrooms, though there were no studios except for the one in Pannónia Street (now Rajk László Street). There was some sort of workshop in Kinizsi Street—on the site of the present Kinizsi Cinema—but that was more of a laboratory; the short instructional pictures of the Budapest Educational Film Company were made here under the direction of Béla Zsitkovszky. Sometimes this place was let. That is how films of a thousand or fifteen hundred—even two thousand metres came to be made by companies which emerged from nowhere only to vanish again a month later.

The French firm Pathé, the largest film company of Europe, also joined the race. Pathé were looking for *couleur locale;* they found it at Kolozsvár. The script was based on a play about peasant life in the villages; Ferenc Csepreghy's popular play certainly provided for every "typical" detail, from fringed wide, white linen trousers (worn by peasants in those days) to rendering meat tender by keeping it under the saddle, as ancient Hungarian horsemen are said to have done a thousand years ago. *The Yellow Foal* (Sárga csikó) had a great success in other countries; it was easy for Pathé to give the film a world-wide distribution, leaving with cinema-goers everywhere a peculiar impression of Hungary; even today in many places Hungarian bravado is thought to be inseparable from flapping, white linen trousers. *The Yellow Foal* was put on cinema programmes between a film about Papuans and a "western".

Of the newly established Hungarian film companies the projects of two provincial firms deserve special notice.

The minor and short-lived attempt was that of Oszkár Damo from Eger with his two films based on the popular novels of Géza Gárdonyi: *The Rose Garden of Ali* (Ali rózsáskertje) and *The Adventures of Gabriel Göre* (Göre Gábor kalandozásai). *The Rose Garden of Ali* was 1,450 metres long, a record length in Hungary in those days. Little information about these works can be found now.

The activities of Jenő Janovics who produced films at Kolozsvár amounted to a more lasting undertaking. Director of the National Theatre of Kolozsvár, he came into contact with filming through Pathé who engaged actors from his company. When he began to make films, in 1914, he had no other ambition than to give his actors work, to make some extra money, and to record for posterity some of the productions that his theatre estimated as good. Of his three screenplays one he wrote himself, *Borrowed Babies* (Kölcsönkért csecsemők), the other two were well-known literary works: a popular play by Ede Tóth, *The Vagrant* (A tolonc) and *Bánk bán,* one of the classics of Hungarian theatre.

To put *Bánk bán* on the screen was a huge undertaking. A national epic and, an additional challenge, originating outside the accepted Budapest theatres. The scenes requiring real locations were shot on a river-bank and in a forest. The king's army marched over the crest of a real mountain. The film was reviewed in *Nyugat,* in a tone of unusually warm appreciation. This film laid down conclusively the trend which had been followed instinctively since 1912, the trend of the national-literary film.

"They did what they wanted with nature. An extensive landscape seen from above, with a sense of air and with a perspective leading into the distance: through a dark frame we look out into sunshine. Sunlight and then moonlight, but in which we clearly can see the white outlines of Melinda. A wide hillside with a tiny corner of sky, lines of men trailing over the dark headland. A narrow strip of earth with the sky above filling the whole image..." wrote Béla Zolnai—a professor of philology—in *Nyugat.*[3]

Gertrudis was played by Mari Jászai—the greatest tragedienne of the time in Hungary—Melinda by Erzsi Paulay. The other roles went to István Szentgyörgyi, Mihály Várkonyi, Jenő Janovics, Adorján Nagy. It is a great pity that this film has been lost.

Kinoriport, founded by Aladár Fodor and János Fröhlich, put on the screen the best hits of the Budapest cabarets. Ferenc Molnár also wrote a burlesque for Kinoriport: *Pufi Buys Boots* (Pufi cipőt vesz). With Károly Huszár (Pufi), the leading man, this was the first time that Gyula Kabos, the later brilliant comedian of the Hungarian sound-films, appeared on the screen. Pál Aczél, who was to play a role later in the Republic of Councils and to write essays for Lajos Kassák's avant-garde paper in the 'twenties, made a film of Sándor Petőfi's *The Apostle* (Az apostol). Years later contemporaries mentioned this film among the best. Photographs that have been preserved of *The Apostle* suggest that the film strove towards a melodramatic effect. It is nevertheless a fact—supported by its subject, the known political convictions of the producer-director, and by contemporary accounts—that this was the first Hungarian film containing conscious social criticism.

The photographer Dénes Rónai appears to have observed astonishingly mature aesthetic principles. Following in the footsteps of his colleague, Ödön Uher, in 1913 he made in his own photographic studio a film entitled *Éva Drághfy.* Before the opening he declared:

"I wanted the scenes, even without moving figures, to evoke the same mood and emotions as those associated with the whole action. With the landscapes serving as background, the masses and lines of architecture act with the actors; they are not decorative backgrounds but equivalent components of the picture. This acting of light and shadow is the actual material of the film."[4]

We do not know how far he was able to realize this artistic programme, for this film, too, has been lost.

The "big, old" firms, Uher and Projectograph, continued along the well-tested lines: they put on the screen the works of successful, recognized authors. Uher secured the co-operation of Sándor Nádas for *Martha* and of Imre Földes for *Captive Soul* (Rablélek). Ferenc Herczeg wrote an original script for the Uher Studio with the title *The Golden-Haired Sphinx* (Az aranyhajú szfinx). Projectograph again commissioned Imre Roboz and Iván Siklósi to write a screenplay: *Slaves of the Night* (Az éjszaka rabjai). In the meantime Kinoriport won Sándor Bródy and Endre Nagy to write an original story—*The Three-Hundred-Year-Old Man* (A háromszáz éves ember)—all the characters of which were aristocrats who, instead of hunting, cultivated the new sport of cinematography!

In this period Hungary was the only film-producing country where ninety per cent of production came from works of well-known authors. Though this attitude of relying on literature became the source of numerous misunderstandings a few decades later, the fact remains that Hungarian films were inspired by classical and contemporary Hungarian literature for a long time to come. Hardly two years had passed and reels of *Bánk bán,* of a Sándor Petőfi poem, of works by Géza Gárdonyi, Sándor Bródy, Ferenc Molnár and Ferenc Herczeg were already kept side by side on the shelves.

The same applies to the artists. With what anxious care the Italians watch over their only film of Duse. And how difficult it was to persuade Duse or Sarah Bernhardt to appear in a film! In Hungary filming was still an innovation when Mari Jászai willingly stepped before the camera. For this, credit must go again to Janovics. In Hungary cinema was thought of as the sister-art of the theatre. Whether they failed, like the Hunnia enterprise of the Gaiety Theatre, or struggled on to success, as did Janovics with his ventures based on the National Theatre of Kolozsvár, film companies grew out of theatrical companies. These artists brought with them another culture and an atmosphere of drama.

The directors came from all professions: from a theatre, as did Mihály Kertész who directed *Slaves of the Night* (Projectograph), *Bánk bán, The Vagrant,* and *Borrowed Babies;* or Gyula Zilahy (*Watch Box in the Carpathians — Őrház a Kárpátokban*), Imre Pintér (*The Militiaman — A népfölkelő*), Ferenc Farkas *(The Golden-Haired Sphinx);* others abandoned journalism in favour of cinema, as did Aladár Fodor or Kornél Tábori *(Pufi*

Buys Boots), Pál Aczél *(The Apostle)*, Oszkár Damo (*Martha* and the films of Gárdonyi's works). Finally there were photographers who came nearest to being experts in the technique of filming, and acted as cameramen and directors of their own products, like Dénes Rónai *(Éva Drághfy)* or Ödön Uher.

Of these men only one was a true director, an actor of the Hungarian Theatre, Mihály Kertész (known from 1919 as Michael Curtiz). Kertész adopted the cinema as his whole vocation. In the summer of 1913, he went to Denmark to study at Nordisk, first as an assistant, then as a cutter; he played a leading role in *Atlantis* and even directed a film for Nordisk. After about six months of this practical study he came home, where his Danish experience helped to become the most popular director: he was offered contracts by Projectograph, Uher and even Janovics. Nordisk's methods, the style of Urban Gad and Asta Nielsen, as transplanted by Kertész, became rooted in the Hungarian cinema for many years. Reviews gave the highest appreciation to the Nordisk films. The poet Ernő Szép even wrote a music-hall song about Danish film production. In 1913 Asta Nielsen, accompanied by Urban Gad, her husband and the director of her films, paid a visit to Budapest. The film industry and the public received them with enthusiasm. Under the dedication on their photograph they wrote: "No silent art has ever had the depth and warmth that filming can have in its best creative achievements."[5] And it was pantomime that began to dominate increasingly in Hungarian films; instead of ingenious cutting—montage—attention was concentrated rather on the expressive play of faces and gestures.

In this connection Kertész stated his views in several articles. While emphasizing the importance of the actor's performance he drew attention to the significance of the director's creative activities: "An actor's success is no more than the success of the director whose concept of the whole brings into harmony the performance of each character on the screen."[6]

In three years about fifty films were made. Film companies were founded at Kolozsvár and in Budapest.

In 1913 as many as 114 cinemas were in operation in Budapest, the largest number in the seventh and sixth districts of the time (27th and 25th at present).[7] Every week millions of people went to the cinemas to watch the miracle. Gradually it ceased to be a miracle and became a habit. That is when it became a real business. It was just then that the First World War broke out.

The Art
Takes Shape
1915—1917

By the end of the First World War forty-five directors had produced films in Hungary. Twelve of the forty-five were professional directors from other countries. Of 'the other thirty-three, fifteen may be regarded as professional Hungarian film directors. The rest, eighteen in number, worked only occasionally in the field of films.

The Art
Takes Shape

The rule prevailing in every part of the world applied also to Hungary: the first film directors were or had been actors or journalists.

By the year 1918 the fifteen professional Hungarian film directors represented a high percentage by world production standards. Of the fifteen Béla Balogh, Alfréd Deésy, Márton Garas, Jenő Janovics, Michael Curtiz, Károly Lajthay had been actors; Oszkár Damo, Aladár Fodor, Eugen Illés, Sándor Korda came from journalism. There was only one cinema proprietor among them, Móric Miklós Pásztory, and one former photographer, Ödön Uher.

Notwithstanding the loss of so many of their films and the passing of time, each of them appears to have had a taste, style and conception of his own. Each of them published his *credo* and his own *ars poetica* in various articles and essays.

No doubt the most outstanding personality was Sándor Korda, to become Sir Alexander Korda. By 1918 he had made nineteen films, four of these under pen names or without credit (*The Duped Journalist*—A becsapott újságíró; *Tutyu and Totyó* with Gyula Zilahy; *Lea Lyon* with Miklós Pásztory; *Officer's Honour*—A tiszti kardbojt, under the name of József Neumann). His career began at Kolozsvár, under Janovics. It was here that Korda directed his first films, from Mark Twain's *Thousand Pound Note* (Az egymillió dolláros banjegy), from plays by Gergely Csiky and Szomaházy, and where he had his first troubles with his actresses and actors. In 1916 Janovics gave his studio the name of Corvin. Not long after he sold the firm and its name to Sándor Korda who moved it to Budapest.[1] Janovics continued to maintain a studio at Kolozsvár and the films he made he presented from 1917 as products of Transylvania. Under his guidance a generation of directors had grown up, cameramen and actors, including Mihály Várkonyi who under the name of Victor Varconi became a well-known actor in Hollywood.

First Korda entered into a partnership with producer Móricz Miklós Pásztory. A gardener of Brassó who became a cinema owner, Pásztory made money by filming several plays about peasants and rural life (*The Deserter—A szökött katona*, *Black Sheep of the Village—A falu rossza*); it was with this money that Korda and Pásztory bought Janovics's firm, Corvin, and moved it to Budapest. Here the company did things on a grand scale: in 1917 they built a film studio at the corner of the present Gorky Avenue and Dózsa György Street; however, since this studio proved to be too small and the city was growing at a rapid rate, they pulled it down six months later and rebuilt it at No 39 Gyarmat Street, then in an outlying suburb. The largest Hungarian motion picture studio is still working there; the stone raven—it was the heraldic animal of the renaissance king Matthias Corvinus and that of the Corvin Film Studio named after him—is still crouching over the gatepost of the entrance in Gyarmat Street.

Corvin did not go in for mass production. While Star made over fifty films, Corvin released only sixteen. These were, however, made with circumspect care. Sándor Korda was not only a good director, but also a first-rate organizer. It was he who devised the method of making films which still underlies film production in Hungary. The system of employing a dramaturge—or literary editor—is a specific Hungarian trait of his method. In Sándor Korda's concept the dramaturge should be well trained in film-making as well as in literature who, while representing the interests of director and studio, guided the writers, who were not experts in films, and at the same time guarding each author's individuality and ideas. The dramaturge of a motion picture studio acts as liaison between the world of films and literature. It is his duty to contact eminent writers and persuade them to write for the screen. Korda was not content to apply the methods followed by Star; in the first place he endeavoured to establish contact with living Hungarian literature instead of screening familiar foreign works.

For this new film position of dramaturge Korda first secured the co-operation of Frigyes Karinthy. Having been an active short-story writer five years before, Korda was personally acquainted with the writers belonging to the circle of the review *Nyugat*. He had published a series of humorous sketches by Karinthy in *Pesti Mozi*. His other liaison was the dramatist László Vajda who later became a well-known scenarist in Germany and England. This highly exacting ensemble began to adapt the best works of Hungarian literature in a planned series, but no longer in order to perpetuate past literature, but to create films. So motion pictures were made from a novel by Mihály Babits, *The Nightmare* [Gólyakalifa] (Korda),[2] from Ferenc

Molnár's play, *The Guardsman* [A testőr] (Sándor Antalffy), from an original scenario by Frigyes Karinthy and Kálmán Sztrókay, *Magic* [Mágia] (Korda), from a script by Frigyes Karinthy, *The King of Reporters* [A riporterkirály] (Pásztory), from a work of Sándor Bródy, *The Woman with Two Souls* [A kétlelkű asszony] (Pásztory). The authors were satisfied with the films, and Bródy spoke of Korda as the only gifted and intelligent filmmaker.

Under the direction of this literary triumvirate the works of foreign authors were also adapted for the Corvin firm: works by Victorien Sardou, Mark Twain and by the popular dramatist Edward Knoblock (*The Faun*— A faun), and the novelist Israel Zaûgwill (*Marian*—Marianne). In Korda's eyes the task of film-makers was to interpret literature on a worthy level. Yet he was aware of the film as a medium having its own peculiar means by which the director could convey the writer's ideas in a specific cinematographic form. Since Korda possessed thorough theoretical grounding and was the first to outline the aesthetic aspects of directing films, and since his works gained success all over the world it is clear that he held to his principles throughout his film-making career.

Incidentally it was not one of his serious films that Korda was the proudest of, but a wild burlesque to a script by Gyula Kőváry and Richárd Falk, *Harrison and Barrison,* also presented with great success in the United States after the war. *Harrison and Barrison* were played by Márton Rátkai and Dezső Gyárfás. Considering the methods of shooting at the time, it seems that with a yearly production of five films Korda had means to prepare his work carefully and thoroughly. Along with his jobs as director and owner of a film studio, Korda kept up his weekly, *Mozihét,* which he edited himself. From a business point of view this was a clever move, for by an efficiently edited paper he could assume control over the whole country's film industry, which he actually did.

Unlike Korda, Kertész did not profess adherence to a programme of "literary films". Although he shot seven versions of novels and plays, these formed part of the studio's programme where he had a contract. This emerges clearly from the circumstance that six of the seven literary versions were produced by Kinoriport and at Kolozsvár between 1914 and 1916 (*The Vagrant; Bánk bán; The Carthusian*—A karthauzi; *The Silver Goat*—Az ezüst kecske; *The Doctor*—A doktor úr; *The Wolf*—A farkas), the latter two by Ferenc Molnár. Throughout his career Kertész resisted the adaptation for the screen of well-known literary works. As managing director of Phönix, formed from Projectograph, he preferred to put on the screen stories of

life, adventure and crime. His scripts were written by László Vajda and
Iván Siklósi with whom he could co-operate smoothly. This was the American style: give the screenplay writer an idea, an outline, and let him work
it out. It was natural for Kertész—as Curtiz—to take root in Hollywood and
stay there until his death in 1962.[3] Korda, on the other hand, always remained a visitor to America, making his headquarters in London.

Kertész had the knack of rendering a plot thrilling. Most likely the
technique of montage brought him success, though not one of his Hungarian films survives in a complete state to verify this. The few scenes which
still exist, for instance, from the film *The Secret of Saint-Job Forest* (A szent-
jóbi erdő titka, written by László Vajda, cameraman József Bécsi) bear
witness to a talent for vivid composition.

Kertész made altogether thirty-eight films in Hungary. In the spring
of 1918, he signed a contract which took him to Vienna. He never returned
to his country again. Foreign encyclopaedias have little to say about his activities in Hungary; some writers have no idea that the great Michael Curtiz
made as many films at home in the years between 1912 and 1918 as during
the thirty years he worked in Hollywood. His most successful films were
Bánk bán; The Secret of Saint-Job Forest; The Colonel (Az ezredes); *Lulu;
Ninety-nine* (Kilencvenkilenc); *Lu the Cocotte; The Lady with Sunflowers*
(A napraforgós hölgy).

Eugen Illés (1877-1951) worked for two years in Hungary in the period
of silent films. After having taken his degree at the Technical University
of Budapest, about 1905 Illés went to Germany where he became a journalist, later a film director (Duskes Litteraria). He came home in answer to
call-up papers. At the front he made several film reportages, then, at the
request of Kinoriport, he was exempted from military service. In two years
he made nine films in Hungary. As shown in the cases of Korda and Curtiz,
five films a year was a good average at the time. Illés's films were either
films dramas of high literary standard—*Monna Vanna, Sulamith, John the
Hero* (János Vitéz), *The World Is Just a Mood* (A világ csak hangulat)—or
Budapest cabaret-comedies, farces, with "little Rott," the most popular
comedian of the day, in the lead—*Better Morals* (Jobb erkölcsöket), *The
Newborn Father* (Az újszülött apa).

Márton Garas (1885-1930) was an actor before he went to Berlin to
study under Illés at Litteraria. Like Korda, he began his career as a film
director with Janovics at Kolozsvár. After 1917 he was the managing producer of Hungaria Studio where *Anna Karenina* was made. Garas directed
what he was commissioned to shoot: a ballad of Arany (*Ordeal of the Bier*

—Tetemrehívás), a scenario by Bródy (*Snow-white*—Hófehérke), a flourishing of the national flag (*Silenced Bells*—Elnémult harangok), a criminal phantasmagoria (*The Secret of the Hieroglyphs*—A hieroglifák titka). He worked correctly and systematically as evidenced by *Anna Karenina* which has survived. By 1918, in four years, he made twenty-three films, about six a year.

A production record was set by Alfréd Deésy who made thirty-four films in the three years beginning late in 1915. Since he produced only one film in 1915 and only two in 1916, he must have shot fifteen or sixteen films a year in 1917 and 1918. This shows the mass production methods of Star.

Deésy was an actor from Debrecen to whom Illés gave a contract for the title-role in *John the Hero*. That is how Deésy got into the business and became the managing director of Star. As a director Deésy concentrated on promoting the business interests of his studio. He liked to act as well. Indeed, he was the only director who appeared in his own films.

The personality, role and methods of Jenő Janovics have been discussed before. In his case it was difficult to separate director from producer, all the more so because, apart from Korda at a later date, Janovics was the only producer who not only provided the financing but was a proficient director as well. In four years Janovics made twenty-two films, an average for that time. The films he directed himself were all versions of literary works, "film records" of successful plays. He had a predilection for superior trash, the writings of Ohnet, Bernstein, Ede Sas. Judging by the few photographs which have survived, his most lasting work seems to have been the cycle of songs by Sándor Petőfi. He filmed six poems by Petőfi, of which *The Innkeeper's Wife* (A csaplárosné) is remarkable for its delicate atmosphere, unassuming sincerity, in pleasing contrast to the numerous film versions of artificial plays on peasant-rural life.

At the outset Ödön Uher worked with his father, later he alone directed those films for which he took some special liking. In the years between 1912 and 1918 he made altogether seven films, much fewer than the German guest-director employed by the company. Presumably this was due to Uher having been in active service at the front; he served as lieutenant, was wounded, and in 1917 no films were produced. A favourite film of Uher's was the screen version of Mór Jókai's novel *By the Time We Grow Old* (Mire megvénülünk).

Pásztory, born in 1875, was the eldest of the film directors then: at the start of regular motion picture production, in 1912, he was thirty-seven.

He specialized in plays with a peasant background: *The Deserter, Black Sheep of the Village, The Red Purse* (Piros bugyelláris), *The Horseherd* (A csikós), with these he made so much money that he could found Corvin together with Korda. The screenplay based on the stage version of *The Notary of Peleske* (Peleskei nótárius) also belongs among his rural films. The secret of Pásztory's success was that he turned his attention to the village spectators for the touring cinemas; the patrons of the latter had little interest in criminal or love stories that showed only city life.

Béla Balogh first appeared in the industry as an actor, a screen actor. Like Deésy, he was employed as director by a newly founded firm. Balogh was a conscious representative of bourgeois progress. His films expressed, more clearly than elsewhere, a protest against the aristocratic-feudal conditions prevailing in the Austro-Hungarian Monarchy. In collaboration with Imre Földes, an eminent dramatist of the period, the plays of the latter were filmed: *The Emperor's Soldiers* (A császár katonái), *Civil Servants* (A hivatalnok urak). But *The "Vengerka"* (Vengerkák), *The Admirable Crichton*, (Egyenlőség), *The Boys of Paul Street* (A Pál utcai fiúk) also formed part of this programme. In the years between 1916 and 1918 Béla Balogh produced seventeen films. Though he appeared only a few months later than the others he may nevertheless be regarded as the first representative of the second generation. Curtiz directed from 1912, Garas and Korda from 1915; Balogh took up work seriously only in 1917, for in 1916 he made only one film. It was Márton Garas who launched Béla Balogh.

From this "second generation" which appeared on the scene in 1917 and 1918, only Antal Forgács, Károly Lajthay, Pál Sugár and Lajos Lázár remained in the industry as professional directors. Lajthay had been an actor at Star, that was how he became interested in making pictures; of his three films *Vorrei morir* had a resounding success. Having entered into partnership with a wealthy cinema proprietor, he made his films as productions of the Rex Studio. Pál Sugár also made his name at Star Studios with three films. Lajos Lázár was a lawyer; he founded a film studio in 1917 under the name of Lux and directed its films himself. Of his twelve films his screen versions of successful operettas found the greatest favour with the public: *Gül Baba, The Slovak Tinker* (A drótostót), *Prince Bob* (Bob herceg). *Typhoon* (Tájfun—by Menyhért Lengyel) was also directed by Lázár.

Aladár Fodor, a journalist, directed a few comedies for Kinoriport, for instance the "aristocratic film" in which every minor role was played by no less a personage than a baroness.

Though not the youngest, for he was almost of the same age as Pásztory, the man who joined the profession latest was Antal Forgács, who in 1918 founded a motion picture studio, Gloria, with a modest capital. Like Lázár, he was attracted by the success of operettas, *The Marriage Market* (Leányvásár), *Count of Luxembourg* (Luxemburg grófja)—it is in these that he saw money, though the silent film knew nothing about incidental music, apart from orchestras and pianists playing accompaniments at performances.

For invariably and ceaselessly a pianist played in the smallest back-street cinema; a performance at the cinema was unimaginable without music. This custom is mentioned so often that one meditates over it, although it is still an open question how the piano found its way into the cinema. As an explanation it has been suggested that it was introduced to relieve the dead silence; to replace speech; to arouse emotions; to suppress the whirring sound of the projector. Maybe. Still, when did it begin? The cinema piano actually raises another fundamental question: has the film always been a sound-film, also in the period of silent pictures, in everything except speech? If projection of a film was unimaginable without music in 1912 it is of little importance whether this music was supplied by a sound track photographed with the picture or by a pianist rejected even by music-halls. The essential point is that there was no cinema performance without music. Yet if we look today at *Intolerance, Battleship Potemkin, Earth, Menschen am Sonntag, The Mother* or *La Passion de Jeanne d'Arc* we don't miss the music, nor does the deep silence lessen our awed absorption. In the sense of the term as it was interpreted in the 'thirties, background-incidental music is also falling into disuse. Did the former director compose to music or was incidental music just added on the spur of the moment? One imagines it as a process of random selection. This supposition is contradicted by the circumstance that young and inexperienced director-businessmen boldly tackled the adaptation of successful operettas of Lehár to the screen, counting strongly on the irresistible effect of vivid memories of waltzes blared out by brass bands in town squares and parks. Indeed, this was what gave new directors the courage to venture making films; that was how approximately two dozen operettas came to be put on the screen in that period, because music, the *memory* of waltzes hummed by shoemakers' apprentices, took the place of other artistic devices.

Old Mr Weiser, who is still willing to play background music as accompaniment to silent films, in connection with a programme of films by Méliès in Budapest, declared before an audience of foreign film experts his deep conviction that the truly artistic production was a film accompanied by piano, which no other experience could surpass. *Music and picture acted together.* Somewhere, in the laboratories of Berlin and New York men were already at work to invent a way whereby the orchestra could be dispensed with, and the same music, chosen beforehand by the director, could be heard at every projection of the film. In fact, this was the first aim—talking was the next step. It was again the cinema-goer who dictated the progress, as at first, when he clamoured for something else, something novel and interesting.

And there sat Griffith at the cutting table, intercutting the film so that various threads of the story might be told simultaneously, whereafter scenes of Babylon, Christ, Saint Bartholomew's night, and demonstrations of American workers appeared in surprising relationships, all enhancing each other, and bound by controlling rhythms. A tubercular film fan, Jenő Török, noticed with great excitement this possibility alien to all other arts, which Béla Balázs was to describe six years later: "...film art understands how to show you at each moment only what you should see. It seizes your hand and takes you commandingly from one character to another... an artist who wants to impress on you the excitement of a trial will not permit you to linger unnecessarily before one picture. He will sweep you on, minute by minute. The director who influences the movement of your emotions... will conceal everything that he does not need, lest even the shapes of alien objects should distract your attention. You may see only a close-up of a girl's face. Tears roll from the corners of her luminous eyes..."4

The audience has grasped the intention of the director. The audience and the creative artist were striving towards the same goal.

A new era had begun.

Towards a Film Theory

It now appears that every film-producing country had its own Ricciotto Canudo. As film literature began to explore its past more thoroughly we learn that Mayakovsky made some perceptive observations about the film medium as early as 1913 in Russia; that tentative film aesthetics were proposed in Italy and in France before the First World War; and that in 1915 the American poet Vachel Lindsay could write his book *The Art of the Moving Picture,* numerous comments in which are still valid. And Hungarian literature can also quote from these early years several remarkable statements about the film as an art which are noteworthy by international standards.

The first film journal, *A kinematográf*, was launched in Hungary in the year 1907; it appeared for three years, until the end of 1909. This journal was followed in 1908 by a second one, *Mozgófénykép Híradó*, which lasted for fifteen years (1908–1922). Up to 1920 seventeen journals were published in Hungarian which dealt exclusively with films. There were almost countless journals concerned with both theatre and films. As mentioned before, Alexander Korda also edited film journals: *Pesti Mozi* (1912); *Mozi* (1913); and *Mozihét* (1915–1919). These journals, as well as the distinguished literary weekly, *Nyugat*, published numerous interesting essays on the film.

For instance, the novelist and dramatist Lajos Bíró, who later emigrated to Great Britain to live in London (where he died September 9, 1948), author of numerous successful scenarios for British and American films (notably *Hotel Imperial*[5]), had declared as early as 1911 that film aesthetics would develop: "The laws of the cinema should be established, and original scenarios, rather than imitations of plays should be written." Also in 1911, in the *Mozgófénykép Híradó* that published Bíró's article, an editorial pointed out that from 1910 the emergence of a new, completely different style had become discernible in the direction of films. In the same year Alexander Korda stated that the film was undoubtedly an art, and this art was created by the director whose task differed from that of a stage-director. To prove his point Korda wrote reviews on Danish (with Asta Nielsen) and American (by Griffith) films.

All this took place in the year 1911.

The number of similar articles considerably increased after the year 1912, and there was hardly any important or outstanding writer who did not express an encouraging opinion on film art.

The article published by the philosopher-psychologist Cecil Bognár, a Benedictine monk, in the *Budapesti Hírlap* of December 5, 1915, is particularly interesting from an international viewpoint. This article not only discusses the film as an art, but also as a form of expression. In 1915 this was unusually perceptive, by international standards. "The film itself is actually only an instrument, a raw material, like paint or type." It furthermore explains that more than poetry is served by speech and the written word, both being indispensable in everyday life; similarly the film may be art, but it may also be the means of scientific communication, of news service, even of perception. It is wrong to do no more than to "translate" literature into pictures and to asseverate the view that the film is an art by comparison to literature and the theatre. These lines of Cecil Bognár presage the more familiar theory that Rudolf Arnheim later formulated.

It thus becomes clear that the book written by the Hungarian author Béla Balázs in the year 1924, *Der sichtbare Mensch,* had Hungarian antecedents. The most important precursor of the theses evolved by Béla Balázs was Jenő Török who died in 1918 of tuberculosis as a young man. Jenő Török had been discovered by Alexander Korda who published his articles in *Mozihét,* Korda's journal, beginning in the summer of 1916.

Jenő Török tried to define the film as an art in the following words: "…A rhythmic alternation of thoughts and emotions brought about by the effect of motion elements." Török emphasized the time-bound nature of the film, its dependence on time; what is more, he denoted time as a not less fundamental element of the film than it is of music. (Compare to similar ideas of Eisenstein.) When we draw the consequences of this recognition— continued Török—it becomes evident that the most important feature of this new art is "the method of linking sequences". Therefore, Török says, the fundamental element in film aesthetics is the sequence. The content of the film may be altered if the same sequences are linked in any other order. There can be no doubt that Jenő Török here made a tentative approach to the concept of montage, defined much later. He wrote phrases which correspond nearly word for word to later statements of Béla Balázs. For instance, Balázs wrote: "Der Regisseur führt deine Augen"; in 1917 Török said: "The director influences the movement of your emotions."[6]

Thus in the years between 1911 and 1917 there flourished in Hungary a noteworthy literature on film theory.

*The Film's Role
in the
Republic of Councils
1919*

By this decree the Hungarian Republic of Councils places under public ownership all film-producing studios, film laboratories, film distributing companies, related factories and cinemas—regardless of the number of employees—as well as their movables and real estate with all their equipment, and the finance required for carrying on production.

The Film's Role in the Republic of Councils

Dated Budapest, April 12, 1919.

From April to August of 1919, for a period of four months, nationalized, socialist film production was carried on, for the first time in history. For it was at the end of this period, in August 1919, that Soviet film production was nationalized.

In these four months thirty-one films were made.

This is an exceptional number, even when we know that several of the films approved and shot in this period were prepared earlier, and some in 1918.

These thirty-one films could be produced only by an enthusiastic group fired by a common will. Had the writer, the director, the producer, the cameraman or the skilled workman wanted to put off the work he might have done so without being noticed or blamed. As a matter of fact four months barely suffice to do the work of organization, to prepare and shoot thirty-one films.

Film actors and workers welcomed the nationalization of the film studios. As early as 1918, impatient voices made themselves heard in the cinema press indicating social irritation. The leader of the film world, Sándor Korda, joint owner and production manager of the largest Hungarian film studio, had been editing a radical bourgeois paper ever since 1912 in which he published sharp attacks against the government. In December 1918, the leading article in Korda's *Mozihét* contained the following lines: "Those who still represent the ruling classes would do well to examine themselves and desist from defending their precarious positions so desperately... No one should struggle against socialism."[1]

Had a miracle come to pass? Did a class of film producers who could amass unlimited wealth as a result of the war-time boom admit the superiority of socialism? Hardly so, even if the progressive and anti-war mentality of the leading film directors—Korda, Balogh, Damo, Janovics—is taken into consideration. At the close of 1918 the Károlyi government appointed Sándor Korda commissioner of film production with authorization to organize progressive bourgeois film production.

The reason why the film industry displayed almost uniform satisfaction over the decree of nationalization issued in April 1919—after having clamoured for it at a meeting held in the Apollo Cinema at the end of March—may be ascribed to economic interests. In the Hungarian film world the classical capitalist methods were represented by distributors and cinema proprietors. The film studios were defenceless and, strange as it may seem, felt exploited. The profit collected by film producers, though not "insignificant", remained far behind the millions pocketed by the distributors. Moreover, the distributors were in a position to dictate terms. As a matter of fact, a situation developed which was similar to that in America ten years earlier: cinema proprietors schemed to keep all power in their hands. Consequently film distributors received nationalization with desperate hatred and did their utmost to hinder production.

An article of Sándor Korda published in *Mozihét,* "Film Distributors against Film Producers", is an important document and proof of the strife between producers and distributors.

Korda accused distributors of suppressing national film art and of acting in a mercenary spirit. A sharp controversy ensued in the press as a result of which the government seriously considered the idea of placing film production under a central state management after the summer of 1918, with censorship and direct state control and other measures. From this aspect the government represented the interests of film distributors, all the more so as the increasingly frequent political demonstrations at cinemas were a danger signal. In the June 12, 1919 issue of *Vörös Film,* Rezső Vári published a letter sent to the Hungarian Ministry of the Interior by a lieutenant-general of the imperial and royal army, who had acted as commander of all factories and mines engaged in war production. In his indignant letter he drew attention to the veritably "…ear-splitting applause of workmen and their families" with which the rule of the people was greeted when allegedly revolutionary scenes in Danish films appeared on the screen of cinemas in the mining district. Those were the factors that led to the nationalization of film production under the Republic of Councils.

Three kinds of leading or social organs were established.

An organization concerned with the interests of the whole industry was set up, the administrative board of which was referred to in the press as the "directory". This institution may have played the role of the Film Art

Association of our days in Hungary. This board included Pál Aczél, journalist and director, Béla Balogh, director, Oszkár Damo, director, Jenő Farkas, projectionist and technician, Lajos Grünfelder, industrial executive, Sándor Korda, director, László Vajda, dramaturge. Béla Lugosi also played an important role in the film life of the Hungarian Republic of Councils. He was an actor in the National Theatre of Budapest and, under the name of Arisztid Olt, a favourite leading-man of the Hungarian silent films. Béla Lugosi, Arisztid Olt, originally called Béla Blaskó, who adopted the name Lugosi—he was born at Lugos—fled abroad after the collapse of the Republic of Councils and turned up first in Vienna and later in the United States. The title role in the film *Dracula* made him famous overnight in Hollywood.

Another directory was also set up, the members of which were appointed by the government—the Commissars' Council. This body was headed by a political commissar, Béla Paulik, who became the managing director of film affairs. In artistic questions his chief deputy was Júlia Komját. The theoretical scheme of nationalization was executed by Paulik and Komját who also carried out the work of reorganization; nothing escaped their attention, from film production to the network of cinemas.

The "routine work" demanded in practice devolved on a third organization which acted under the control and competence of the commissariat of education, not like Paulik's office which was responsible to the government itself. In essence this third institution corresponded to the Hungarian Film Board of our days. The chief of this body was László Márkus—later director of the Opera House—while István Radó acted as his deputy in economic matters.

Occasionally controversy flared up between the elective representative organizations and the appointed bodies; the paper *Vörös Film* published an article in which it was strongly emphasized that the film centre was "...not a parliament where elected men could get in, but an office."

This office did energetic work.

Minor film studios were merged. Work was controlled and directed from one centre. Six studios were operated, those in Pasaréti Road and Gyarmat Street by separate managements, with plants of the merged firm at the studios of Tomori Square (Astra), Ráday Street (Uher), Szövetség Street (Hunnia), and at the corner of Pannónia and Sziget Streets (Phönix). A central department was organized which provided for scripts. Four leading dramaturges were appointed: Pál Aczél (who had produced *The Apostle*), István Lázár, Ede Sas, and Iván Siklósi. All of them were experienced scenarists. Scripts were criticized by an art council which decided also the schedule of production. The members of the art council were Béla Balogh, Mihály Kertész, László Márkus, József Pakots, László Vajda, i.e. the head of the Central Management Council of Socialized Motion Picture Industry (László Márkus), two highly respected directors (Balogh, Kertész), and two dramaturges (Pakots from Star, Vajda from Corvin).

The question of actors was also settled. Forty-one film actors and actresses were registered. These were entitled to play leading roles. To a certain degree these arrangements served to safeguard individual interests: the film actors who had no contract with a theatre did not have to share their fees and success with colleagues who played also on the stage. The forty-one film actors included, of course, the stars. In addition thirty-seven "film actor candidates" were registered, as well as forty-five "juvenile film actor candidates"—Géza Bolváry among them—and a hundred and thirty extras.

These 253 persons were distributed by a central office to meet the requirements of various projects. Thus work proceeded quickly and in an organized way, though along rather bureaucratic lines. For instance, an actor registered on the film-actor list and paid on this basis could not move ahead, even though he did his best; unless he was promoted on the list he could get no other parts than those assigned to his category. It is true, Oszkár Dénes, a film actor candidate, nevertheless got the lead in the film *Yesterday* (Tegnap), a few weeks after his registration. Ilona Mattyasovszky was the elected head of this group. The central literary board planned to put on the screen memorable works of Hungarian and world literature. From this grand programme the following works were chosen:

Russian literature	Gorky	*Mother*
	Gogol	*The Government Inspector*
	Tolstoi	*The Power of Darkness*
	Artsybashev	*Passion*
English literature	Shaw	*The Devil's Disciple*
	Wells	*Exchanged Lives*
	Dickens	*A Christmas Carol*
French literature	Stendhal	*Le Rouge et le Noir*
	Zola	*La Faute de l'Abbé Mouret*
	Hugo	*L'Homme qui rit*
	Verne	*Mathias Sandorff*

German literature	Heinrich Mann	*Die Armen*
	Hauptmann	*Die Weber*
		Hanneles Himmelfahrt
	Sudermann	*Sodoms Ende*
Scandinavian literature	Ibsen	*Rosmersholm*
		Ghosts
Hungarian literature	Sándor Bródy	*Doctor Faustus*
	Géza Gárdonyi	*Anna Fehér*
	József Eötvös	*The Village Notary*
		(A falu jegyzője)
	Kálmán Mikszáth	*A Strange Marriage*
		(Különös házasság)
		The Ghost of Lublo
		(Kísértet Lublón)
	Ferenc Molnár	*Liliom*
	Jenő Heltai	*Family Hotel*
	Andor Gábor	*A Millionaire*

These were the titles that were planned but not realized.[2] This plan was adjusted also to the natural development of Hungarian film production—with due regard to the popularization of literature but still more consciously to a criticism of society.

Nevertheless thirty-one projects were realized. Part of them had been put on schedule by some film studios in 1918, only shooting had not yet been started. All the thirty-one may be looked upon as films of the Republic of Councils, since every one of them was discussed by the Art Council.

Sándor Korda directed three films:

1. *Ave Caesar!*
2. *Yamata*
3. *White Rose* (Fehér rózsa).

White Rose was a screen version of one of Mór Jókai's stories. The scripts of *Yamata* and *Ave Caesar!* were by László Vajda. *Yamata* is the story of a Negro slave's revolt. His master flogs him so cruelly that Yamata's body is covered with blood. His miserable plight arouses the pity of a marquis who buys him and treats him well, though he, too, exploits the man, but more subtly. Finally Yamata gets involved in a murder as in most versions of this old tale. *Ave Caesar!* is the story of a profligate Habsburg prince, actually a variation of *Le Roi s'amuse*. The prince gets his aide-de-camp to kidnap a gipsy girl who is branded for life by this adventure. Obviously the film was directed against the feudal class. In both films the lead was played by Gábor Rajnai who was borrowed from his theatre for the occasion.

The films of Béla Balogh were

4. *The Doll* (A baba)

5. *Nantas*

6. *No Kissing* (Tilos a csók).

The theme of *The Doll* was by Sándor Bródy, the screenplay was written by Richard Falk. A young man on the point of becoming a monk inherits a vast fortune on the condition that he gets married; in the monastery the monks construct a machine-bride for the novice to marry, in order to acquire all his wealth for the order. However, instead of a machine the doll introduced into the cell is alive. The novice falls in love with her; so the story has a happy ending. In all probability this film was put into the plan as an anticlerical piece. *No Kissing,* a burlesque, was the stage success of József Pásztor. In an imaginary country kissing is prohibited by law, which leads to amusing complications, because nobody obeys the law. *Nantas* was a film version of Zola's novel *Nana.*

The films of Márton Garas were

7. *Samuel the Seeker*

8. *Oliver Twist*

9. *The Greatest Sin* (A legnagyobb bűn).

As a "literary" programme, that of Garas is certainly the most exacting. *Samuel the Seeker* is a screen version of Upton Sinclair's novel. *Oliver Twist* has been adapted to the screen in more versions than any other novel by Dickens.

The Greatest Sin was also based on a recurrent theme. One of the pupils of a convent school is seduced by a Hussar officer billeted at the place in wartime. A baby is born—and this is "the greatest sin". The theme provided opportunities for social criticism and its filming would not have been possible earlier. Margit Makay played Sister Mary, Mihály Várkonyi the Hussar officer.

Oszkár Damo's programme was very serious, well considered, and truly aimed at social criticism. Since the *Cave Dwellers* (Barlanglakók)—which he presented with peasants and not with actors—he has belonged to the most modern Hungarian directors.

The two films of Oszkár Damo were

10. *The Nurse* (A dada)

11. *Conscience* (A lelkiismeret).

The Nurse was based on a play by Sándor Bródy. The very fact of putting this play on the screen was an achievement. Contemporary reviews emphasized the remarkable beauty of the scenery where the film was shot as well as the brilliant representation of a Hungarian village and the life of Hungarian peasants. It is a pity that the film has been lost; it is an equally great pity that, consequently, it is difficult to rescue the name of Oszkár Damo from oblivion. Indeed, not only *The Nurse* and *Cave Dwellers* were significant feats, but also another short story of Tömörkény, *Conscience*. This film gave a version of Tömörkény's minor masterpiece in which a peasant, while shopping, steals a mechanical tin soldier that persists in standing up reproachfully each time it is knocked over; the peasant, brought to feel remorse, smuggles the toy back to its place, having become aware of his "sin". This film must have been remarkable, if for no other reason than it rested not on a complicated plot but on an inner conflict.

Alfréd Deésy produced his usual mediocre films:

12. *Cupid* (Ámor)
13. *The Burglar* (A betörő)
14. *Eva.*

Eva was a version of Lehár's operetta; *Cupid* a sentimental story "based on an English novel", *The Burglar* was a comedy. That is all we know about them; furthermore that the censorship of Horthy had nothing against them... "unless we take exception to the scene in which a woman appears in a rather scanty attire"—this may have been the director's reason for denoting the film as progressive.

Pál Aczél also produced a comedy:

15. *Farmer Máté and the Dwarfs* (Máté gazda és a törpék).

After *The Apostle* it was odd to choose such a peculiar theme; it was from among the midgets of the Lilliputian theatre that Franciska Gál started on her career.

Ödön Uher had only one film,

16. *Night and Morning* (Éj és virradat)

based on Edward Bulwer's novel. The sets were designed by József Pán.

The two films of Károly Lajthay were

17. *The Commissioner* (A kormánybiztos)
18. *Miss Julie* (Júlia kisasszony).

The film version of Strindberg's *Miss Julie* was given a first-rate cast headed by Gizi Bajor and Gyula Csortos. Unfortunately this is all we know about it. *The Commissioner* was based on the adaptation of one of Soma Guthi's works to the screen.

Pál Sugár also directed two films:

19. *The Statue* (A szobor)

20. *Tragedy in the Alps* (Alpesi tragédia).

The screenplay of *The Statue* was written by Pál Forró. In connection with the shooting of *Tragedy in the Alps,* the leading lady, Bella Muzsnay, wrote: "In this film I played an unfaithful wife who was to be crucified for her deception. For shooting the scene I was actually tied to a cross and as long as one of the company supported my feet with his hands I experienced no particular pain. But when I was left to myself, like a soldier tied to a tree, with toes just off the ground (a military punishment) and I was hanging in the air, beads of perspiration ran down my face and I wailed loudly, shrieking 'Take me down, Take me down!' Well, they did take me down—for the film. The director saw my despair which was by no means put on and reflected the agony of the crucified woman so truthfully that shooting was started at once."[3]

Móric Miklós Pásztory made a picture of Hall Caine's novel,

21. *The Prodigal Son* (A tékozló fiú)

with Oszkár Beregi, Margit Makay, Ilona Mattyasovszky in the leading parts.

It is worthy of note that the German film directors who were active in Hungary before the bourgeois revolution of 1918 remained in the country and continued to work; so did the Italian Carmen Cartellieri. They agreed with the general policy.

Cornelius Hintner made two films:

22. *Stolen Luck* (Az elrabolt szerencse)

23. *Marion de Lorme.*

Both films were adaptations of novels. One, Susa Grassi's novel, treats the recurrent theme of the twins, a beautiful girl and a plain one; of course, the doctor marries the dancer... Victor Hugo's novel, *Marion de Lorme,* is the story of a French prostitute who, being unable to realize her desire for a pure life, commits suicide.

The three films of Joseph Stein were

24. *Tiny Tot* (A csöppség)

25. *Francillon*

26. *Gentlemen Gangsters* (Úri banditák).

Tiny Tot is based on a gay peasant play by Samu Fényes, an eminent writer who deserves to be better remembered. *Francillon* was adapted to the screen from the novel of Dumas. The title of *Gentlemen Gangsters* is exceedingly high-sounding, but even the censorship of the white terror period could find no fault with it and pointed out that it was really a harmless tale which "...did not serve to propagandize for social change," because it was simply a criminal story of gentlemen dressed up as gangsters.

These films were produced by directors who had worked regularly in Hungarian film production before the year of 1919. Moreover, the government of the Republic of Councils made it possible for gifted assistants to produce their first films. Such directors of their first films were Béla Gerőffy (1889–1925), assistant of the Uher Studio; Gyula Szöreghy (1883–1942), actor and assistant in the permanent company of Star; Sándor Pallos, assistant cameraman of Corvin; Dezső Orbán, an author.

Béla Gerőffy made two films written by Ede Sas. Only their titles have survived:

27. *Infamous Honour* (Becstelen becsület)

28. *Children Prohibited* (Tilos a gyerek).

Gyula Szöreghy adapted for the screen Daudet's novel giving a charmingly humorous picture of social resignation; it may have been supposed to exercise social criticism:

29. *Fromont Junior and Risler Senior* (Ifjabb Fromont és idősb Risler).

Sándor Pallos made the most significant venture. He planned a series of films from Gorky's stories, but got no further than the first:

30. *Chelkash* (A pénz).

The leading role—the old "sea-wolf" Chelkash—was played by Lajos Gellért. This film was remarkable, but its director suffered a terrible punishment. Few directors have paid with their lives for a film which in this instance expressed a political conviction. In the autumn of 1919, Sándor Pallos was tortured to death by Horthy's gendarmes. It is a pity that the memory of Sándor Pallos has not been preserved by his film which has been lost. This was the first film-version of *Chelkash;* the only other, as far as I know, was made in 1956 and directed by Fedor Filippov.

Only one feature film has survived from the thirty-one motion pictures made under the Republic of Councils:

31. *Yesterday* (Tegnap)

written and directed by Dezső Orbán, in collaboration with Lajos Lázár.

The story of the film is silly and unnatural. After the festive *première* a contemporary review stated: *"Yesterday* differs from the average failure by its bad taste, lack of culture and high-flowing but confused naiveté. It is simply a poor film, based on an impossible script, produced without any artistic flair.[4]

"We try to break away from the stage. But here, in all the scenes we found

them to be direct imitations of the stage. Every rule of direction and setting
has been identical with those followed in the theatre; characters and crowds
move as they would on the stage. The only difference was that we saw them
not in reality before us but in a series of pictures... Our ambition for a film
is that it should convey the effect of pictorial compositions."[5]

The Proletarian Academy and the production group finished the shooting
in eight and a half days that the picture might be presented sooner. Were its
faults due to haste? No. It was its unfortunate story that brought about
the failure of the film. It deserves all the censure that it received.

A skilled workman lives in a room rented from the director of the factory
where he is employed. Of the luxurious villa and lovely park he has only
one corner. This obviously absurd situation was most likely intended as a
symbol by the makers of the film: the workman exploited by the capitalist
who lets him have only crumbs of his residence and his wealth, for he is
master of the world.

The workman-lodger falls in love with the capitalist's neglected wife.
The woman is only an object used by the husband, for he has only loved
her body and never her soul. Having tired of her body he is encouraging his
factory manager to seduce his wife; if caught in the act she could be divorced
and deprived of financial support. But his elaborate scheme is not necessary:
while the husband enjoys the carnal pleasures offered by a sumptuously
furnished brothel, the lodger begins to court the neglected beauty who
allows him to keep her lace handkerchief which is subsequently found by
a valet in the lodger's room, inevitably causing a scandal. The workman is
driven out of his paradise, while the lady is to be divorced ignominiously.

The only consolation of the hero is his revolutionary propaganda at the
factory: he organizes his companions, prepares them for a strike, provides
for the printing of pamphlets, and forms a study group the members of which
regularly attend ideological lectures. Obviously this is also meant to be a sym-
bolic activity. Meanwhile, whenever he can get away from his revolutionary
work, the workman meets the beautiful persecuted lady in a lonely corner
of the churchyard. She tells him the vicissitudes of her childhood and youth
when she was a seamstress and her mother, in hope of a better life, per-
suaded her to marry the rich manufacturer. She had to choose between poverty and bourgeois prosperity; she chose prosperity but now she could see
reality clearly. Scorned now, she had to endure knowing about her husband's mistress and the pain of being separated from her little son.

The hero, in emotional turmoil, returns to the factory where he sees
the failure of the revolt: in vain do white leaflets flutter down to the workers,

the army is called in and the workmen are defeated. In a paroxysm of despair the workman-hero kills the manufacturer and escapes from the country with a revolutionary (who has a distinct resemblance to Marx). Here is the climax of the film's blunders. The revolutionary hero of a socialist film commits a love-motivated murder and then simply escapes abroad. Is this the mentality typical of revolution?

The method used in producing the film, as promised by the makers of the film in a statement, was partially vindicated. The film has several remarkable sequences.

The sequences showing the factory are of special importance. A little old woman is allowed to pass the suspicious guards; it is she who smuggles the leaflets into the factory at the bottom of her lunch-basket. This episode from Gorky's novel, *The Mother,* is used in a Hungarian film of 1919, with touching awkwardness. Then the factory interior. Subdued lighting. A conscious endeavour to use the effects of light and shadow. White leaflets come fluttering down from above, perhaps from a factory bridge.

Shots of the mobilized military force and the workmen assembling for their demonstration alternate in parallel contrasting montage. These may have been the first Hungarian experiments in montage. Close-up of the factory siren cuts to a close-up of a soldier blowing his trumpet, i.e. sound montage has been achieved in a silent film through images.

It is with the gesture of the familiar worker-symbol that the hero-workman raises the large hammer to his shoulder. It is an awkward symbol, but it is the first time a workman appears on the Hungarian screen.

In the scenes shot in the villa and the park the camera moved boldly and ingeniously. The panning camera was relatively—and unusually—frequent; the camera angles and composition show much ingenuity. Efforts at originality may be appreciated even if they sometimes make a scene funny: in her elaborate boudoir the manufacturer's wife can be seen in a mirror, alongside the reflection of the cameraman.

Hence, as regards the efforts of the director, *Yesterday* was a noteworthy achievement. It was recovered in 1959 through the courtesy of the Soviet Film Archive.

Yesterday is a living memory of the cinema during the Republic of Councils of 1919.

Dead Silence
1920—1929

The 'twenties brought bankruptcy to the production and art of Hungarian films.

This failure was caused chiefly by the counter-revolution, the white terror, though the lost war, inflation and distrust by big capital were also factors. At any rate, the soldiers of Miklós Horthy singled out the art of film to be honoured by their special

Dead Silence

attention. Directors (particularly) and actors who remained active under the Republic of Councils were summoned and arrested one after the other. Sándor Korda fled to Vienna. Mihály Kertész (now Michael Curtiz) had earlier signed a contract which required his presence in Vienna, too. Jenő Janovics became a citizen of Rumania. Pál Aczél and Pál Sugár also chose Vienna for their exile. Sándor Pallos, the director of the film version of Gorky's *Chelkash,* was tortured to death. Hungary lost its best directors one after the other as a result of systematic persecution by Horthy's men. The white terror raged. Cinemas were given as rewards to soldiers wearing crane-feathered caps—symbol of the counter-revolutionary army; war widows, leftist citizens, Jews were driven out of their cinemas. An English adventurer using the name of "Colonel Stead" was presented by Horthy with a profitable cinema to add to the money that he accumulated in various dubious ways during this dark period.[1]

Film production was in trouble, because directors could not be found. Now the film distributors could triumph over the film studios, and made the most of their opportunity by establishing a new organization. The old studios, Corvin, Star, Astra and Uher, continued to function, and, in the hope of another boom, some new firms were founded. But who were to direct their films? A "second-line" set came forward, just as a steady flow of the American, French and Italian films that were held back in 1914–15 began to reach Hungarian screens. These films differed in quality from the pictures made before 1915. However, in Hungary film production proceeded along the old lines. In the autumn of 1919 eleven new films were made. Before leaving forever Korda hurriedly finished *No. 111,* a screen version of Heltai's novel. The balance was upset by his departure.

Of the eighty-six Hungarian feature films produced from the downfall of the Republic of Councils till January, 1922, the most outstanding achievement was *The Fascinated* (Megbűvöltek), directed by the actor Gyula Gál, member of the National Theatre. The script was written by László Gál based on Dostoyevski's short story *The Hostess*. On the evidence of the few preserved photographs and the memories of István Békés, it must have been a carefully composed film, with a conscious endeavour to create effects of light and shadow. Its fine cast featured Gizi Bajor, Géza Abonyi, Károly Sugár, László Bakó. Gorky's play, *The Lower Depths,* was filmed by Star Studio during the First World War.

Nevertheless, this Dostoyevski film by László Gál appears to have been far above average, especially when its surviving photographs are compared with the Russian film of the same story made in 1916 by Chardinin *(Ilya Murin)*. Five years had also gone by between 1916 and 1921, five significant years in the history of film art. In Chardinin's film Ilya Murin stretches out his hand to seize the sword with a theatrical gesture, with a background set swimming in even, placid stage lighting, while Katerina tries to dissuade him. This scene bears the typical mark of early silent films.[2] As for the qualities of *The Fascinated*, the memories of István Békés are substantiated by the picture of Ordino walking slowly from the sunshine into the dim church amidst a swarm of beggars, by photographs of a servant with an ecstatic countenance (Károly Sugár), and the horrified, brooding face of Gizi Bajor (it is her bobbed hair alone which is not in keeping with the period). Békés has spoken with much affection about the enthusiasm evinced by the makers of this film who had been prisoners of war in Russia, praising their local knowledge and stressing the film's artistic composition: "This was the first film to be shot in a darkened studio, in artificial light throughout, using semitones and effects of deep shadows. Sometimes work was continued until late in the night. Then the young actors, Gizi Bajor, Géza Abonyi and we young writers remained together until the small hours, to analyze and discuss what had been accomplished."[3]

The films seen by the public at that time were much more grand than those to be seen during the war. After *Intolerance,* mediocre directors applied the methods of Griffith. Spectacular films were made with enormous capital using vast crowds. A Hungarian director would never have even dreamt of such expensive crowds. The film had become a truly spectacular show. When nothing happened on the screen it was still fascinating to see hundreds, thousands of dancers, fighters, Indian riders, and gigantic structures. At the beginning the mere fact of motion had been an overwhelming spectacle, now films that were produced on a grand scale, mobilizing huge crowds in their mass scenes, became the most attractive. No theatre could offer a similar experience.

Hungarian motion picture producers could not compete with films of this scale, though the latter depended on talent as well as on money. But our gifted film men had been driven from the country; many of the German films applauded by serious audiences had been made by Hungarians.

Most of the eighty-six films made in Hungary during this period employed the old impulse, to bring cinema to the status of an art by linking it to literature. However, this literature was worthless, far from the previous sources of Sándor Bródy, Mihály Babits, Dickens or Gorky. About one-third of the films produced still consisted of adaptations from novels (thirty-two), but apart from the Vörösmarty film (*Fair Helen*—Szép Ilonka), two adaptations of Jókai, two of Eötvös, three of Jenő Heltai (*No. 111, The Milliner*—A masamód, *Father Sebastian*—Pater Sebastian), only contemporary fiction was put on the screen. These books were sold in the bookshops; though much read and discussed they had no literary significance. Version of novels of Bithia Mary Croker, Gaston Leroux, Edouard Pailleron, Ethel May Dell, Nataly von Eschruth, Helen Mathers, Florence Montgomery were presented on the screen. A few attempts were made to use the works of Hungarian authors whose writing had not been filmed before, but these ventures proved unlucky. The film based on Dezső Szomory's *Friday Night* (Péntek este) failed; Tamás Kóbor's film was unable to reproduce the wry humour and bitter irony typical of this author (*In the Name of Decency*—A tisztesség nevében). The detective story of Tamás Moly, on the other hand, was a success (*The Robin*—Vörösbegy).

The fact that literary quality was relegated to the background was really a natural process rather than an unfortunate circumstance. Most directors abroad—particularly in Germany and France—strove to present their own themes and to convey their own messages. In Hungary, directors had no message of their own; this void was filled by trash and melodrama.

The war was over, the boom was over. A tragi-comic situation arose: the Hungarian film industry had to wait for another war before it could rise economically again to the 1915–1918 level.

By the mid-'twenties only a few directors were available, but not first-class men. Béla Balogh and Alfréd Deésy were also working in Germany. Béla Gerőffy committed suicide. In 1923 Pál Fejős made a last effort: he acquired capital and began to shoot *The Stars of Eger* (Egri csillagok). However, instead of finishing this work he emigrated to the United States.[4] In Corvin Studio German directors were making UFA films. Good Antal Forgács alone continued to produce scenarios of peasant themes for the villages in distant districts.

In the years from 1922 to 1930 altogether thirty-five films were made in Hungary, that is to say, four films a year.

But in 1925 all activity had not yet come to a standstill. Béla Balogh, Károly Lajthay, Béla Gerőffy, Antal Forgács, Pál Fejős, Artúr Lakner, Béla Gaál, and two foreigners, the Danish–German Uwe Jens Kraft and the Italian Renato Bulla del Torchio, made films. Sándor Korda's younger brother, Zoltán Korda, directed his first film (until then he had worked as assistant), *Prodigy* (A csodagyerek); having this achievement to his credit he hurriedly left the country to join his brother abroad. On the evidence of contemporary reviews Béla Balogh's film, *White Pigeons in a Black Town* (Fehér galambok fekete városban), may have been a valuable work. It strove to show Budapest's hectic whirl of inflation which was deeply affecting the film world.

The true tragedy of Hungarian films in the 'twenties was that the same years brought the first golden age of cinema to the world. It was in the 'twenties that six of the world's twelve best films were made, which are still considered to be masterpieces: Stroheim's *Greed* in 1924, Eisenstein's *Battleship Potemkin* in 1925, Chaplin's *Gold Rush* in 1925, Murnau's *Der letzte Mann* in 1925, Pudovkin's *Mother* in 1926, Dreyer's *La Passion de Jeanne d'Arc* in 1928. It was at this time that the first "schools" and trends of style emerged in film art: the German *Kammerspiel,* the bold Soviet socialist style, the French avant-garde; and the first theoretical works were written on the growing art by Dziga Vertov, Béla Balázs, Louis Delluc.

The tragedy is that in 1919 Hungarian filming started at no disadvantage compared with German or Soviet conditions.

Contemporary literary periodicals also took up the issue of Hungary's lagging behind in cinema. *Nyugat* introduced a permanent film column, and film reviews were written by Lajos Kassák, Józsi Jenő Tersánszky, and by the aesthetician Iván Hevesy. There was also film industrial progress abroad at an almost incredible rate. In Germany the number of active film studios was 245 in 1919, 230 in 1920, 270 in 1921, 360 in 1922.[5]

In the late 'twenties the cinema developed significantly all over the world, both in spectacular display and in psychologically true human characters. In the theatres of Budapest cinema-goers could see important works of the French avant-garde in addition to the best German and American films; they could not see Soviet films (except for one—Pudovkin's *Storm over Asia*), though they heard about them, even from enthusiastic reviews in the Hungarian press. The film claimed a place among the arts, no longer on the ground of photographing literature—as had been the rule in Hungary as well as in other countries before—but by virtue of its own message conveyed by its own means of expression.

In this situation, when stimulating essays were published in Hungary on the aesthetic aspects of motion pictures—notably *Aesthetics and Structure of the Film Drama* by Iván Hevesy—when articles dealing with films appeared regularly in the periodical *Nyugat,* Hungarian film production was on the verge of bankruptcy. Those years were an irreparable loss, the effect of which—without exaggeration—may be said to be still felt in Hungarian film production. As if ten years had dropped from the history of a nation's literature, as if no books or periodicals had appeared for that long a time. The few films made in the second half of this barren decade provide a sad proof.

On closer inspection another appalling feature may be noted: not only few and poor films were made, but of the six directors of the thirteen films produced between 1925 and 1929 only two had been active in the film industry before 1920, in the period of regular film production when training and experience could be acquired. These two had also been working only from 1918. Forgács, generally known as a modest and efficient craftsman, was a poor director; Lázár returned from abroad only in 1929. Though the Hungarian film industry had been producing feature films regularly since 1912, by 1925 there was not one of the old experts, not one of the directors who made their names in the initial period between 1912 and 1917. Four out of seven directors had not made any picture before 1925: Letzter, Vanicsek, György, Rajháti were certainly keen and painstaking workers in their profession, but they were not creative artists. Béla Gaál, on the other hand, relied on the safe background of his theatre and directed a film only occasionally.

The prime minister's wife also wrote a scenario, but this was not much help either. There was something to be proud of: the wife of a prime minister took an active part in Hungarian film production, but in vain. Hungarian film production had irretrievably failed.

Apart from the white terror which raged in the early 'twenties, in the age of consolidation under István Bethlen, the cinema proprietors were also responsible for this development. The country having become smaller, there were fewer cinemas to make a firm market, whence the inclination to produce films also subsided. There was no war, the boom was over. Import of the films made by the competing producers was no longer prohibited. Hungarian films ceased to be profitable. There was no one to insist on the necessity to maintain Hungarian film production for its own sake. Béla

Balogh emigrated in 1925 after spending a year seeking an exhibitor for his film, *The Boys of Paul Street,* finished in the spring of 1924. A total lack of interest was encountered by Hungarian films. Distributors vied with one another in making contracts for the best foreign films, renting them to exhibitors at a high price. As a matter of fact, from the business point of view, it would have been senseless to produce films: finished films bought for a song were more lucrative.

In the meantime it seemed that the government intended to take steps. In 1924 the Ministry of the Interior called a conference "...to reconcile the interests of cinema proprietors, distributors and film producers". But these efforts were futile.

This stage was followed by co-production programmes. These brought no improvement either. *Die Tschardaschfürstin* was no success; these German films were directed by adventurers who had no ability. Arzén Cserépy, the director of *Fridericus Rex,* a Junker film which had an enormous success in German nationalist circles, fed the public with promises of producing a film on Attila, king of the Huns. Cserépy fancied himself in the role of saving Hungarian film art; the regent granted him an audience and Cserépy sold the film to seventeen countries before the scenario was written; then he went back to Germany, leaving the film unmade.

In the late 'twenties Hungarian film studios became bankrupt. Of the major companies with studios of their own, both Phönix, the enterprise of Mór Ungerleider, the doyen of the industry, and Hungaria had closed down as early as the autumn of 1919; Uher had followed in the early 'twenties. At the time in question Ödön Uher sat on the board of a German company. Astra practically collapsed, only the largest, Star and Corvin, struggled on.

Corvin failed in 1925. The bankrupt estate was wound up by the state, and after lengthy wrangling and many delays a Film Industry Fund was established for the management of the studio; later, in 1929, Hunnia Studio was founded. Thus after 1929 Corvin went under the name of Hunnia Studio, but no films were produced.

Star was liquidated in 1929. It contrived to avoid bankruptcy, because it manœuvred more skilfully and had a distribution branch to support it, but finally it too was compelled to go out of business. It was revived in 1940 by the new boom brought by the Second World War. In 1929 Hungarian film production ceased, as if it had never existed.

While the Hungarian film barely existed in the early 'twenties, the literature of film theory flourished amazingly.

Film Theory in the 'Twenties

While Béla Balázs, living in exile in Vienna and Berlin, published his book *Der Sichtbare Mensch* (Wien—Leipzig, 1924), in Budapest Iván Hevesy wrote film reviews and his book *A filmjáték esztétikája és dramaturgiája* [Aesthetics and Structure of the Film Drama] (Budapest, 1925). It is remarkable that Hevesy's book shows film art in the process of its development, giving detailed attention to the phenomena which Béla Balázs was to note as a "pictorial grammar" in their historical growth. Hevesy makes an interesting study of the reasons why it was that fundamental aesthetic rules took shape in connection with burlesque films, and, in general, why it was in such comedies that the first appearance of the fictional scenario followed the first news films.

Hevesy begins the preface of his book: "Notwithstanding its extreme youth, the film scenario has progressed beyond the first phase of being satisfied with itself as an art and being patted condescendingly on the shoulder, and it has reached the stage where its literature may be expected to give us more than generalizations or witty reflections. Film aesthetics should be based on the iron rods of logic and constructed in regular form."

His comments on the captions of silent films are exceedingly interesting. In Hevesy's view, the apparently obvious explanation that captions were intended to replace the dialogue of the theatre and to provide the necessary information which images alone were unable to convey was by no means acceptable. According to Hevesy, captions were much more depended upon to support clumsily constructed montage, covering some change of mood or the passage of time which might have been conveyed by well-planned images. About montage Hevesy says: "...the mode of connecting sequences may evoke associations; moreover, it may even amount to a certain code." His comments on the audience are of equal importance. He claims that the film as an art had developed into its existing form through the categorical demands of the public.

From an international viewpoint, *MA,* the journal of the avant-garde painter and poet Lajos Kassák, is even more interesting. This periodical is a veritable treasure for art historians. As Kassák had contacts with every important modern artist from Picasso and Léger to Eggeling, he printed many original writings from these men in his Hungarian journal. Cinema also figured among his interests. For instance, he published Ivan Goll's "film poem" on Chaplin, Viking Eggeling's essay "Analysis of the Principles of Motion Pictures", as well as an important film idea by László Moholy-Nagy. As this script may interest readers abroad—(I have already published it in the Roman journal *Bianco e Nero,* 1962, No. 11)—and as it clearly antedates Ruttmann's *Berlin, Sinfonie einer Grossstadt* (1927) and Dziga Vertov's *Man with the Camera* (1929), as well as a host of other "city-symphonies", the text of Moholy's script is given below. The published text was illustrated with his numerous drawings and diagrams. The script, dated 1921–22, appeared in the September 1924 issue of *MA.*

László Moholy-Nagy: A Film Sketch
Dinamics of a Metropolis

Building construction with an iron crane (Use of special trick effects—line drawings—melting slowly into the filming of nature)
Crane for construction:
    shot from below
             diagonally
     from above
     elevator for bricks
     revolving crane
This movement is continued by an automobile racing
    to the left. The same house is always seen
    in the centre of the picture.
(The house should always be re-photographed to place it in the centre.)
    Another automobile appears which tears along at the same speed,
but in the opposite direction.
    Tempo, tempo!
One row of houses rushes by in the same direction, always allowing the house in the middle to be seen. The row of houses runs past and comes back.
    Rows of houses race transparently in opposite directions, and so do the automobiles. Faster and faster, so that the spectators are made dizzy.
    A tiger, TIGER walks about in his cage
    walks back and forth angrily.
High up, clearly visible traffic signals.

Moving automatically
a-u-t-o-m-a-t-i-c-a-l-l-y
   (Close up)
  up   up
     down   down
up up up down down
 1   2   3   4   5

Goods-station.

Shunting yard.

Warehouses and cellars   Dark   Dark
                            DARKNESS

Railway

Highway with vehicles. Bridge. Viaduct. Ships passing below. Above an overhead railway. (Elberfeld)

View of a train from a high embankment, shot diagonally.

A track-watchman salutes standing at attention.

Eyes become fixed. (Close up)

Train seen from a bridge, from above.

From below: from the ditch between the rails the belly of the train as it rushes along. The turning wheels—so fast as to be an indistinct vibration.

       TEMPO
         TEMPO
          TEM
          TEM   PO
          TEM
              TEEEM
                M
               M POOOOO
                       DOWN

In a department store glass-enclosed lift with Negro children.

Obliquely.   UP
                                 UP

Distorted perspective.

Longshot.   A CROWD

At the entrance tethered dogs

Beside the glass lifts glass telephone boxes with callers

Filming from the ground floor through the glass

The FACE of a caller, painted with phosphorescent paint (so as to produce

no shadow) turns slowly to the right, directly beside the lift.
Over his head a distant aeroplane spirals in the air.
View from a slight altitude: a square where
many streets converge.

Masses of vehicles. Tramways, motorcars, lorries, carts, bicycles, buses
drive fast from the square.
Suddenly all of them go backwards.

They pile up in the centre of the square.
The square opens in the middle and swallows them up.

(The camera is at an angle to create the impression of falling.)
underground
cables

TEMPO

Gas-tank
Sewers. (deep beneath the town)

Light reflected on water.
Arc lamp.
Sparks *spraying.*
Highway at night, gleaming city streets.
Gliding automobiles from above, diagonally.

For five seconds only a black screen
Electric advertising with flashing letters:

MOHOLY   MOHOLY

Fireworks in the amusement park.
Riding on the roller-coaster.
SPEEDing.
Ferris-wheel.
Fun-house.
Distorting mirrors.
Other jokes.
Picture of exhibition in a railway station.
The camera moves in a horizontal circle,
then in a vertical circle.

Taut
telephone wires and telegraph cables
between houses.

> Towers of porcelain insulators.
> Radio-aerials on roofs.

Factory.

> Wheels turning.
> An acrobat twirls and turns somersaults.

> Pole-vaulting. A fall shown 10 times in succession.

Variety show. Frantic activity.
Football match. Rough. Fast tempo.
Women wrestling. Kitsch!
Jazz-band instruments. (in Close-up.)

POINTED AT THE PUBLIC

A hollow, shining metal funnel is fixed on the lens of the camera.
Immediately:
a man jerks away his head in a flash. (Close-up.)

A glass of WATER.
(only the surface of the water, in Close-up.)
Gushing like a fountain.
Jazz-band, *with its sound.*

FORTISSIMOOOO

Wild dance caricature.
Prostitutes.
Boxing, Close-up.

> ONLY gloves.
> With slow-motion (Zeitlupe) camera

A cloud of smoke. (Coming through a bridge, as a train runs under it)
Chimney-stack, aslant.
A diver plunges down into water.
Propeller turning under the water.

Opening of drain above and under water.
Filming from motor boat along the canal to

RUBBISH dump.
Utilization of rubbish.
        Hills of scrap iron.
        Mounds of old shoes.
        Stacks of tin cans.
Perpetual motion lift, with view. All around.
        From here the whole section, back to the JAZZ BAND
        (also reversed), should go from
        fortissimo to PIANISSIMO
Mortuary. From above.
Military parade.
March-march.

        Women riding horses.
The two shots are superimposed, so that both are visible.

Slaughter-house. Oxen.
Machinery of a cold-storage plant.
Sausage machine. Thousands of sausages.
A LION'S HEAD snarling. (Close-up.)
Audience.
A LION'S HEAD snarling (Close-up.)
Policeman with a rubber truncheon in the middle of a crowded square.
The TRUNCHEON (Close-up.)
Audience in a theatre.
Snarling LION'S HEAD (Close-up.)

    For a few seconds total darkness.

      CIRCLE
Circus.
              TEMPO
Trapeze.
            LION,   Lion
        CLOWN.
            LION,   Lion

Clowns
clowns   **LION**
clowns
Slowly. WATERFALL: with sound.
A body floats on the water.
Soldiers.
March—march.
A glass of **WATER**
with moving surface.
A brief,
rapid jet of water upwards.

THE END

Berlin, 1921–22

Remarks for those who refuse to understand the film immediately.

This film mostly flowed from the possibilities offered by the camera.

My aim was for a film to produce an effect by its own action, its own tempo and rhythm, instead of the still fashionable plots that force cinema to ape literature or theatre.

The speeding autos are necessary for a shocking introduction. To show the breathless rush, the turmoil of a city. The tiger is used for contrast. And so that the audience would get used to such surprises and inconsistency from the start.

The purpose of this film is not to teach, nor to moralize, nor to tell a story. Its acting is purely visual.

Bridges, trains, ships, etc. are here to illustrate the services and conveniences of an urban civilization.

The belly of the train: this is a visual experience that we would not normally encounter.

The phosphorescent face that slowly turns away: reminding us of fatiguing telephone conversations. A dream-like state. (Glass, glass, glass) —the direction of the movement prepares us for the spiral course of the pilot.

The rushing of a roller-coaster: many things escape your attention. Many things pass unnoticed, because the senses are unable to perceive everything, rapid motion, moments of danger, etc. On the roller-coaster almost all passengers close their eyes at the great downward drop. But the camera does not close its eye. We rarely watch objectively babies or animals because our attention is taken by the apprehension of numerous other circumstances.

The metal funnel: is to frighten so terribly that it should almost hurt. The surface of the glass of water: should be brilliant.

The frequent recurrence of the lion's head is a nightmare. (Again, again, again.)

The audience of the theatre is gay, but we are still conscious of the lion's head.

In general one should understand more from a rapid reading of the manuscript than can ever be expressed by explanations.

László Moholy-Nagy

This "sketch for a film" has several fascinating aspects. Its author, though familiar with photography at the time he wrote it, had not yet had the opportunity to work in films. Thus his scenario now tells us what an alert graphic artist captured from the films that everyone was then seeing, to be brought together in his vision of a city, his dream for a film. Here are suggestions gleaned from documentary films (the river and rail traffic), newsreels (the actions of planes and parades), instructional films (slow-motion photography), early sound-film experiments (often shown as novelties on film programmes), the exaggerated images of adventure films (superimpositions and the "belly" of a speeding train), the photographic gags of fantastic comedies—perhaps a recollection from Moholy's childhood of Pathé or Gaumont burlesques (the square swallows up the converging traffic)—but only Moholy could put it all together in this way, always combining these with his own observation of the city's movement. He also took a step (at least on paper) beyond the experimental films that he saw in Berlin in 1921, for Eggeling, Richter and Ruttmann then aimed at linear abstractions that could be fully controlled through the stop-motion camera. Moholy's abstraction was to be made of fragments of reality, and that was the direction the international experimental film was to take in the second half of this decade.

As published in *MA* in 1924, Moholy's sketch is a key document in the history of the experimental cinema.

The Dream Car
Decade
1930—1938

On September 20, 1929, *The Singing Fool* was presented in Budapest, in the Forum Cinema. Sound-film had arrived in Hungary.

The Dream Car Decade

In the year that witnessed the triumph of the sound-film all over the world, 136 cinemas were in operation at Budapest and there were 496 in the whole of Hungary. There was hardly any change in this figure until the outbreak of the Second World War.[1]

The programmes of these 496 cinemas had to include films that were liked by the largest number of movie-goers, otherwise the cinema proprietor would be ruined.

In the 'thirties more than half of the feature films presented in Hungary —51.5 per cent—were American pictures.[2] Another twenty per cent were German. In 1930 the rest were French, Austrian, English and Italian. There was not one Hungarian film.

Even though the public wished to see Hungarian films, their production did not pay, because they would have had to compete with American, German and French pictures. A foreign market would have been welcome; but who would look at a Hungarian film, particularly a talkie, in America? Therefore foreign markets could scarcely be counted on.

Fortunately there remained one film studio which was in working order, the former Corvin Studio in Gyarmat Street, bought by the state and re-named the Hunnia Film Studio. Its newly appointed manager, János Bingert, spared no effort in his attempt to make this state film studio pay. It was fitted out with modern camera and recording equipment and proper insulation. In 1930 Hunnia stood ready for producers as a relatively modern sound-film studio. The idea was that businessmen would rent the studio space and equipment. However, nobody evinced any such interest, for in the meantime American companies began multi-lingual productions in Paris and London; Hollywood scenarios were re-filmed there in the major European languages with actors of various nationalities.

In the first years of talkies audiences were supposed to want to hear films only in their own language; producers wanted to avoid using captions as it reminded people of the silent films. Hardly had the former Corvin Studio been put into working order and converted into Hunnia when Hollywood chose Paris for its headquarters and invited some of the best Hungarian actors to work there. The Paramount company made two Hungarian versions, *The Laughing Woman* and *The Doctor's Secret,* with Gizi Bajor and Artúr Somlay in the lead. In the face of this János Bingert resorted to the tactic of offering to rent Hunnia to foreign film producers. He contrived to conclude agreements, so that a fair number of German, Austrian, Czech, French, and even American films were made in Budapest. This, however, proved to be merely a half-measure, for the foreign producers did not use the studios to full capacity. (Some of these films were produced in Hungarian version too.)

A way had to be found that films might be produced by independent enterprise.

Bingert introduced the idea—but, according to some experts, following a German pattern—that in addition to ordinary taxes, special taxes and customs duty should be levied on foreign films presented in Hungarian cinemas; moreover, after twenty foreign films one Hungarian production had to be shown. These were the preconditions of being permitted a licence for the presentation of talking pictures in Hungary. Since several hundred films were presented in Hungary every year, this scheme provided for the production of approximately ten new Hungarian films each year.[3]

This decree pinched Hollywood disagreeably. American firms threatened to apply severe financial sanctions, which they were ready to carry out, and financial threats were supported by political pressure. In his book *Die Traumfabrik* Ilja Ehrenburg has described these events.[4]

They succeeded in having the decree modified. It no longer stipulated the production of one Hungarian picture for every twenty foreign films but required the payment of a certain excess amount over and above the usual taxes: one thousand pengős to a Film Industry Fund instituted for the purpose. At the time the production costs of an average film amounted to a hundred to a hundred and fifty thousand pengős. At the established rate only twenty thousand pengős were paid into the Fund after twenty films, and thus the considerable sum of money collected every year in this way sufficed only to assist rather than support the production of films.

These new circumstances created a peculiar situation. These contributions of several thousand pengős made it possible to revive Hungarian film production, and for this the credit must undoubtedly go to János Bingert and to the decree issued by the government. As a result Hungary was soon the only small European country to produce films regularly. On the other hand, the Film Industry Fund held all the money allotted as subsidy which no film-maker could do without, for owing to exorbitant production costs,

1. SÁNDOR KORDA
   —SIR ALEXANDER KORDA—
   1916, BUDAPEST
2. SÁNDOR KORDA: THE DUPED
   JOURNALIST, 1914, HIS FIRST
   FILM

3, ILLÉS: THE WORLD IS JUST
  A MOOD, 1916.
  LEONTINE KÜHNBERG,
  ARTÚR SOMLAY

4–5. LAJOS LÁZÁR–DEZSŐ ORBÁN:
  YESTERDAY, 1919. A FILM OF THE
  HUNGARIAN REPUBLIC OF COUNCILS

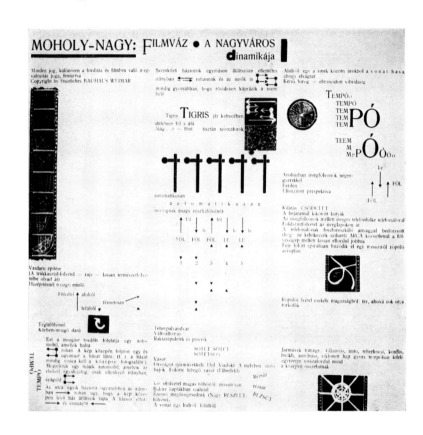

6. LÁSZLÓ MOHOLY-NAGY: DYNAMICS
   OF A METROPOLIS, 1921–22.
   AN ILLUSTRATED SCRIPT

7. GYULA KABOS

8. IMITATION OF HOLLYWOOD:
   THE VAMP. EMIL MARTONFFY:
   BLACK SHEEP OF THE FAMILY,
   1942. BEA GOLL
9. IMITATION OF HOLLYWOOD:
   THE *FEMME FATALE*.
   LÁSZLÓ KALMÁR:
   THE FATAL KISS, 1942
   KATALIN KARÁDY

10. JÁNOS SZÉKELY–JOHN S. TOLDY
1901–1958. ACADEMY AWARD WINNER
FOR THE BEST ORIGINAL SCREENPLAY
IN 1940: ARISE, MY LOVE
11. LÁSZLÓ (LADISLAS) VAJDA, 1962.
12. SIR ALEXANDER KORDA, 1955.
HIS LAST PHOTOGRAPH BY
ALEXANDER PAAL

13. ISTVÁN SZŐTS: PEOPLE ON THE ALPS, 1942

no film could be made to pay without this financial aid. A subvention or credit was granted by the Film Industry Fund only to the producer who guaranteed that his film would be made in a spirit acceptable to the Fund, i.e. the government. Therefore the script had to be submitted for approval simultaneously with the petition for a subsidy.

A curious situation. There existed, on the one hand, an independent film production in Hungary. The producer could make what he chose; whether his film was a flop or a success was his affair, his luck or misfortune. On the other hand, there was a state film company which rented studios, and no other studios were available because there was no other company; in close connection with this company there was a Film Industry Fund, in the last analysis a government organization, which actually censored, accepted or rejected scripts. Films could be made only on the basis of scripts approved by the state. Yet film production was not nationalized, the state itself did not produce films, refrained from giving guidance concerning the kind of films it wanted to be presented, and exercised censorship by refusing what it would not permit to appear on the screen. Of course, anybody who decided to go to work without applying to the Film Industry Fund for a subsidy could produce what he liked, but there was no producer who commanded such capital. In an article published in its December 15, 1937, issue the *Esti Újság* was justified in complaining that "...a studio is made available only for the production of a film whose scenario has been approved by the Film Industry Fund."

The modification of the original idea thus helped to develop a film production of a small-scale industrial type which required a modest capital, subsisted almost completely on subsidies and was dominated by a censorship of shallow, bureaucratic taste. Contemporary papers never tired of objecting to the Fund's limitations: shots of roads enveloped in clouds of dust raised by the hoofs of galloping horses had to be omitted, as our roads could not be dusty; shots of important public figures running up the stairs had to be omitted, as a Hungarian official must never be undignified, and so on.[5]

The scared obsequious small producer who risked his capital every two years by making a Hungarian film took good care to present to the official of the ministry a script which did not contain anything objectionable. From the very outset all matters and details were omitted that might be considered controversial. The producer preferred to play safe, avoiding everything that might cause trouble or displease the gentlemen who granted the subsidy.

The Hungarian talking picture was born in this atmosphere smelling of ministerial antechambers and clerks' oversleeves, where every word was controlled by the "national" policy of the moment.

Of course, we are still speaking of the existing possibilities. A film studio existed, and subsidies could be obtained by enterprising producers. But were there any cinema-goers, audiences willing to pay for tickets to see a Hungarian film? If it attracted no audience, exhibitors and distributors would not take the film; despite all the work and worry, the reels would be left in the tin cans of the studio. Did it depend on cinema-goers whether one, two or ten films were made in Hungary a year? Ten films a year meant a Hungarian *première* every month except for the summer. There can be no doubt that it was the masses of cinema-goers who made it possible to produce Hungarian talkies by buying their tickets. However, they also decided the taste, style and subject of the films; they added a word to the dialogue between the producer and the civil servant; sometimes their taste agreed with that of the government official, sometimes it was the opposite. That is how the style of Hungarian films developed in the decade of *The Dream Car* (Meseautó).

The cinema-goer wanted Hungarian talkies because the film spoke in Hungarian. Had sound-films been introduced later, the depression in the silent 'twenties would have continued in Hungarian film production into the 'thirties. Three quarters of the Hungarian cinema audiences consisted of youth from sixteen to eighteen, workers seeking simple and inexpensive entertainment, soldiers having a day off, shop assistants, minor clerks, servants. These people did not like to read captions. The mere fact that a film could be made to speak the mother tongue decided the fate of Hungarian films.

The next issue was the subject-matter of the films. Cinema-goers voted for Hungarian talkies because they liked their stories. In the very first year it was definitely decided which trend Hungarian audiences chose of the two offered to them. Their choice is quite instructive, because at the moment of decision the progressive elements were more numerous than might be supposed from later films or from this whole period.

Just as in the autumn of 1912, now in the autumn of 1931 two Hungarian films competed for first place: *The Blue Idol* (A kék bálvány) and *Hyppolit the Butler* (Hyppolit a lakáj), the first two Hungarian talking pictures. The first, the shooting of which was started on April 29, 1931, when two cabinet ministers spoke to celebrate the event, was first shown on September 25, 1931, at the Royal Apollo. The film was an aftermath of the age of silent pictures, an atmosphere charged with passion, with the scene laid in aristocratic circles and an action which might have taken place in any fictitious film world. The scenario told of the adventures of a Hungarian nobleman in the U.S.A. and was based on a story by Adorján Bónyi, an editor and author who wrote entertaining stories on the life of the bourgeoisie in Budapest. The film was made by Lajos Lázár, one of the best-known and most experienced directors of the silent films. The money—one hundred and fifty thousand pengős!—was advanced by the tycoon Miksa Schiffer, while no less a personage than Count Géza Lipót Zichy, member of the Upper House, the *administrateur délégué,* assumed responsibility for the actual production, bringing together representatives of big capital and the aristocracy. The cast was good: Pál Jávor, an actor of twenty-nine, who had lately come to Budapest from the country, made his first screen appearance in it; other parts were played by the best actors of the silent film, Oszkár Beregi, Gyula Gózon, etc.

The Blue Idol was rejected by the public. However, another Hungarian film, *Hyppolit the Butler,* made with much less fanfare, and without ministers or any member of the Upper House, had the greater success. Its first night, held two months after that of *The Blue Idol,* on November 27, marked the beginning of a succession of successes in the following decade; its latest revivals in 1957 and 1966 brought undiminished success. *Hyppolit the Butler* was financed by Emil Kovács, in the business of film distribution since 1912. The scenario was written by István Zágon and Károly Nóti, and the film was directed by István Székely (Steve Sekely), a thirty-two-year-old former journalist and assistant-director who had returned after several years' apprenticeship in Berlin.

The sweeping success of this film determined the subject-matter and acting style of Hungarian sound-films for many years to come. The principal endeavour of Hungarian film production in the period between the two wars was to achieve at least one more success like that of *Hyppolit the Butler.*

Why did the film audience choose *Hyppolit?*

This film was a comedy and the spectator wished to laugh. He chose comedy rather than tragedy. This comedy was a typical local comedy, with turns of speech, scenes and characters typical of Budapest. A story borrowed from Molière's *Le Bourgeois Gentilhomme,* reduced to a simplified form—the blunders of newly rich imitating the nobility—to which the authors lent the colour of easily recognizable local elements. Not only did the film speak in Hungarian, but the action took place against familiar backgrounds. This created a veritable sensation, Óbuda pubs, shop-keepers and drivers having a game of cards: a familiar world. Not Hollywood, not Paris, but Óbuda. And the way these lower middle-class people talked while playing cards: genuine Budapest slang, Budapest humour. Suddenly the breath of Budapest had entered the cinema.

The characters deserve the closest inspection. The film-goer recognized his neighbours rather than himself. And this aroused the heartiest laughter. Moreover: this wealthy bourgeois was not even his neighbour, but his boss. Boss to half of the audience: to the shop assistant, the minor clerk, the servant, the unskilled worker, the mechanic. Now they could see this boss stumble about on the screen and speak Hungarian. This Hungarian *bourgeois gentilhomme* was filled with life by a brilliant actor, Gyula Kabos.

This upstart merchant has somehow made money and grown rich. Now he begins to live the life of the gentility, not for his own sake, but at his wife's command, to satisfy social conventions, for the sake of his marriageable daughter. As for himself, he likes comfort, to play cards and sit around with his friends, and he loathes tight clothes. He makes you laugh, but you can't help liking him. The cinema-goer laughed at Gyula Kabos as his boss, yet liked him; as if seeing himself fidgeting in his best Sunday clothes and bowler. Kabos winked at him from the screen, conveying to him not so much the thought of his wealth and the power of money, but giving him to understand that he, too, was human, that his most ardent wish was to be left alone. For the sake of peace he was capable of revolt. He rebelled and it was delightful to watch this revolt from a cinema seat. For the moment it was immaterial that it was a rich man who rebelled against the well-deserved cage he had built for himself. Kabos convinced his audience that here the chief point was revolt itself: to sit in the kitchen in his shirt-sleeves, eating roast beef with onions, dipping bread in the gravy and being rude to the finicking, refined butler who, from the moment that Kabos has winked at the audience, is transformed from a paid servant into a detestable gentleman who wrinkles his nose, the same unpleasant person whom the film-goer will later meet in the shop, or in the big flat as his master.

Thus the source of humour is twofold; the honey of laughter flows from two springs. We laugh at the newly rich upstart, but share his loathing for the moneyed world of those who wear bowlers and starched shirts. And see, the wife, the shrewish spouse, sides with the world of the bowlered; watch her well: she will come to grief and come off worse than her husband. She is worsted by the butler because she tries to conform to his standards and to adopt his manners. It is therefore agreeable to watch her blunders and humiliations. But how far inferior her simple interpretation is to the thousand colours and grimaces of Kabos when he speaks to his daughter; when he is intimidated by his wife; the way he shows his hatred for his butler—even Gyula Csortos, the great hero of tragedies, only played second fiddle to Kabos—and with what superior self-assurance he moves about in his own sphere. So Kabos triumphed. The cinema-goer accepted him, made a note of his name and was going to look for it in the cast of other films.

Though Csortos in the role of Hyppolit did not generalize the butler's characteristics, he nevertheless gave a shining caricature of official pomposity. Hyppolit enjoys his position in the house of the newly rich family, for what was normal in his earlier posts, has here become a miracle. There he was an attendant, in this new domain he rules. This petty reign, this glory of liveried power, shows the audience new perspectives and conveys the preposterousness of a state of affairs where film production is superintended by a Count. It is worthy of note that the story and the script meant the public to take the side of Hyppolit; cinema-goers should have laughed with Hyppolit, should have laughed from above at the petty bourgeois wishing to become rich, and thinking foolishly that money alone was enough to achieve rank and distinction. This is suggested also by the title. Even though enjoying the superior, distinguished and fine acting of Csortos, one cannot help feeling sympathy for the figure of Kabos and laughing heartily at the silly regulations dictated by the butler. This laugh is also the laugh of Molière who, while poking fun at Monsieur Jourdain, sympathized with the bourgeoisie, because that was where he belonged himself. This laugh was the sound of democracy.

All these are positive features to the film-goer's advantage; to the advantage of the audiences who have determined the subject and style of a film production in the making.

However, the film goes on. The dialogue between Hyppolit and the parvenu is interrupted ever more frequently by the cooing of young lovers. Pál Jávor appears on the screen, in his second part after *The Blue Idol;* he appears and conquers. Prince Charming in disguise: the handsome engineer falls in love with the newly rich girl; as a matter of fact he condescends to her but to make the situation more thrilling, he disguises himself as a workman. And here is the silly young lady giggling song hits, making dates, and spending papa's money. How nice to forget daily cares for a moment or two. An engineer in disguise, a pretty young girl. A pleasant world. With resigned elegance Gyula Gózon kisses the hand of Mici Erdélyi while giving up his place in the smartest possible style to Pál Jávor for the next fifteen years. Incidentally all this was imitation: gestures of Hollywood, cocktail parties, ravishing evening gowns, artificial eye-lashes. Hollywood knew much better how to carry off this sort of thing. However, there is no getting away from it: the audience positively liked it. Everyone liked the tall, dark and handsome young man who won hearts in the cinema on Sunday evening, making conquests that the cinema-goer had been long-ing for in vain in the past week. And the beautifully dressed charming young girl whose only concern is to make her choice among the eligible men who vie for her hand.

> The recipe had assumed its final shape:
> take people of the lower middle classes;
> in a Budapest milieu;
> let them tell good jokes;
> let them experience all the adventures
> that happen to the man in the street in Budapest;
> let it all end as people would like it to end,
> and not as it usually does.
> And the comedian should be Gyula Kabos.

Let there be in the film lovers who deserve a better fate, a handsome man and a pretty girl who overcome obstacles and difficulties while humm-ing songs that the radio has made popular.

These obstacles and difficulties should merely be indicated but not al-lowed to assume tragic proportions. Audiences wanted to see a comedy.

All the more so as the Film Industry Fund would not tolerate the pre-sentation of any picture with social content. The Film Industry Fund preferred and approved only the make-believe products of the dream factory, the serene, falsified world of a happy nation living in prosperity and coping with minor cares. Workman, peasant, even real middle-class people were to be kept off the screen.

Who was to write these stories, these scripts?

Those who wrote the script of *Hyppolit*.

The scripts of half of the Hungarian films produced in the 'thirties were thus written by or with the collaboration of Károly Nóti.

Who was to be the director of these pictures?

Why, of course, the man who directed the successful *Hyppolit*.

One quarter of the Hungarian films made in the 'thirties were therefore directed by Steve Sekely.

There was no escape: the well-proven success had to be copied, the businessman with a small capital wanted to be on the safe side. And the film-goer also liked to be sure of being entertained just as he was last Saturday or Sunday. So the promptly launched production of talking pictures soon adopted a uniform pattern, leading to the development of a style characteristic of Hungarian films in the 'thirties.

It is interesting that Steve Sekely stated it as his opinion that it was the avowedly Budapest character of the film, the home environment, that attracted the audiences. Yet he thought it undesirable to concentrate Hungarian film industry on this one kind of merchandise, because such a course might lead to overproduction and bankruptcy.[6]

Only an independent film studio carrying on uninterrupted production after a programme of its own might have undertaken to make pictures of a different kind for the education and guidance of the public. A precedent for this was the Corvin or Star Studio between 1910–1920. But no such studio existed in 1931.

The sixteen films made in 1931–1933 were produced by ten concerns. In these three years there were altogether four companies that were willing to shoot two films each. After *Hyppolit the Butler* Emil Kovács made another picture, *A Night in Venice* (Egy éj Velencében). In 1932 the Paris company Osso shot two films, *Flying Gold* (Repülő arany) and *Spring Shower* (Tavaszi zápor). Phöbus, with a manager who called himself Berci Fodor, was a well-established old firm that distributed films, as did the producer of *Hyppolit*; the films of Phöbus were *The Verdict of Lake Balaton* (Ítél a Balaton) and *Piri Knows Everything* (Piri mindent tud).

City Studios alone made an attempt to carry out a more extensive programme of film production. City Studios was founded by a stockbroker, Sándor Winter, in 1933. The moment appeared to be auspicious, for sound-film production had been pursued with some regularity for over two years in Hungary, and of the eight films made in this time some—such as *Hyppolit the Butler*—had had success; the world economic crisis was being overcome. Only comedy appealed to the public. The French company Osso had lost interest in the Hungarian market altogether after the failure of *Spring Shower*, though it had been made by Paul Fejős, an internationally known director brought home from the United States for this film.

So Sándor Winter bought the Hungarian interests of Osso, acquired credit, and founded the firm City Studios. He went to work very tentatively, producing inexpensive and very safe films, feeling his way cautiously. *The Ghost Train* (A kísértetek vonata) was really hardly more than an imported film, bought by Winter for a song, then synchronized, recut and completed with a series of additional shots. As Andor Lajta writes: "Originally the film was made in London in English, but at the cost of a few hundred metres of additional film, Lajos Lázár converted it into an entirely new Hungarian talkie."[7] (*The Ghost Train,* 1931, directed by Walter Forde for Gainsborough from a stage-comedy thriller by Arnold Ridley, starred the British actress Anna Todd, in one of her first appearances on the screen.) The second attempt, *Kneel to Women* (Mindent a nőért), was shot in Hungary; this was a series of three comedy episodes. This form was used as a measure of precaution: if the whole film failed, the three short films could be presented separately. The titles of the three parts reveal the nature of the whole scheme: *Night in the Pharmacy* (Éjjel a patikában), *Bull of the Pampas* (A pampák bikája), *Love is Everything* (Jaj de jó szeretni).

The first full-length City Studios production was *Aunt Iza* (Iza néni). The box-office draw of this film was to be the star Sári Fedák and a nationalist evocation of the good old times. The script was, or was alleged to have been, written by Sári Fedák herself. The film had a moderate success: in the capital it failed, in the country it was liked. Reviews proved how astutely Sándor Winter had gauged the situation. Even *Filmújság,* a very outspoken and aggressive periodical, did not dare to deal harshly with a film which enjoyed official support owing to its political leaning.

The next picture of City Studios made such a "hit" that the firm was almost justified in looking upon itself as nearly the first and most serious Hungarian film company. In November 1933 *The Rákóczi March* (Rákóczi-induló) was presented, with resounding success. Two large theatres vied for the right to present the film. The first night, raised to a gala evening, was attended by Miklós Horthy himself.

The screen version of Ferenc Herczeg's work at Kolozsvár in the era of silent films, *The Daughter of the Nabob of Dolova* (A dolovai nábob lánya), directed by Jenő Janovics, became a veritable vocabulary of film policy in the Horthy period: handsome hussars, Hungarian military bravado, rides, duels, revelries, women, serenades, happy old peaceful times in Hungary before the Treaty of Trianon, swimming in a haze of rosy clouds, giddy with champagne. The name of Ferenc Herczeg vouched for the literary subject. The direction of Steve Sekely guaranteed public enjoyment, the incidental music of Pál Ábrahám, a congenial atmosphere. Compared to other films made after 1931, the cast was magnificent, starring Pál Jávor, Ferenc Kiss, Gyula Csortos (who had played also in the silent film version of 1916), Oszkár Beregi, Gyula Gózon, Ida Turay, Margit Dayka, Tibor Halmai. City Studios closed the year with the triumph of *The Rákóczi March.*

Four films were produced in 1933 (one-third of the Hungarian talkies made by then) and one of the four, *The Rákóczi March,* captivated the village notaries, landowners, civil servants and the middle classes in general in addition to the lower middle classes won over by *Hyppolit.* Though *The Rákóczi March* with its openly reactionary spirit was a backward step after the modest bourgeois virtues of *Hyppolit the Butler,* there can be no doubt that City Studios had done their business shrewdly.

A sober and circumspect businessman now would have waited, kept his eyes open, gathered strength and capital while these films were running in the several hundred Hungarian cinemas. It would have been all the more reasonable to sit back and wait since by 1934 only about half (207) of the over four hundred Hungarian cinemas were equipped for sound-films.[8] These 207 cinemas were unable to market the film crop produced by any Hungarian studio working on a grand scale, in addition to presenting a large number of foreign pictures.

City Studios nevertheless continued to produce at the old rate and full capacity, relying on former success, especially on foreign markets. Winter hoped to create a demand in Austria, Germany and Great Britain. Therefore he made two more films in quick succession in 1934, one for home consumption, the other for foreign markets in two versions, in Hungarian and German. The screen version of the play of László Bus Fekete, which was having enormous success in the Hungarian Theatre, *Cornflower* (Búzavirág), was intended for Hungarian audiences (starring Antal Páger, Irén Ágai, Márton Rátkai and Kálmán Rózsahegyi, directed by Steve Sekely); a screen version of Pál Ábrahám's operetta, *Ball at the Savoy* (Bál a Savoyban), the first Hungarian variety musical, was to be launched on the foreign market.

But abroad the project failed. Winter did not succeed in selling the film in England, and negotiations in Germany also took a long time. In the meantime the banks gave notice and recalled their capital, demanding cash payment, whereupon City Studios went bankrupt in a few days. Hints in *Filmújság* as well as hasty financial manipulations at home during Winter's trip abroad suggest that some hostile competitor may have started rumours hoping to stir up trouble by prying into excessive and perhaps wasteful investments, and City Studios may have been ruined by a well-organized plot. At all events the fact is that a host of creditors, from the fruit dealer to the tobacconist, all started to claim their money, from amounts of ten pengős to sums of several thousand pengős.[9]

As a matter of fact, *Ball at the Savoy* was by no means inferior to the average product of the period.

Steve Sekely, this versatile craftsman, who may have served his masters
with too much modesty and alacrity, showed wit and a good grasp of the
lessons to be learnt from the first German and American revues in basing
his film on the music of Ábrahám, the voice of Gitta Alpár, the wry humour
of Felix Bressart, and on the good looks of Hans Járay. As the only Hungarian revue film for a long time to come, *Ball at the Savoy* deserves a certain
attention. All the more so as with the spectacular failure of City Studios
the revue form itself failed and no one dared to revive it, perhaps because
it was this genre that had terminated the activities of City Studios. In the
relatively small but well-designed studio of Hunnia the sets of Márton
Vincze—who was to die of an injury sustained during work in 1939—provided a favourable background to the group of ballet-dancers and the appearance of Gitta Alpár. It is noteworthy that Sekely paid little heed to the
depiction of character or the thread of the action, conveying thereby his
intention to offer no more than variété. The foolish story of the film thus
differs from those of other films of the period by being merely suggested—as
are also the sets and the hotel built up in the studio.

By the year 1934 we thus had already a bankrupt firm, and this failure,
together with the bitter experience of Osso, marked the further path of
development to be followed by the Hungarian film industry and its art. The
kind of Hungarian talking pictures to which people like to refer as the "old,
pre-war" Hungarian films, actually took shape in 1934. In this instance more
blame must go to the petty-bourgeois middle-class film-goer than to the
producer who put out his product and left the choice to the buyer or the
creditor.

It is remarkable that in the years between 1931 and 1934 the film industry
had a wider range of goods to sell than there were customers to buy. It offered comedy in the silent film style *(The Blue Idol)*; lower middle-class
comedy with some realism in representing social conditions *(Hyppolit the
Butler)*; a realistic film which endeavoured to depict Hungarian peasant
life in a credible though stylized manner *(Spring Shower)*; a nationalist
picture *(Aunt Iza)*; the screen version of a play valued as a classic in Hungarian literature *(Wine)*; the hussar world of the good old days
(The Rákóczi March); the revue *(Ball at the Savoy)*; the screen version of
a mediocre but successful play *(Cornflower)* and so on. Even a popular
writer of melodramatic scripts expected a deeper experience from the film
than did the cinema-goer, as shown by the article of István Mihály on film
stories: "In choosing film themes today the Russians have shown the best
road... Their theory, brilliantly confirmed by practice, is worthy of par-

ticular interest in connection with the Hungarian pictures to be produced in coming years."[10]

It is strange and sad that of the above-mentioned strongly mercenary trends, certainly the lower middle-class comedy was the most progressive and the most valuable, though we still have to fight against its sentimental tricks and false attitude to life, for they still recur as living mementoes of old and reprehensible traditions.

In 1934 there was only one film which ventured to join in the experiment of looking for new paths and—failed. It was *Purple Acacia* (Lila akác), made by Manó Guttmann's old film-distributing firm, Pátria, under the direction of Steve Sekely. Sekely himself spoke of this picture as his favourite work in 1938 when he looked back upon his career at home in a melancholy statement of farewell to journalists upon his departure to fulfil a contract in Hollywood.

Upon closer inspection of *Purple Acacia* and the two films shot by City Studios in 1934, together with the first Hungarian talkies, it is found that every film of progressive aspirations with a claim to a relatively artistic treatment of its subject was doomed to failure.

The most discouraging fiasco was experienced in connection with the most exacting task, one of the finest pictures in the history of Hungarian films, *Spring Shower* (Tavaszi zápor).

In the mid-twenties Paul Fejős had emigrated to the United States under adventurous circumstances; by the late twenties his modest films *The Last Moment* and *Lonesome* had given him the opportunity to make large-scale films, including European versions of important early sound-films (such as *The Big House*) and, at the invitation of the Paris firm Osso, he came home to direct two films. Fejős knew exactly what he wanted to achieve. He chose a popular legend which, in his opinion, was Hungarian while having universal appeal. The author of the screenplay was Ilona Fülöp, one of the most important Hungarian writers in the USA. She had been living in the States since 1913, and published novels (*The Child of Storm,* 1918; *American Village,* 1919), poems, essays. She died in Hollywood in 1953, whilst employed as a continuity girl. As the legend has it, in old times the unwedded mothers of young girls besought heaven for heavy showers to drive away unwanted would-be lovers and spare their daughters from shame. Ethnographically this is not a typical Hungarian legend; the background lacks characteristic traits, evoking a studio atmosphere, and is over-accentuated by spurious "Hungarian folk costumes". The film exposes, however, the bailiff, the landlord's farm overseer, effectively and with great artistic power, showing this figure—hitherto unassailable in Hungarian films—in his true character, as an exploiter of the people. The film represents the peasant girl driven by her shame from the village into the town, into a brothel, where the prostitutes show more kindness on her than had the richer peasants of her village. "It is not true that the people of a Hungarian village disown a girl who let herself be seduced, that people with sympathy and understanding can be found in Hungary only among the patrons of disreputable cafés, and it is untrue that the state ruthlessly tears away the baby from its mother's breast to take it to an orphanage," remonstrated the critic of the *Budapesti Hírlap* in the November 5, 1932, issue; this vexed defence itself bears witness to the virtues of the film. Fejős's severe criticism of society was motivated by his own earlier experience of village life.

Spring Shower was the only Hungarian film that not only carried on the finest tradition of Hungarian silent films, but actually tried—and that on the eve of the accession of German fascism to power—to continue in the spirit of Hungarian film art inspired by 1919 which, among other factors, had started Paul Fejős, though indirectly, on his career. Fejős had appeared on the scene as a stage designer at the time of the Republic of Councils. The militant though occasionally naive romanticism, the revolutionary verve, the clever stylization and symbolism, the cruel social criticism yet somewhat over-simplified story which were as characteristic of the over thirty films made under the Republic of Councils as the animated debates of the time, reappeared in *Spring Shower*.

Fejős applied montage, the value of which had been proved by Eisenstein and his associates: little text, more extensive use of sound, symbolical allusions by series of parallel and contrasting pictures, carefully composed sets, slightly stylized acting based on effects accentuated by the interplay of light and shadow. This delicate style, this omission of words—there is no audible dialogue in the film—contributed to failure, though Annabella convinced the audience that she was a Hungarian peasant girl who had got into trouble, and wore the gaudy, imitation-national costume naturally and gracefully. The acting of the rest of the cast was full of subtle nuances and more thoughtful than was usual in Hungarian films. István Gyergyai, Ilona Dajbukát, Erzsi Bársony, Margit Ladomerszky and Gyula Gózon played the supporting parts.

It was only abroad that the director's endeavour to tell the world about Hungary elicited spontaneous response. In the international history of film *Spring Shower* (it was shown abroad as *Marie*) has been given a better place than at home, where it was received in a sly silence.

The other film made by Fejős in Hungary, *The Verdict of Lake Balaton* (Ítél a Balaton), has been lost. The choice of its theme may have been induced by similar motifs as in the case of *Spring Shower*: a drama reflecting the lives of fishermen on Lake Balaton. It was with this picture that the film career of Antal Páger began; the cameraman was István Eiben. "This film has astonished everybody by its brilliant technical execution. Particularly the scenes taken in storm are striking, any director may be proud of them. The photography is excellent," says a contemporary critic in his review and then proceeds to censure the film for too much revelry, dancing, gipsy music, shirts with very wide sleeves (worn formerly by peasants and herdsmen), and for its romantic, far-fetched story.[11]

The failure of *Spring Shower* and *The Verdict of Lake Balaton* not only sounded the knell of a homogeneous artistic trend; it also discouraged Hungarian directors who had contracts abroad when they felt inclined to come home. Indeed, Fejős was received at home like the prophet who, while respected elsewhere, is rejected in his own country. The Hungarian film world made no secret of its gloating over the fate of Fejős's films; self-important, pompous criticism and protests of "I told you so" were the order of the day. The only director who had dared to come back to Hungary was as good as driven away, and the slogan of *extra Hungariam non est vita* was again in full force.

Two more experiments have to be mentioned, both of which foundered hopelessly. István György, a director who had worked in the "popular-national" line in the last years of the silent film, made a film version of *Wine* (A bor), a play by Géza Gárdonyi. In connection with this venture the most remarkable point is that the director went to a rural district to shoot the picture, employing provincial actors and actresses (with Pál Jávor and Kálmán Rózsahegyi in the leading roles). Notwithstanding compliance with the false nationalistic tone and philosophy of the age, György endeavoured to give art in his own way, according to his own lights, and strove to depict the reality of Hungarian village life. This attempt, which drew on the traditions of the silent film, failed. For many years to come only a few reviews referred to it.

When he made a screen version of Ernő Szép's *Purple Acacia*, Steve Sekely had the ambition to produce a literary film. He gave an honest and courageous criticism of the "good old days" which had been praised indiscriminately in *The Rákóczi March*. In this instance a real peace-time atmosphere emanates from the screen peopled with the stupid little prostitute of the park who unwittingly finds herself in the clutches of cunning white slavers; the flirtatious married lady choosing her beaux carefully and using her financial independence to live a life of leisure and frivolous love affairs; the bank clerk with a small salary thinking himself generous while members of the upper class make a fool of him.

Sekely gave his audience to understand that the sentimentalism of these stories was not to be taken seriously, only their lyrical element. He laughed with them at the emotional crises of his heroes and heroines, and counterbalanced every touching turn of events with an anticlimax amounting to a grimace, one directed against contemporary society. Irén Ágai's performance was delicate. Acting, even in her case, was nevertheless allowed to retain a theatrical character as a result of which it was felt to be slightly affected; the actors could almost be detected giving one another their cues. Even so this film was a fine poetical work. It is an exceedingly rare event in the international history of films that Sekely, the director of the first version, was asked to direct the remake of *Purple Acacia* in 1972 in Budapest. This commission was a gesture of homage on the part of the Hungarian film industry to the 73-year-old Hungarian director living in Hollywood.

A Ride
in the
Dream Car

On December 14, 1934, the twenty-fifth Hungarian sound-film was presented at the Forum Cinema by a newly founded distributing company, under the title of *The Dream Car* (Meseautó).

The new firm undertook to present a Hungarian film as a duty, as did similar other firms: in two years this firm had put on the market so many imported films that it seemed worth while to risk the production of a new picture instead of playing one thousand pengős per film. Mrs. Miklós Vitéz, secretary of Metro's Budapest office, set herself up in the industry and, having good business relations, she founded the firm named Reflektor. The plot of the firm's first Hungarian film was the idea of her husband, Miklós Vitéz, a dramatist, friend of Frigyes Karinthy; the script was written by László Vadnai, the author of several successful film comedies *(Kiss Me, Darling)*.

The cautious producer did not engage the services of the fashionable

Sekely, but chose Béla Gaál to direct the film, though he had a less successful record. At the time Béla Gaál taught at a private dramatic school, and
he put one of his pupils, Kláry Tolnay, under contract to play in the unassuming little film. Jenő Törzs, the exceedingly popular and justly celebrated
hero of numerous silent films, was to be the leading man, while the female
lead went to a completely unknown young actress, Zita Perczel. To have
another good name in the cast besides Jenő Törzs, Gyula Kabos, who had
become indispensable since *Hyppolit,* was also given a part.

The film was also to contain a hit song, so Alfréd Márkus, a popular
composer, was commissioned to produce one. The music of the song was
encouraging and the words deserve full quotation:

In a dream car
We slip past the silver trees,
Hearts ablaze in the springtime breeze.
From heaven the angels watch us, and from afar
His hands on the wheel, Destiny steers our car...
Stark reality will laugh at us tomorrow.
But in a dream car, today,
We rush on, slipping past silver trees,
Our hearts abloom in the morning breeze!

It seemed lucky that the *première* was in December when any fairly
successful Hungarian film could have a run of two weeks. But hardly ever
longer than that. It was under such conditions that the day came for the
first night of *The Dream Car.* The film had an incredible success. It remained
on the programme of the first run cinema for many weeks and was played
for years throughout the country.

The firm Reflektor had found the key to success: popular lower middle-
class comedy was mixed with the sentimentalism of Hollywood career
stories, lending an air of touching drama; from films on hussars teeming
with handsome, valiant peace-time officers it adopted the calm superiority
of the ruling classes, of the wealthy, the pleasant world of general managers
floating in Olympian serenity above the heads of the whirling multitudes
of cinema-goers "happening by some stroke of fortune to be having a hard
time owing to a transient spell of bad luck," a dream world where any typist
may conquer.

"Stark reality will laugh at us tomorrow," ran the words of the song;
but the cinema-goer, though aware of the truth in these words, did not
mind in the cinema, in the darkened auditorium, but watched with pleasure

the adventure of Prince Charming, modernized to appear as a general manager, in pursuit of his Cinderella.

For the story was a variant of the Cinderella theme which, in the course of time, has been put before the public in more than a thousand versions. The penniless typist gets to know a gay Lothario of a general manager who is on the point of buying the latest marvel in motor-cars. Having pretended to be the chauffeur—see Pál Jávor in *Hyppolit the Butler*—the manager is happy to be liked for himself. Still pretending to be the chauffeur, he elopes with the pretty young lady to Lillafüred, a place very highly praised in many other films about Hungarian high life. Misunderstandings; the impecunious young girl is offended by the advances of a rich man, but the chief accountant settles everything. There is a wedding. Fate has taken hold of the steering-wheel, and in heaven the angels watch over the democratic union.

Cinderella has always proved a successful figure, but when this theme was coupled with distinguished acting and sprinkled with some irony—as in the case of Jenő Törzs—and the earlier type of wide-eyed innocence is replaced by a delightful young woman who, far from being naive and inexperienced, is quite adult and mature, even a flirt, who likes to get into motor-cars but can always take good care of herself—played by Zita Perczel—this theme was readily accepted even by middle-class cinema-goers who claimed to have a preference for films of a superior standard.

Moreover, the whole idyll was made somewhat less than idyllic by the Hungarian type of city turned gentleman, introduced in *Hyppolit,* who appeared in this instance as the chief accountant whose very clumsiness, awkward courting, but excellent flair for business invested the screen with the colour of reality that was Budapest itself. This strange character, tailored to fit the personality of Gyula Kabos, is the real value of this inane imitation of Hollywood films. All that is connected with Kabos, the dull office atmosphere emitting a stale, sour smell, with the rubber stamps, the oversleeves, the Sunday excursion to Zugliget, belongs to the reality of Budapest which may be lower middle-class but is nevertheless healthier and more realistic than the world of the general manager.

Here the cinema-goer saw himself at the swimming-pool, in the park, on the hills surrounding Budapest, in fact in every place where the camera followed Kabos. And Béla Gaál's camera, having escaped from the studio into reality, shot scenes more interesting than those of the lovesick general manager sighing on the studio set. The idea of this fascinating montage of Sunday as it was spent by the man in the street could have come to Béla Gaál from the German film of 1928, *Menschen am Sonntag.*

By showing Budapest in this way, Béla Gaál emphasized that the action was taking place here and in no other city. No hope of placing the film on the international market anyway. The film-goer, on the other hand, was glad to see the Danube embankment, the Chain and Elizabeth Bridges on the screen. It was in this café at the corner on the Danube embankment that the neighbouring grocer usually had his breakfast, and the man scribbling away at the other desk, Gyula Kabos, was familiar to young and old in every quiver of his eyelids, every gesture of his hands, and in every remark he made. The energetic, fat secretary, Ella Gombaszögi, was his worthy partner with her funny blinking and her worried, fussy pedantry. It is in the dialogue of these two that Vadnai was really brilliant: their jokes and arguments are still alive, quite apart from the film.

It is interesting that the scenes of Kabos and Gombaszögi were a sort of peculiar *pas de deux* with their own special flavour and special rules, with a life independent of the plot. These two talk in a corner of a cheaply furnished office: a writing table, a door, a filing cabinet. The camera did not even take the trouble to shift from one to the other: they talk in a pleasant semi-close up (or American close-up as it was referred to at the time), as if the spectator had been sitting quite close to the stage of an intimate cabaret. They scarcely exist apart from each other; the fun recommences with flashes of humour when they resume their endless dialogue; when Kabos has to go to the country, in this instance to Lillafüred, he rings up Ella Gombaszögi, and the dialogue is continued on the pretext of telephoning. Of course, the more important party is Kabos; but even when he obviously performs a monologue, with hardly any text, he must have his partner.

The extraordinary success of the film had a fatal effect on the Hungarian cinema. Everybody wanted to produce, to direct, to see such films, in the hope of sure success and first-class entertainment. From this time, almost every Hungarian film made in the second half of the decade contained motifs of *The Dream Car*. Kabos as a half-witted clerk, lawyer, employee; Gombaszögi, his energetic, stout partner; handsome general manager, landowner, or hussar; a penniless pretty young girl; a hit song hummed in an intimate corner of a Budapest night-club; the jovial policeman as he watches over his charges, with an indulgent smile, in the name of the state. The producer bought the story ready-made: the only thing required of him was to present the story with the greatest possible ingenuity at the lowest possible cost.

It is now clear that the first decade of the Hungarian sound-film bore the stamp of *The Dream Car*. Even British Gaumont remade it in August 1935 with the title of *Car of My Dreams*.

Every work of art is a mirror of the society by which it is produced, appreciated, or rejected. The Hungarian public of the 'thirties sometimes enjoyed, sometimes rejected Hungarian films, but at all events cultivated them. In the first eight years of its life the Hungarian sound-film represented and interpreted society; of course involuntarily and virtually in its wishful aspirations. These old Hungarian talkies conjured up pictures of the ruling classes and the petty bourgeoisie as they longed to see themselves, their past, present, and future. Images of their desires.

In the period between May, 1931, and December, 1938, 132 full-length Hungarian feature films were produced in Hungary. These screenplays included 98 comedies, 96 of which were set in contemporary Hungary. In 75 per cent of these, the action took place chiefly in Budapest. The great majority of the comedies were adapted from novels or plays. Of the 132 films, 88 were based on a novel or short story, 54 were screen versions of contemporary plays. There were only 44 original film scripts, 34 of them comedies. In fact, it was the Hungarian stage which became the life-giving spring of the Hungarian film; all that film-makers actually did was to reproduce on celluloid plays which had proved to be hits before audiences of several ten-thousands of theatre-goers, that hundreds of thousands or even millions might buy tickets for the cinema.

Hence *the great majority of films were screen versions of successful stage comedies, with the scene set in Hungary, principally in Budapest.*

Who were the heroes of these films?

In the first place, men. Women were only necessary concomitant complements. Ninety per cent of these men were gentlemen, members of the ruling classes; only ten per cent represented the "people", but even these were rich farmers. In none of the Hungarian films from the period under review does a workman, a poor peasant, a cotter or even a craftsman appear as the hero. The majority of the gentlemen are landowners, aristocrats, officers—in 39 cases; in most instances the officer is also a landowner and vica versa; men possessing landed estates are almost invariably aristocrats. Manufacturers, managing directors, bankers as heroes are much fewer, occurring only in 17 films. In 34 films the hero belongs to the so-called middle-class intelligentsia: an engineer, teacher, or lawyer who has also come into landed property or is related to the aristocracy. Artists, such as writers, composers, painters or actors number no more than ten. It is striking and characteristic that none of the heroes is a merchant (however wealthy!). Therefore it is clear who and what the ideal was: a landowner who is a regular or reserve officer, preferably a baron, if not of higher rank. It is simply unprecedented in the film industries of other countries to declare so peremptorily the clear-cut provoking declaration: we certainly *are* a "feudal" country, and that in the third decade of the twentieth century. In several films this statement is loudly proclaimed in words, boasting-bragging of the backwardness of the Hungarian social order (*The Old Rogue* – Vén gazember, *The Rákóczi March* – Rákóczi-induló, etc.). The strange fact has to be emphasized again that no merchant, tradesman, agent or businessman, typical representatives, of capitalist society, ever appeared as the hero of a screenplay.

In 63 out of the 132 films—that is in nearly 50 per cent—the leads were played by only three actors: Pál Jávor, Antal Páger, or Imre Rádai. They personified ideal manhood. Curiously enough, the favoured type of leading lady emerged much later, while the principal male stars the public was to fall for were established by the first few talkies. From *The Blue Idol* (A kék bál-vány) Pál Jávor played a landed-gentry-officer in 28 films, a member of the middle-class intelligentsia, engineer or lawyer, in nine; a painter in one film, a rich peasant in two, an acrobat performing in a circus in one, and in one instance a young woodcutter. Jávor never played the managing director of a factory, an industrial magnate or a banker; he was gentry to the core, even when he appeared in the role of an unemployed engineer-inventor (*The Chairman's Daughter,* Az elnökkisasszony), or as a lawyer.

From January 1932, Antal Páger could be seen in as many films as Jávor, but he was given the leading part only in 21; Pál Jávor alone was granted the privilege of appearing only in starring roles; the rest, including Páger as well as Rádai, had to be content now and then with subordinate, comic parts. Antal Páger—being a better actor than Jávor but not so much the ideal hero incarnate—was cast not only as a gentleman; it was only in seven leads that he played a landowner or officer, in five the director of a bank or a manufacturer. In five he came from the middle-class intelligentsia, in other films he was an actor, a tramp, or a jack-of-all-trades.

In his 14 leading parts—apart from comic secondary characters in 3 other films—Imre Rádai played a gentleman in 12 films, whether a general manager, a landowner or an engineer, an engaging habitué of night-clubs or a charming bohemian who was to abandon the primrose path under the influence of an earnest wife and an exacting, responsible job (perhaps after having cleared the affairs of his estate or come into a legacy). He was the jolly good fellow who inspired cinema-goers with feelings of indulgence for the promising offspring of landowners, so they forgave him his weaknesses in the pious hope that the hero would sow his wild oats and settle down in time.

It is interesting that the social picture of heroines is slightly more varied than that of heroes; interesting but not peculiar, for it fits into the pattern. Actually "only" 70 per cent of heroines were kept ladies, such as daughters of landowners, wives of engineers or physicians, etc., and 30 per cent earned their living, mostly as actresses or typists; however, they were bread-winners only until they contrived to catch a husband. A girl rarely took a job just to make a living, more often she became secretary to the boss in the hope of marrying him. But even so it is a fact that among heroines there was a maid-servant (for which reason Paul Fejős's *Spring Shower* [Tavaszi zápor] was boycotted), a photographer in the amusement park (*Keep Smiling* [Barátságos arcot kérek], the script by Frigyes Karinthy), a waitress, a charwoman in a shop, even a factory hand (the daughter of an impoverished civil servant). Lajos Zilahy's script was based on his own play *A Girl Sets Out* (Egy lány elindul).

On the other hand, it is remarkable that in this eight-year period of the Hungarian sound-film none of the actresses aroused such general admiration as did the trio of ideal heroes, Jávor, Páger and Rádai. As a matter of fact, in the same number of films in which the lead was shared by 3 actors, 9 actresses were cast as leading ladies. Irén Ágai came out top, but her 11 leads fell far behind the 14 heroes played even by Rádai. Ida Turai came next with 9, Margit Dayka and Klári Tolnay with 8, Zita Szeleczky and Éva Szörényi with 7, while only 6 leading roles went to Mária Lázár, Rózsi Bársony and Zita Perczel respectively.

Apparently, the public were unable to agree regarding the ideal type of woman. None of the actresses represented the female ideal cherished at the time by Hungarian society in general: the diligent house-wife and "Hungarian mother" who accepts her defencelessness with good grace.

Who were the authors of these films? There can be no doubt that in our case the *screenplay writers* have to be regarded as the authors. Indeed, praise is due to the script writers for having invented such varied turns of events set off by colourful scenic ideas and for having created such opportunities for actors and actresses to display their talents despite the existing, strictly limited possibilities, under *a priori* fixed conditions, and confined by restrictive rules. The script writer was second only to the actors, also because he was commissioned long before the director. By the time the approved script was handed over to the director, everything was ready, and in most instances the cast had also been selected.

Who were these writers?

Sixty films—45 per cent—were written by seven men: Károly Nóti, István

Mihály, László Vadnai, István Békeffi, Ottó Indig, Miklós Vitéz, and Miklós Lőrincz. Three of them collaborated in writing the scripts of more than ten films; they were the decisive personalities: *Károly Nóti, István Mihály,* and *László Vadnai.*

All wrote for small theatres, entertainers and cabarets; they were quick and clever in their vivid reactions to the events of political and social life, judging feudal Hungary with the eyes of the bourgeois longing for progress. Hardly any of their works appeared in print; in youthful years all had tried their hands at "highbrow" literature, but they soon gave up these experiments. In contemporary literary life no one took any notice of them. Plays and librettos of all the seven had long runs and resounding success on the stage in Hungary, even on Broadway, and a few of their scenarios were bought by Hollywood.

The 132 films in question were made by 31 directors; however, 101, i.e. about 80 per cent of the whole crop were directed by ten men: István Székely (Steve Sekely), Béla Gaál, Ladislas Vajda, Viktor Gertler, István György, Béla Balogh, Emil Martonffy, Ákos Ráthonyi, János Vaszary, and Márton Keleti. Forty-four films, i.e. one-third of the total

Directors and Works

(33 per cent) were directed by Steve Sekely (24 films) and Béla Gaál (20 films). Of the other 21 only Paul Fejős, Artúr Bárdos, Géza Bolváry and László Kardos made films which were to survive.

Where did these directors come from?

Sekely, a young, successful film expert, returned from Berlin to Budapest, having signed a contract to direct *Hyppolit the Butler* (Hyppolit a lakáj). (Before *Hyppolit* Sekely had directed some German films and had also worked as the Paris correspondent of several high-class German newspapers.) In commissioning Sekely it must have been decisive that he had directed successful films before, that he was young and therefore did not expect to be paid enormous fees, and, last but not least, he could speak Hungarian. At the time only directors active in Germany could be taken into consideration, since the men available at home had no experience in making sound-films; moreover, preferably the film was to be produced in two versions, in Hungarian and in German, which promised better chances of high returns.

Of Hungarian directors Béla Gaál—who had made silent films from the early 'twenties and was the head of a motion-picture training school—was the first to make his way, but not easily. For two years, in 1932–33, he made so-called skits, sometime in collaboration with others. It was only after he had been "apprenticed" to Steve Sekely and worked as his assistant that Béla Gaál received his first commission to direct a film in 1934, *The New Relation* (Az új rokon), to make his career with *The Dream Car* (Mese-autó), shot in the same year, and rise to the position of the second most important director, ranking after Sekely.

Compared to the two masters, the others made much fewer films at far longer intervals. Having returned from Berlin, where he had worked as a cutter, Viktor Gertler began to make films in the summer of 1933 at the State Documentary Studio which was not yet equipped for the production of screenplays. After the flop of his film which he completed at the Hunnia Studios *Stolen Wednesday* (Ellopott szerda), Gertler did not receive his next assignment, *Sister Mary* (Mária nővér), until November 1936. This hit, however, brought further commissions to direct another seven films in quick succession.

István György, a moderately gifted director and cutter of silent films, with his seven screenplays, produced from 1933, and Béla Balogh, who had to wait upon his return from Berlin until the summer of 1935 when he was finally given an opportunity to start work on what was to total seven films (though he had directed Hungarian silent films from the year 1916), did not come anywhere near the two past masters, Sekely and Gaál, in numbers, which in terms of producers implies that the latter had much less confidence in their abilities.

Ladislas Vajda jun., son of the eminent script writer and drama critic, directed ten films in Hungary in the period between 1935 and 1938, yet never permanently settled in the country. Working in England and France, he came home for a month or two to shoot a film and never appeared at the first night of any of his films, because at the time of the première he was always engaged in some other part of the world.

Of these directors Steve Sekely, Ladislas Vajda and Béla Balogh seem to have been the most original artists. It is interesting—and can hardly have been by mere chance—that all three were relatively progressive-minded directors, who, with due regard to the rules of bourgeois decency, gave expression to their censure of Hungary for flaunting her feudal leanings.

Café Moscow (Café Moszkva)
After nearly a year of inactivity, Sekely set to work in autumn, 1935; in the modernized premises of the State Documentary Studios he directed István Tamás's original screenplay, *Café Moscow* (Café Moszkva), the first wartime film. A serious theme. It did not glorify war, representing the sufferings of

A Few Valuable Films

Russian and Hungarian soldiers alike. It showed how war distorts human character and undermines virtues, how it prevents and destroys happiness. The writer, István Tamás, was a remarkable personality: known for his childrens' books, reminiscent of Erich Kästner, and by his translations of Franz Werfel and Hans Fallada, he was regarded as a noteworthy young author, perhaps the first "real" author who came forward with a script. He was interested in films; in the 'twenties he acted as an assistant in Paris, after emigrating he worked for American film companies from 1939 onwards.

The story of *Café Moscow* is as follows: the Austro-Hungarian army occupies a small Russian town from which the wife of the Russian czarist general Suharov and his aide-de-camp have failed to escape. The woman fends for herself by singing at a night-club; with the intention of slipping across the front line she tries to attract a Hungarian officer who, however, takes no notice of her though he invites her for a meal. The tables are rapidly turned: the Russian army recaptures the town; this time it is Lieutenant Szilágyi, the host of the general's wife, who is left behind. The Hungarian officers are caught while they are concocting a daring plan to escape. It is now the turn of the general's wife to help the Hungarian officer. This story, illustrating and condemning war for playing senseless havoc with private lives, is coloured by conflicts of jealousy in the eternal triangle of the Russian general (Gyula Csortos), a passionate gambler enthralled by roulette, the pleasure-loving wife, a flirt (Anna Tőkés), and Baklyushin, the aide-de-camp (Ferenc Kiss). The acting is splendid: Csortos is excellent as the Russian czarist general, ceaselessly fingering his pocket-size roulette, while concealing his anxieties with an iron self-control behind a mien of forced calm. His performance brings it home that he is already aware that not only the war is lost, but a whole class; the Russian aristocracy is to be swept from the scene of history, virtually within a few minutes' time.

Affair of Honour (Lovagias ügy)

The film criticizes the lower middle-class of Budapest. The petty-bourgeois hero of this film has to suffer more concrete grievances from Hungarian society than does Hyppolit. The character is played by Gyula Kabos.

Of course, for financial success the film relied not on its vague social criticism, but rather on László Vadnai's humorous quips and on Kabos's ability to present them effectively.

Kabos plays a respectable lower middle-class book-keeper working for a respectable firm. In a moment of rashness he manhandles his boss's relative, a frivolous young man who has offended him on several occasions. The outcome is that he must fight a duel, but he lacks the courage. He dares not say a word at home; he sulks and absents himself from office hours. His defiance is nourished by the fear of losing his job. The other feature of the story, the well-proven recipe of *The Dream Car*, the love of an "absolutely decent" gentleman with a department store and motor-car, for a lower middle-class girl, is hardly worth mentioning. On the other hand, the characterization of the lower middle-class household with its tiled stoves, with the grandmother in arrears with the rent, and with the indispensable lodger, of whom everybody is ashamed, is very good. This apartment has an excellent atmosphere with well-observed details. The picture of office life is also good. For instance, in the café near the office there sits an unemployed book-keeper every day for hours on end. He is watching for the moment when one of the staff is discharged. Without a moment's hesitation he turns up and applies for the vacancy with awkward humility. Both the direction and Béla Salamon's performance are memorable; the audience must realize that this is no joke, but sad reality.

All this Sekely produced on a very low budget. Here, too, are the office corners, so typical of Hungarian films of the period. In one corner Ella Gombaszögi is typing, and Kabos, the managing clerk, courts her. At home, in a corner of the apartment, Szeréna Sziklay is the housewife; Kabos, as the husband, does not court her, but they nevertheless create humour from the situation. The Beau makes love to the Damsel in a corner of a restaurant, and even here the witticisms are numerous. As a rule, a good anecdote or humorous repartee is delivered every few minutes. And yet the tension of the period is felt to vibrate in every corner of the studio, whatever locality the set may show us. It only vibrates, however, but does not rise to any heat; problems are not exposed openly.

Man under the Bridge (Ember a híd alatt)

The film, a screen version of Ottó Indig's successful play presented in 1933, was directed by Ladislas Vajda in February, 1936.

András Visky, a physician, is unable to find a job. He is unemployed. In his misery, on the brink of suicide, he loiters about on the steps of the Danube embankment. A burglar named Smirgli, who lives under the bridge, prevents the fatal plunge and takes the semi-conscious, mentally resigned young man to the villa of a professor of medicine. With the passive support of his new-found friend, Smirgli is absorbed in trying to pry open the safe when an unexpected visitor arrives, a patient with heart disease. Smirgli escapes while Visky examines the patient, gives him an injection and advice. The patient, a draper, who does not know the professor personally and rang his bell because it was the nearest doctor's brass-plate he could find when needing medical help, gives the young man a fee of ten pengős and is on the point of leaving when the host gets home. The professor believes Dr Visky's story and employs him. However, the professor's beautiful, neglected wife sets her eye on the young assistant. The elderly husband becomes suspicious and refuses to go with her to a concert; however, later he nevertheless goes, in order to watch his wife unobserved. Visky is invited to the professor's house for a party at which he declares his love to his hostess while the guests listen to a chamber music ensemble. The woman admits that she feels neglected, that she cares for Visky, yet, in her own interest and to avoid any possible inconvenience, she would never be unfaithful to her husband. The professor cannot hear these words but, having seen them talk so intimately, he reproaches Visky of having robbed him more despicably than he might have done by cleaning out his rooms with the burglar. In the meantime Smirgli is caught by the police. The criminal implicates Visky and detectives come for him. The professor exonerates Visky, then orders him to leave, forbidding him the house. The young physician leaves to work in India for five years. The action takes place in a financially independent, carefree stratum of society; it is the first time that unemployment and social conflicts are treated seriously. Moreover, the protagonists are not landlords, aristocrats, or officers, not even general managers, or tycoons, but intellectuals who gain their livelihood by work.

Decisive Moment (Döntő pillanat)

This film on a remarkable theme was directed by Ladislas Vajda; the screenplay was written by János Bókay, based on Andor Zsoldos's play, *The Great Scene* (A nagy jelenet), written in 1922 and published in 1923.

Notwithstanding several confused or unjustified turns of events in the action, *Decisive Moment* was a valuable work. The main points of the story are that the secretary of a Budapest theatre (Gyula Kabos) organizes a company and rents a theatre in a provincial town; "a Paris on the River Sajó". He takes with him an enthusiastic young couple, an actor and an actress, both beginners. However, his efforts fail; when his acquaintance, the renowned Tőrös of Budapest, engaged to play as a guest star, refuses to appear on the stage because he is not paid his fee in advance and the angry public clamour for the return of the money paid for their tickets, he runs away, gives up the struggle and returns to Budapest to his former post, to resume his duties as secretary.

The two novices also return to Budapest. The young actor begs the celebrated Tőrös to give him a chance to show what he can do and let him replace the great actor in the lead on a single night in the play which is running at the time. Tőrös consents; on a plea of illness he phones to cancel his appearance that evening. However, when his young colleague gives a splendid performance of the great scene in an audition, he flinches. He keeps his change of heart to himself, thinking that he would go to the theatre in time and play the part himself. The young actor is in a fever of excited preparation to make the best of his great opportunity. In the meantime his wife, who has learnt what Tőrös is up to, goes to the actor's flat and pretends to be in love with him, for she has noticed his admiration for her. So she contrives to play for time. When Tőrös reaches the theatre the young actor is already on the stage, having a tremendous success.

This story contains three arresting elements handled excellently not only by the director but by the actors as well.

First: this is the only dramatic role ever played by Gyula Kabos in films. He experiences bitter disappointment as the founder of a theatre in a provincial town. His failure is not humorous but tragic, and that is how it is played in the film. Kabos gives a magnificent portrait of the man who encourages himself with high hopes and is then unable to cope with the difficulties resulting from them. His dreamy, slightly snobbish, artistic mentality is defeated by the harsh realities and he takes refuge in his modest but comfortable job as secretary of a theatre to which he is accustomed.

The other element is the world of provincial theatres. For some time Hungarian film directors enjoyed presenting provincial companies and did so on a higher than average level. However, Vajda surpassed them and put before the public a more profound, more artistic interpretation of the tragicomic episodes.

The third motif of lasting value is the young actor's appearance in the capital when, in the role of an unemployed man, he shouts to the audience in a passionate speech, "I want to work, after all I am human".

Here Ladislas Vajda displayed the virtues which later brought him well deserved fame as a film director.

Keep Smiling (Barátságos arcot kérek)

Keep Smiling is the first and only Hungarian film satire. The performance is opened by Frigyes Karinthy's puppet figure, as if we were at a puppet show in the town park. "Excellencies, wits and half-wits, hysterical, pampered females, countesses and lounge-lizards, puppets of a vanished world" will appear in the film.

As it happens the girl, a young photographer in the amusement park, does find a husband, a rich engineer, but it is equally true that at the bitter-sweet ending of the film we see the figure of the barker who, resigned and disappointed, buys lemon-drops.

Burlesque scenes of Szakáll Szőke and Vilma Medgyaszay at an evening party, conjuring tricks and misunderstandings were all attempts to create a kind of film farce unknown in Hungary, following in the footsteps of the Laurel and Hardy films, without imitating them. The unassuming naturalness of the amusement park scenes are a credit to the director, and so is the bold usage of the camera.

Szakáll Szőke's acting is first-rate. He impersonates a petty bourgeois who believes resolutely and stubbornly, through thick and thin, in the triumph of virtue over vice, in the goodness of mankind, who gets involved in the most absurd situations with serene innocence; a stout tight-rope dancer who teeters along on a thin taut wire stretched out over hair-raising abysses, because he has implicit faith in his ability to perform his stunt which is really not so difficult and anyway he *has to reach* the other side.

Jenő Gerő, appearing under the name of Szakáll Szőke, was given many opportunities by producers to let his clumsy charm and humanity shine in dozens of walk-on parts in German and American films. A few of his Hungarian films have survived; they owe their significance to having preserved the art of this eminent comedian in leading roles.

The Henpecked Husband (A papucshős)

In May, 1938, Gyula Kabos and István Mihály, the actor and the script writer without whom a Hungarian sound-film was practically unthinkable, were invited to appear in a benefit performance, the first attempt of Photophon, a company recently established in the modest studio of the State Documentary Studio. The screenplay was István Mihály's original work; the part was Gyula Kabos's forty-second sound-film character in the 111th Hungarian talkie; it was the first time that Kabos played the lead and title-role. Eight months before his departure from Hungary, after 44 hits, Gyula Kabos was finally cast as the principal lead, for the first and only time in his life.

The film was directed by János Vaszary, the popular, successful playwright, during his excursion in the film industry in the period between January, 1937, and May, 1938. Except for another towards the end of World War II, this was the last adventure of his excursion.

The Henpecked Husband, a comedy—in the style of René Clair—is unique of its kind in our country. (It is possible that Vaszary, who spent the late 'twenties in Paris, may have been influenced by this French director.)

Consistent adherence to this style was executed with wit and ingenuity. In the representation of events, photography in 1913 differed considerably from that of 1938; the former recalls the *"Chapenn de paville el'Italie"* tricks in the treatment of the camera, whilst the latter avails itself of the technique of American comedies, radiating optimism with its balanced light effects. Jests and banter are always moderate and in good taste, never banal or extravagant. Kabos is also superb because it is not he who makes the jokes, but life and society who play the jokes on him. Therefore, like truly great clowns, he is always sad; only his audiences are gay, for they cannot help roaring with laughter.

It Was Me (Én voltam)

Among the varied shades of colour which brought heartening tones into Hungarian film production after the film law of 1935, the film based on Rose Meller's play and directed by Artúr Bárdos, with the assistance of Viktor Gertler, was an outstanding phenomenon.

The appearance of Artúr Bárdos, the eminent theatre-manager and director, in film production was so astonishing that even experts in the branch could hardly believe it: it was not some formal pseudo-excursion—with Viktor Gertler actually directing the film in the background—but Bárdos professed a profound interest in the cinema even though, for various reasons, this was the only film he ever directed. When shooting began, he gave the following statement to *Színházi Élet* (No. 17, 1936):

"I am fully aware of the artistic laws of the film and I have spared no effort to make the screen version of this play as cinematic as possible."

The script, written by Jenő Szatmári, recently returned from Berlin, was a film version of Rose Meller's *Confession* (Vallomás) which had been staged at the Belvárosi Színház, managed by Bárdos, with great success in 1934. The scene is set in Vienna, the characters have German names, in an Austrian milieu.

The story of *Confession*.

A large sum of money disappears from a designing office in Vienna. Wanda Huber, the secretary, formerly an actress (Elma Bulla), is horrified to see that the grim detective (Ferenc Kiss) suspects Erwin Köhler, an engineer, with whom she is in love. The other engineer, Bornemann, is also suspect, but in her anxiety for her lover, Wanda confesses to the crime, thinking erroneously that Köhler may have taken the money in order to run away with her. However, Köhler (Jenő Törzs), being innocent, has not the remotest idea that Wanda believes him to be the culprit and by admitting her crime sacrificed herself to save him. He thinks that she is really guilty and, feeling jealous, he suspects her of having committed the theft for the sake of another engineer in the office. Wanda is sent to prison, but Köhler does not visit her, because he is bitterly disappointed. Wanda, on the other hand, feels that her sacrifice has been unnecessary and senseless. She becomes so confused that a psychiatrist is called in to examine her (Gyula Csortos). While Wanda suffers in prison, Köhler tries to "forget" at a night-club in Bornemann's company. After a few years Wanda, having served her sentence, comes out of prison. Bornemann would like to console her and give her a present, therefore he uses some of the long-hoarded, stolen money to redeem his silver cigarette case from the pawnshop. The pawnbroker looks at the number of the banknote, because he had copied out the numbers of the stolen notes from a newspaper which reported the theft at the time. He hurries to a lawyer, then to the police; Bornemann is found out and denounced as the perpetrator of the theft. All tragic misunderstandings are cleared between Köhler and Wanda.

This occasionally melodramatic story is transformed into a genuine artistic experience by Elma Bulla's superb acting and by the high standard of Artúr Bárdos's (and Viktor Gertler's) direction. It was as though Bárdos had been guided by the rules laid down in his study on Film Aesthetics (Filmesztétika) written for *Nyugat* in 1913... "a truly good screenplay is almost a consecutive projection of emotions". In a film everything depends on the actor or actress; Asta Nielsen's brilliant use of her face and hands is an illustrative case in point. Twenty-three years after the publication of the study, these ideas of Bárdos were carried out: Elma Bulla's acting was simple, accurate and profound; her gestures, her quivering face are worth remembering. When Wanda frankly says to the uncomprehending, indifferent psychiatrist "...but it wasn't me who stole the money", Bulla's spontaneous gesture clearly reveals not only her innocence but also her motives.

*An Artist
of the 'Thirties:
Gyula Kabos*

He was forty-three years old when he played his first role in a sound-film; he acted in films for eight years, appearing in 45 talkies; six months after his fiftieth birthday he was forced to leave the country which he had comforted and entertained with his films for eight years. He died in New York at the age of fifty-three, on October 6th, 1941, a desolate and lonely man.

On March 15, 1936, in an interview with a reporter of the *Színházi Élet* who asked him questions about his Hollywood engagements Kabos replied:

"This is my fourth invitation to America, but so far I have been unable to bring myself to sign a contract. We have had talks, we have come to an agreement, they have got my landing permit... but in the last minute I refused to sign. God knows why. I was born here, in this town, it was here that I became somebody, here people like me and like to laugh at me... I am to leave at the end of April and cross the Atlantic on board of the *Ile de France*. First I am to appear on the stage in New York, then go on a tour, after which I am expected at Hollywood. I must tell you frankly that I did not want to accept this offer either... Now I am waiting only for the consent of the Vígszínház. Secretly I cherish the hope that—with God's help— perhaps they will not let me go."

He did not leave; he remained at home and presented us with another 26 films, including *Three Dragons* (Három sárkány), *Affair of Honour* (Lovagias ügy), *Decisive Moment* (Döntő pillanat) and *The Henpecked Husband* (A papucshős). Had he left at the time, in 1936, only 19 films would have been made. But he remained at home and waited until he was shamefully dismissed. He could choose between two forms of death; a heart attack in New York and collapse on a small shabby stage or a death camp, a gas-chamber, a mass grave, with a forced labour unit at the front. In New York death was more humane though also tragic; it is good that he left, on nearly the last boat, in 1939.

Of his 45 films only six have perished: *A Car and No Money* (Ein Auto und kein Geld), *Piri Knows Everything* (Piri mindent tud), *Flying Gold* (Repülő arany), *I Have Married for Love* (Szerelemből nősültem), *Billeting* (Beszállásolás), *The Fehérvár Hussars* (A fehérvári huszárok). So his career as an artist is appraisable.

Kabos's development, his steadily deepening and always analytical study of the characters he created are unmistakably apparent. What was a jest in 1932, became grim reality by 1937, sometimes appallingly so: he must have observed himself, though contemporary reviews never went into any thorough analysis of his performance—except for bursting into lyrical transports of delight. Yet apart from buying their tickets, audiences failed to stand up for him, even when he had to flee his country. Kabos nevertheless continued to form his life-work with dogged perseverance and artistic ambition.

Closer inspection reveals that in *Hyppolit the Butler* he gave no more than an amusing, telling caricature of an upstart. One can believe everything he says and does, his ways and demeanour, but his wealth and prosperity have no atmosphere or background; indeed, we are left in the dark as to how this clumsy little fellow could have managed to amass a fortune so close to the disastrous year of 1931. He understands business and knows what's what on the market, but perhaps no better than a managing clerk.

In the roles he played in the years of 1933, 1934, 1935 he was still a nice, facetious fellow who made funny remarks and bungled everything, but he was no longer a rich man; nobody would have accepted him in a series of films as a man living in affluent circumstances. *Honeymoon at Half Price* is a typical fruit of this pleasant period; here he plays the managing clerk— his favourite role—simply as a dear idiot. In *Purple Acacia* he appeared in an entirely different profession: in the role of a white-slaver, a night-club pimp, and a female impersonator. Where he cannot give vent to his feelings of human sympathy and compassion, he is out of place. In *Confectionary of Buda* he was better, but he still hovered over the surface: here he could make gifts, dispense the milk of human kindness as the landlord's agent and an antique dealer, though he isn't above swindling a little now and then.

Within this pattern of a managing clerk a mask slowly took shape: a slightly awkward carriage, a wry face with stealthy, cunning glances and Schweik-like stupidity, for these looks betray some deeper human shrewdness notwithstanding a faintly apparent touch of imbecility. This Schweik-like attitude is good but, as indicated by the epithet, it still smacks of imitation. Kabos could assimilate no uncongenial role; he cast it off: hardly any vestige was left of the cynical, sensuous procurer of *Purple Acacia,* the jocose female impersonator popped up instead in cheap and loud colours. In his creative period that followed, *The Dream Car* is the medium of transition: here Kabos created his beloved character of the managing clerk. He hangs about his boss like a half-witted minor clerk, but finally proves to be the more astute, and it is he who solves the conflict, in the general manager's love affair, smoothing things out with his human composure and lower middle-class knack for adjustment.

Then come the films of 1937–38, in the best, final period of Kabos's maturity. At this time he played worried lawyers, managing clerks, country doctors. Why did his face always look so startled? The scripts themselves, the roles, give no clue to this question. The roles were not even precisely defined; it was enough to put down some witty remarks, to provide opportunities for cracking jokes, for carrying on a humorous dialogue; that was Kabos's role. This petty bourgeois—(though he had never been actually poor or destitute like Charlie Chaplin) who is well off, who enjoys a modest independence—seems to be at a loss, to be frightened, though there is no pecuniary reason to explain his uneasiness. The attempt to present a more profound delineation of society, as far as Kabos could draw such a portrait —and sometimes he certainly did, without ever consulting his director— can be regarded only as a partial motivation of this anxious demeanor, or of the humiliating dependence of civil servants, however wealthy or prosperous, on the provincial gentry. The true cause is to be found in the imminent, increasingly audible, rumbling approach of fascism in the mid-thirties. In a short time those heavy boots will step down from the screen to crush everything in their way...

Both aspects deserve closer inspection. In Kabos's interpretation of his characters no one could overlook this criticism of an obsolete—but even in its anachronism dangerous—feudalism in a Hungary where no real bourgeois revolution had ever been carried out with success. The characters he played were ominously and completely at the mercy of the gentry. In *Three Dragons* he appears to have the upper hand as the lawyer of three old maids of the village. Nevertheless he has to dance attendance on, to fawn upon the ladies, the three dragons, and their favourite nephew. In *Vicki* (Viki) he played a country doctor who is called in to be present at a duel. Kabos was never content with the hollow jokes contained by the script. He lived his part and formed the character of a man who profoundly despised the whole of this feudal society, but who wisely kept his opinions to himself (in his own interest), being aware of the fact that it was only when they wanted something from him that the gentry treated him as one of their set.

His portrayal of the managing clerk of *Affair of Honour* is superb. Most likely this artistic performance, abounding in subtle nuances, contributed to the kindling of nationalistic indignation among racist undergraduates who forthwith staged a demonstration against the film. The way he sits down by the stove when he gets home, as if he actually needed the warmth of the family hearth to encourage him to give a piece of his mind to his bosses there and then for the wrongs he has had to endure; the way he puts his hand up to his cheek, as though expecting another blow, when the young gentry who has insulted him, apologizes; the way he makes an entirely hopeless attempt to give orders to his daughter and energetic wife; the way he shows his efficiency in business matters, for the very gesture with which he picks up a document is evidence of his thorough knowledge of all that concerns the issue in question; the way he prepares himself for fighting a duel and goes to a fencing-master; the way he tries to screw a monocle into his eye and lends new content to this long outdated gesture which in the course of time had become a paltry, ingrained theatrical trick eliciting the same conditioned reflex; when he is moved by the apology offered in the name of the whole staff, he knows that he counts not as an individual but only as a man who is good at his job; when he talks to his deaf mother-in-law, with whom even he dares to use a superior tone, he gives not only a carefully drawn character: this is conscious criticism of an age in which every citizen who is not of the nobility or gentry leads a precarious existence. In his compilation of Kabos scenes Pál Kertész wittily juxtaposed shots to show the frightened lower middle-class nobody raising his hand to avert a blow, followed by a shot in which he is seen bowing humbly, a cowering expression on his face.

So much for social criticism. However, as we have mentioned before, the characters that Kabos played convey something more: the horror of menacing fascism and complete uncertainty of existence. It is by no means accidental that Gyula Kabos achieved his artistic maturity when fascism reached Hungary. I do not think that Kabos feared fascism as the future victim of the impending anti-Jewish laws: it is felt that he brought to the screen a universally shared human fear and horror. This explains his terrified gestures and stammering half-way through a joke, his desolate loneliness. For this man, the managing clerk, physician, or lawyer of the screen was quite friendless. He wanted to love and longed to be loved, but, instead, everybody laughed at him—not only film-goers but also the people who worked with him—laughed and then turned their backs on him. For long periods of his life he was single, and when he was married—as in *Affair of Honour*—in his greatest trouble he could count on nobody, not even his wife. Terror-stricken, he dreaded some fatal calamity; sadly, history justified his fears.

He was good enough for a ticket to the cinema, yet contemporary Hungarian society did not hold him in high esteem. Kabos fled from Hungary; he toured America and appeared in all sorts of worthless shows. Hollywood did not open its doors to him. In October 1941, he collapsed on the stage and a few days later he died.

One more point. The public *liked* Gyula Kabos and the figures he created. As a rule, audiences laugh at comedians and are amused by their antics; but the kind of comedian which film-goers really like is exceedingly rare. This liking did not go deep enough for the audience to identify with him (as with Charlie Chaplin or Heinz Rühmann); they simply took a fancy to him. It is good to know that such people exist. So Kabos gave them back their faith in humanity. He never does anything evil and helps everybody. While the lovers find happiness and wealth due to his cunning connivance, Kabos remains in the background and has to resign himself to being denied the small poultry-farm he had longed for so ardently (*At Eighty Miles per Hour*). He makes up for his selflessness by chuckling and sniggering a little as if he were thinking... you wait, I am sure this will not lead to any good. Trees don't grow sky-high! There is gentle pride and slightly mocking forgiveness in his attitude, but this never turns to cynicism. The way he begins to court the secretary in his rash, exuberant flare-up of manly passion (*Affair of Honour*), to turn away the next moment and shyly wipe his pincenez; the way he stoops to ingratiate himself with the theatre manager in Budapest at the end of *Decisive Moment* after having failed as a theatre manager himself in a provincial town; as he becomes fed up with the endless compromises of his miserable life in *The Henpecked Husband;* the way he performs stunts on his bycicle along the road to Lake Balaton when no one is looking (*Address Unknown*); when, as the family lawyer, he gives cunning advice to others while he himself remains stranded (*Three Dragons; Emmy*) or as the husband who lives on his wife's fortune and hides behind a children's book with an apologetic air; but secretly watching men on the Danube embankment carry sacks he vows to himself that he will rather go and carry sacks than tolerate his wife's terrorism again (*My Daughter Is Not That Sort*), every detail contributes to the grotesque picture of the opportunist bourgeois who longs to perform great deeds but is afraid to lose the smal amount of inner harmony and balance that he still possesses.

Were the scenes in which he appeared cut out from his surviving 39 films and the reels of approximately twenty-five thousand meters long joined together and presented on the screen, they would yield a more accurate picture of Hungarian bourgeois life in the 'thirties than could any scientific research work.

Guns Direct
the Muse
1939—1944

Once before, the war had saved the Hungarian film industry: the French, Italian and American films that were prohibited between 1914–1918 had to be replaced by Hungarian products to keep business going. The same thing happened in the new war.

Wartime Boom

However, in the First World War Hungarian cinema served neither the government nor the war, and there was no film that supported the war; whereas the film industry of the Second World War became a humble servant of the government and the policy of war.

French, British and American films were gradually superseded, and in 1942 American films were altogether stopped in Hungary. Distributing companies went out of business, one after the other.

The proportion of compulsory showings of Hungarian films was increased: by the early 'forties, of every one hundred films thirty had to be Hungarian productions in all cinemas.[1] At the same time cinemas increased in number: Hungarian films were shown in the picture houses of the Northern Region, Transylvania, and the Southern Region.

A Balkan market also became accessible. The important American market was certainly lost, but Yugoslavia, which had held strictly aloof from the Hungarian film market—even in the brief months of the treaty of friendship—later Bulgaria, also Italy and Scandinavia bought Hungarian films in large numbers. The Balkans and Italy became permanent buyers who made satisfactory payment. In 1940 alone Yugoslavia accepted one hundred and fifty films, while Italy purchased the whole production of a year.[2]

It is interesting that Germany, on the other hand, almost completely refrained from buying Hungarian films, as in the time of the First World War. Neither the spirit of the comedies which were void of politics, nor Hungarian nationalist and military films satisfied German principles. In his article "Hungarian Films Abroad", János Bingert, director of Hunnia, complained: "A separate chapter ought to be devoted to an investigation of the reason why the import of this commodity (i.e. films) to our friendly neighbour, Germany, has thus far failed, although... the occasional sale of a Hungarian film to Germany would bring the owners of the films a surplus exceeding the income derived so far from export areas."[8]

This situation did not change during the war; however, it was arranged that at the Budapest meeting of the supreme council of the International Film Chamber, controlled by the Germans, held in December 1940, in the Grand Hotel on Margaret Island, a considerable part of the Balkan market was allotted to Hungary.[4]

The further increase in the number of films to be shot necessitated the building of new studios. Twenty-eight major Hungarian feature films were made in 1939, 38 in 1940, 41 in 1941, 45 in 1942, 53 in 1943. So many films could not be produced at the two existing establishments, at Hunnia Studio in Gyarmat Street and at the studios of the Hungarian Film Office in Könyves Kálmán Boulevard. Therefore the studio built by Star in 1917 in Pasaréti Road was modernized and used as the second plant of Hunnia. In September 1941, work was started at the former Star Studios.[5] Now the Hungarian film industry had three modern establishments. Hungarian sound-film production thus began to flourish, as a result of the war boom.

With an annual output of 40 to 50 films a national festival was organized at Lillafüred to reward the best films and to establish some kind of grading. These film weeks at Lillafüred remained mere curiosity shows without any true interest for public opinion or the industry, despite the various prizes awarded. The two-hundredth Hungarian film was presented amidst gala festivities. This distinction fell to *Pista Dankó* (Dankó Pista); not as if this film had really been the two-hundredth in order of appearance, but because it was the film chosen by the government for distinction, holding it up as worthy of the highest award and as a model to show the public the kind of subject, spirit, atmosphere and execution deemed exemplary by the Hungarian state. The *première* was honoured by the presence of Regent Horthy himself, making this resemble the occasion ten years earlier at the first night of *The Rákóczi March.*

The Hungarian state now took over the control of film production openly and avowedly. A National Film Committee was organized to replace the Film Industry Fund. This body decided every question concerning films, while exercising the strictest censorship and political control. The producer was only permitted to advance the capital, the rest devolved on the National Film Committee. The chairman was Baron Gyula Wlassich who had already been active on the three-man interdepartmental committee assigned to control the Film Industry Fund as the representative of the Ministry of Education. László Balogh, appointed secretary to the National Film Committee, was the head of the Film Department of the Ministry. Practically all matters concerning film production were managed by Balogh. Scripts were submitted to a board presided over by Balogh and Wlassich, and the members of the board—authors, critics, public figures—gave their opinion on the script and scheduled it for production, after having pocketed their fees for the evening.

All decisions concerning film production were thus made by incompetent men who knew very little about films, such as László Balogh and Gyula Wlassich, though Bingert had been the first to organize Hungarian film production and, as a former police officer, ought to have been considered politically reliable. Owing to amateurish measures and inexpert arrangement of production, Bingert came up against the National Film Committee, as had the Hungarian Film Office earlier. A contemporary report summarized the activities of the National Film Committee: "The producing firms are obliged to submit to the National Film Committee the script of the film to be produced, a list of the cast and the technical staff, as well as an estimate of the costs. The producing firm may start to shoot the film after having obtained the Committee's approval and is expected to proceed in accordance with the schedule set up by the Committee."[6]

Since this took place in a capitalist country where the state itself did not go in for production, gave no money and did not incur any risk, the situation was preposterous. If somebody wanted to make a film, he had to pay the price of a whole script, remit the rights and dramatic fees, and, having taken this financial risk, he had to wait until he was granted or refused a permission. He could not engage a director until he obtained his permit, and then it was prohibited to change the script. Therefore he had to pay a director in advance to work on the shooting script. This, too, augmented the financial risk.

Baron Wlassich and the departmental head László Balogh did not give their decision on all the scripts submitted to them at the same time; those they liked were classified for production at an early date, while the rest had to wait, pending their judgment. Consequently no plan could be made either by the studio or by the producer. This state of affairs often led to superficial, inconsistent, overhasty execution, because protracted work was said to occupy the studio too long while others awaited their turn. An atmosphere of haste developed. Moreover, it was not the best scripts that the Film Committee selected for approval, but those that were "the least likely to cause trouble".

Thus the Committee favoured the kind of commonplace comedy which had become popular in the 'thirties. For instance, in 1943 it approved *The Siamese Cat* (Sziámi macska), a script by László Kalmár, to be directed by the author himself. On the other hand, the script written by István Szőts in collaboration with László Ranódy, *Song of the Cornfields* (Ének a búza-mezőkről), based on the novel of Ferenc Móra, was rejected. This refusal coincided with the award of a medal to Szőts at the Venice Film Festival. However, it was not Szőts who had directed "the two-hundredth Hungarian film" (*Pista Dankó*), but László Kalmár. A script of Szőts about Lajos Kossuth was also rejected and a scenario of Endre Rodriguez, *Madonna of Kalotaszeg* (Kalotaszegi Madonna), was accepted instead. No film was produced on the script of Áron Tamási's *Abel Alone* (Ábel a rengeteg-ben), or of Mihály Babits's novel, *Nightmare* (A gólyakalifa), filmed once before in 1918 by Sándor Korda; nor on *Kakuk Marci,* a script by Jenő Józsi Tersánszky; nor of Molière's *L'Avare.* Yet the door was opened to films about the gentry and themes fanning fascist warmongering.[7]

The other price to be paid by Hungarian film production and the war boom was the issue and enforcement of the anti-Jewish laws as a concession to German and Hungarian fascism.

In its issue of July 14, 1937, the *Új Magyarság* began an open anti-Semitic campaign. In November the fascist organization of undergraduates called Turul held a general meeting; it was at this juncture that the name of the later fascist director, Viktor Bánky, was heard for the first time. This younger brother of the film actress Vilma Bánky was a fascist film cutter who had been biding his time. In October 1938, the "Christian film industry" was founded in the beer-house of the Officers' Club; those present decided that from that time every film was going to be better, every film was going to be more artistic, and all those who were present were going to make much more money.[8] Fascist initiatives and methods were given the power of state decrees in the laws of 1939. Several eminent directors were banned from film production; they went abroad where they became highly appreciated directors—like László Vajda and Steve Sekely—or fell on evil days and privation in Hungary to die a bitter death, as did Béla Gaál.

According to the view proclaimed by the National Film Committee, spread by the press, and swallowed by the public, it was the "Jewish film people" who were responsible for the low standards of Hungarian films. Instead of great national stories they had shot banal comedies; they were ignorant of the glorious deeds of the Hungarian past, and so on. These stupid accusations are refuted not only by the fact that such films as *The Rákóczi March,* directed by Steve Sekely, and *Confectionary of Buda,* directed by Béla Gaál, had been extolled in the 'thirties as "national" films, but also by the later products, the still poorer, still emptier, and still cheaper commonplace comedies and career stories put on the screen during the war.

The boom provided possibilities for founding larger and more permanent firms than were those of the preceding decade, but they were short-lived and followed a programme curtailed by the National Film Committee.

The Producers

The most important film producing company was Kárpát Films founded in 1936 by István Erdélyi, owner of the cinema of Pestszentlőrinc, who filled various posts in the Cinema Association, to general satisfaction. He started with a piece of atrocious melodrama, *Tommy, the Frozen Child,* which actually brought in a great profit. However, he also produced a major historical film (partly in colour), *The Talking Kaftan* (A beszélő köntös). Some of his seventeen films testify to efforts towards a higher standard, others were cheap plays chosen to find favour with the wider public, such as, for example, *No Thoroughfare* (Behajtani tilos) and *Flower of Perdition* (A láp virága). Erdélyi tried to hold together the best men of the profession. First he invited film critics and film producers to his house; later he arranged debates connected with the projection of films. These meetings on Wednesdays and Fridays were so successful that in 1943 they were referred to by many people as "Erdélyi's academy". He asked well-known aestheticians to conduct the debates. As a rule, films not publicly shown, including some Soviet films, were projected at these meetings. Erdélyi, who had visited Italy in 1942, may have been stimulated in this direction by the ferment of that time in Italian film life and culture.

As a matter of fact, Erdélyi did not have a very high opinion of Hungarian directors. In one of his writings he declared that the available ten to twenty film directors were not enough; their taste, if they had any at all, made the annual fifty films monotonous; there was no competition and no perspective. In his opinion there were not more than two or three among them who really knew their business, and perhaps one, if at all, who was a true artist. Erdélyi called for a special cinema school to correct these inadequacies. How right Erdélyi was is shown by the declarations of some highly respected directors. One of these stated at his debating evenings that film making was no art but an industry whose products were destined only to entertain people. Erdélyi spoke his mind also against producers, saying that there was not one capitalist with a truly wide horizon.[9]

Therefore it was logical for Erdélyi to try to use the works of two valuable writers, *The Abyss* (Szakadék) and *Song of the Cornfields*. Both were rejected. *The Abyss* had promised to be a remarkable undertaking. It would have been the first film of the young assistant László Ranódy based on the novel of József Darvas. Ranódy intended to have the leading parts played by peasants, without actors. He even went to the village of Türje to choose locations. In November 1943, an extensive, country-wide competition was initiated among popular amateur theatrical companies to end on December 31, 1943. The careful preparations for making the film began to assume the proportions of a popular movement. Its political character began to come into prominence, apart from the person of the writer József Darvas; eventually the film had to be dropped. If shooting had been started, the German occupation, which came a few months later, would have prevented its conclusion in any case.

Erdélyi's other project, *Song of the Cornfields,* had a similar fate. In its issue No. 24, 1943, *Moziújság* said: "In the near future Kárpát Films will start the shooting of *Song of the Cornfields*. The script based on the novel of Ferenc Móra has been written by the gifted young author László Ranódy. Antal Páger is to be the leading man, Alice Szellay the leading lady. The film is to be directed by István Szőts..."

One month later, at the end of July, the unexpected news came that the script had been rejected. In an interview the leading man told a journalist: "To my greatest regret the film will not be realized."[10]

Besides Erdélyi the firm Hajdú, active since 1933, and the firm of József Daróczy showed business abilities and a tendency to work on a grand scale. Daróczy, who had been in films since the mid-twenties and owned a cinema, also directed films himself. He liked to put on the screen plays dealing with topical social problems, and the public of those days were delighted with *Fidelity* (Férfihűség) and *Too Late* (Késő). He directed and produced *The Song of Rákóczi* (Rákóczi nótája), a highly successful picture, the first truly major historical film made in Hungary, to give a characteristic description of its period—like *The Talking Kaftan*—featuring historical figures.

During its existence the firm Hajdú produced fourteen films, the Mester Film seventeen, as many as Kárpát Films. The firm Mester Film worked under the aegis of an influential rightist politician, Miklós Mester. Mária Hausz, the clever former secretary of Hunnia Studios, produced at least ten commonplace films. The firm Hamza belonged to an educated producer who took up direction: Ákos Dezső Hamza; as a capitalist he preferred to finance comedies; so did Palatinus and the firm of Antal Takács.

These were the really big concerns. It must be remarked that they were rather cautious: no openly fascist, inciting films can be found among their products; their chief objective was to amuse their audiences. Only the heads of the firm Atelier—not mentioned so far—were open fascists personally; strangely enough, there is not one fascist film among their pictures. On the contrary, they produced several noteworthy films, those directed by Géza Radványi after his return from Paris: *Hearing in Camera* (Zárt tárgyalás) and *A Woman Looks Back* (Egy asszony visszanéz). The managers of Atelier tried to imitate Erdélyi's large-scale methods; they started a journal which was important because no film paper had been published since Korda and Ungerleider edited their journal. The new paper was the *Moziújság*, but their self-advertising did not bring much benefit to the owners of Atelier.

Among the minor companies mention has to be made of Lajos Zilahy's firm named Pegasus, which was active from 1939 to 1943, but went out of business in 1944; with its six films this firm tried to gain ground for the production of literary pictures. It is interesting that the two studios Hunnia and Hungarian Film Office, which in the 'thirties had been maintained only to be rented to producers, began to make pictures of their own during the war. In the years from 1941 to 1944 Hunnia produced seven films, including a version of Zsigmond Móricz's *Judge Sarah* (Sári bíró). During the same period the Hungarian Film Office, drawing on its own resources, produced ten more films. Most of them were comedies.

Truly militarist and fascist propaganda films were produced mostly by small firms, with one or two films on their record, whose owners seized the opportunity to exploit violent subjects. A firm named Pannonia produced the shame of Hungarian films: *Changing of the Guard* (Őrségváltás); a company named Vörösmarty, *Unknown Adversary* (Ismeretlen ellenfél), etc.

As in the 'thirties, the closest connection was maintained with writers. Stories were ordered from, supplied by, and discussed with them. As a rule the director received a completely finished script and signed a contract for its shooting. Often the director discussed matters not with the producer but with his manager or assistant. The script writer was still a craftsman; a tradesman who came when he was summoned, who threw together a scenario that could be sent on to the Studio.

Who were these script writers? Their names have remained still more obscure than the identity of those who were active in the preceding decade. Script writers under a cloud for political and other reasons submitted their work under the names of others, names that sounded better in the ears of the National Film Committee. A look at the official list of titles, particularly at the list of amusing "apolitical" comedies, does not bring the reader any nearer to the truth. It is quite impossible to see through this maze, and it is, indeed, unnecessary to make any effort to do so. The author who wrote the script was as poor a writer as the one who allowed his name to be used.

Danse Macabre

Notwithstanding the strict control exercised by the National Film Committee over releases, so many films were made during the boom that a few inevitably escaped the attention of censors who aimed at a timid middle course and favoured aggressive nationalism. This explains how it came about that the war years witnessed the launching of a few healthy initiatives. There were directors who made it their task to serve the cause of progress in art and in social development.

Of course, most films followed old paths under new directors. Commonplace comedies were still superior in numbers (90 out of 227 films) but, as the war went on, they began to be superseded by sentimental-tragic, pseudo-social drama, the hero fighting against destiny and a *femme fatale,* the old motif of the woman longing for love. *One More Day* (Egy nap a világ) sang the *femme fatale* in the film hit of the same title, as though prophesying the decline of a whole society. Kabos had disappeared from the commonplace comedy, and so had the old offices and clerks of Budapest. The world of pretty young ladies from the country took possession of the screen.

The fashionable directors of comedies were Ákos Ráthonyi, trying to keep conversation on a sophisticated, upper-class level—*Come on the First* (Jöjjön elsején), *One Kiss and Nothing More* (Egy csók és más semmi), *The Left-Handed Angel* (A balkezes angyal)—and Emil Martonffy who tried to fill the vacuum left by Kabos with Kálmán Latabár, reviving the ancient, long-forgotten burlesque. Unfortunately, he did not show enough intelligence in tackling his genre, because he took over only its apparently wild confusion, but none of its philosophy: *One Fool Makes a Hundred* (Egy bolond százat csinál), *A Slap, a Kiss* (Egy pofon, egy csók). Baron Félix Podmaniczky favoured comedies in noble circles. He built up a veritable myth around the revelries of the landed gentry to gipsy music: *Seven Plum*

Trees (Hét szilvafa); *The Bailiff* (Az intéző úr); *A Nest of Nobles* (Gentry-fészek); *Queen Elizabeth* (Erzsébet királyné).

There was no specialist to develop a certain line: Ráthonyi sometimes directed a "serious" film while the pampered pet of the system, Viktor Bánky, occasionally abandoned the lofty atmosphere of his national themes, and condescended to direct a comedy.

The number of actors and actresses increased with the output of films. A certain primitive but tough cult of stars developed among fans. The most popular actresses, to be seen in the largest number of films, were Klári Tolnay and Zita Szeleczky. Szeleczky usually played roles of the captivatingly foolish *ingénue,* while Tolnay, an actress of genuine talent, having achieved success at the Gaiety Theatre in difficult parts that demanded full dramatic concentration, became the lucky star of the film studios, playing the heroine in *Katie* (Katyi) and in *Sunshine on the Snow* (Havasi napsütés) with equal excellence.

Parts like that played by Tolnay at the beginning of her career in *The Dream Car* were now filled with the frequent duo of Erzsi Simor and Éva Szörényi. In the greatest hit of the war years, *The Marriage of Mara Szüts* (Szüts Mara házassága), the two of them played piano duets and caught husbands subtly but firmly, with the sweet aggressiveness of provincial young ladies.

Mária Tasnády Fekete represented an entirely different type: a reserved lady, an earnest beauty of town life, a personality the Hungarian screen had lacked before. She makes her own decisions, she thinks, and, what is still more unusual, she reads: *A Woman Looks Back; No Answer from Europe* (Európa nem válaszol). The more fateful and more sensuous woman of this kind was played by Margit Lukács: *Black Dawn* (Fekete hajnal).

The Transylvanian actresses Alice Fényes and Alice Szellay became popular in the middle of the war; both played women from the people with great understanding and success: *The Daughter of the Mountains* (A hegyek lánya); *The Golden Peacock* (Aranypáva); *People on the Alps* (Emberek a havason).

A new colour was introduced on the Hungarian screen by two young actresses, owing to their individuality and character, rather than to any special gifts. Bea Goll tried to imitate the Hollywood vamp of the 'thirties and to create—with scant success—a Budapest variety of the loose modern woman of the type introduced by Jean Harlow. Vali Hidvéghy, on the other hand, liked to appear in the role of the calm, intelligent, independent girl earning her own living, a kind of Hungarian Claudette Colbert or Irene

Dunne—however, without the talent of these. At all events, the variation of types indicated livelier interest for the cinema in general.

The most remarkable development in this sphere was the sudden appearance in 1939 of a dark-haired actress with a deep, sensual voice, Katalin Karády, and her rapid rise to popularity. The secret of her success may perhaps be explained by people seeking to forget the horrors of the war with the enjoyment of sensuous pleasures. There can be no doubt that she was a poor actress. Her appearance was almost provokingly vulgar, while her movements, gestures and glances were reduced to a few fundamental means of expression. She nevertheless had an enthusiastic public of raving fans who sent her showers of letters, and a club was founded in her honour. "She is possessed of every biological ingredient of a great actress," wrote László Németh in one of his reviews on a stage performance, "a sombre, dramatic body, eyes flashing with passion, a sensual smile. Artistic consciousness and the power to form a character are, however, lacking. She is a medium for acting, rather than an actresss. A great director may mould her into an excellent tool; left to herself she is bound to collapse."[11]

Another actress with a similar stature, Eszter Szilágyi Szabó, also tried her luck, but without success, though she was played off against Karády in *Maria's Two Nights* (Mária két éjszakája); *You Are Mine* (Enyém vagy).

The young hero was played by István Nagy, or the handsome László Szilassy who debased himself so low as to become a fascist and member of the SS. Of the four actors employed the most frequently, Antal Páger alone was truly gifted, a real actor capable of extraordinary achievement.

After Kabos nobody could conjure up true humour to brighten the screen. The wooden grimaces of Kálmán Latabár evoked idiots of a non-existent world at whose jokes the film-goers laughed with the satisfaction of the healthy. The secret of his success was to prove to this lower middle-class audience how much cleverer they were than he, but he did not show anything of the social reality which Gyula Kabos could convey in his most modest roles. In view of his peculiar sense for funny pantomime and his talent for comedy, Kálmán Latabár might have done much more. However, the directors and the ideologists of the period did not expect him to do more; perhaps they did not even allow him to display his talents. So there is nothing to say about the war-time variants of the commonplace comedy developed in the 'thirties. A new kind of screenplay, the sentimental drama of manners, though reactionary and cheap, deserves more attention as a typical product of the period. First, a few words about the few comedies which strove towards some sort of progress.

The comedy of Endre Tóth (otherwise André de Toth), *Six Weeks' Happiness* (Hat hét boldogság), based on the script of Zoltán Várkonyi, is the satirical emotional story of a safe-breaker who gives his daughter the education of a lady. At the end of the film the good old convict sings in the church choir at the wedding of his daughter. The whole set-up would seem to have been an attempt to emulate in a Hungarian milieu the type of comedy developed by Capra. However, Capra's films confined themselves to pulling faces at society, exposing now and again, in a flash, the essence of social reality; this modest imitation of Capra moved only on the surface. It is nevertheless exhilarating to see the cheerfully active camerawork in the town, on the platform of a tram, in the traffic of the shopping district, and it is a pleasure to see how André de Toth, home from America on a visit for one year, taunted a hypocritical society with his mild fillips.

An excellent stage director of progressive mentality, Árpád Horváth, who was to take part in the resistance, to be murdered by the fascists in 1944, directed a comedy based on changing clothes, in the French style: *White Tie* (Estélyiruha kötelező). Eszter Réthy, the charming singer of the Vienna Opera, was the leading lady. The names of Árpád Horváth and László Cserépy stood side by side on the play-bill. This friendly gesture of László Cserépy shows his human attitude, of which more hereafter.

White Tie is the only Hungarian attempt to utilize the lessons learnt from the French film comedy. The action takes place somewhere on the Riviera, in order to avoid any possible cavilling by the censor: a man, having been detained by mistake, is released from prison in broad daylight, wearing the evening clothes in which he had been arrested. His dress suit provides an entrance everywhere, and wins for him the love of a lovely singer. A new complication arises when he is mistaken for somebody else, this time for a well-dressed notorious criminal. Clothes are changed, people are chased all over a hotel until, finally, all is resolved.

This primitive story is rendered interesting by subtle observation and well-prepared, bold direction. Such subtle observation is shown in the scene where the newly rich family boasts of its jewels; when the camera moves about the apartment, presenting all the members of the family while dressing for the theatre: the silly daughter, the father who has no manners, and the mother who swoops down eagerly on the wealthy suitor. Well planned, clever camerawork helped to avoid the painful sensation of airlessness, apt to make more sensitive film-goers fidget at the sight of many a Hungarian comedy. While the most outstanding virtue of Pál Jávor was that he knew how to wear a dress-suit, Sándor Pethes and László Misoga, in minor roles, followed the director's intentions in their efforts to breathe life into types derived from French comedies, a prepossessing thief, and a scatter-brained detective in disguise.

László Cserépy made an attempt to adapt another form of French comedy, a chamber piece for two, in his film *We Two Alone* (Kettesben) on the holidays of a misanthropic clerk, spending his leisure on islands of the Danube in the region of Süttő. For the expert, the significance of astonishingly valuable solutions of detail is weakened by the meagre action and the languid flow of humour. But even so it is pleasant to discover in this chamber piece the Hungarian precursor of a trend held to be modern.

After the 1934 flop of *Ball at the Savoy* the musical comedy verging on the revue was neglected, until an attempt was made to revive it in *They Are Seven* (Heten mint a gonoszok), directed by Endre Rodriguez. As can be gathered from the producer's statements, he tried to break away from the usual pattern followed in Hungarian films: he was going to put on the screen the story of seven penniless young musicians who set up an orchestra. This was again a motif from Hollywood. The co-operation of an eminent foreign musician, the still highly popular Michael Jaray, was secured at enormous cost. The film shows Budapest suburbs, dismal streets, a merry-go-round, a bar... These scenes are remarkable as exteriors, but the story, the plot is false. One feature was stolen from Molnár's *Liliom*—the showman's wife is secretly in love with the park tough wearing a sailor's jersey, who, however, chooses the lonely little servant girl; the other idea was derived from several German revue films. In his double role Tivadar Bilicsi was alternately shrewd and sheepish.

Some attention should be given a peculiar phenomenon of the period, the sentimental drama, a genre in which the largest number of films were produced. In the 'thirties the film-goer dreaded tragedy, but five or ten years later, under the influence of the war, the blackout, anti-aircraft guns, air-raids, ominous news from the fronts, frequent bereavements in the family and among friends, the same public began to conceive a strange liking for tragic stories on the screen. These stories sometimes even endeavoured to delineate social reality, making a show of giving an objective account of social conditions, as in the films of József Daróczy, extremely popular at the time. Sometimes the tragic love story conceived in the fantasy of a *femme fatale* was put on the screen, as in the Karády films of László Kalmár or Béla Balogh, sometimes mingled with comedy, but with some "sweetly-sad" humour, like the scene in the churchyard in the top box office draw of the period, *The Marriage of Mara Szüts*.

Efforts were made to attribute some serious, profoundly human, fundamental philosophical significance to these films. Moved to tears, film-goers wiped their eyes and left the cinema with the feeling of having seen something very deep drawn from Life, and next Saturday bought their tickets with a relieved conscience to the farce *Checked Coat* (Pepita kabát) to have a good laugh.

The *Danse Macabre* (Haláltánc)—in which the *femme fatale* was a cynical, immoral teenager, Bea Goll—*Sentenced to Life* (Életre ítéltek), *Black Dawn, At Crossroad* (Keresztúton), all pretended to raise some important social issue. In *A Renounced Life* (Kölcsönadott élet) a plain girl writes letters to an unknown soldier who falls in love with the writer of these letters; she sacrifices herself and lets a pretty girl have credit for the letters and get the boy.

In *Vision on the Lake Shore* (Tóparti látomás) the director takes the audience to the Enchanted Castle of Art, revealing the strange traits of Genius. How elevating is the lesson taught by *Spring Sonata* (Tavaszi szonáta); the young lady, a landowner's daughter, is not impressed by the young man of good family who plays the saxophone at the dance given at the manor-house. No, she feels an affinity to the simpler noble-minded son of the village school-teacher. They send messages to each other through Beethoven sonatas. *Love Fever* (Szerelmi láz) is the heartbreaking story of a once great singer dragged down by dissipation to the level of a clown. It is with horror mixed with envy that we see him go for a walk after his performance at the circus. Of course, his evening stroll is a mere pretext; what he really goes out for is a couple of drinks in the tavern at the corner, while his daughter, who has just come home unexpectedly from abroad, wrings her hands in vain.

In addition, these dramas were usually plagiarisms. They presented to the Hungarian public the stories of American, French and German films of twenty years before, as proofs of the gifts of Hungarian directors marked out for a brilliant future. *The Way Back* (Vissza az úton) is a typical example. The story was taken from an American film with Emil Jannings *(The Way of All Flesh),* and this became so evident at the *première* that even Andor Lajta, a very cautious man, allowed himself to remark that the film "...certainly walks along beaten tracks, for it follows an old picture with Jannings, in a slightly changed setting."[12]

The story is about a bank clerk who, after having lived an exemplary life, becomes sick of bowing and scraping, of being honest, of being treated with condescension; suddenly he breaks out. He embezzles, gambles, lives high, keeps mistresses, and enjoys himself. When the money is spent, he goes to work as a labourer in the building trade. Then he sinks still deeper and finally becomes a regular boozer in low taverns. Before he is completely ruined he wakes up from his tormenting dream—for it was only a dream—to learn with senile bliss that the general manager has promoted him to the rank of managing clerk. A managing clerk! A recurrent wish-dream of Hungarian films. Poor Kabos also used to play the role of a managing clerk, and, behold, now Csortos has been promoted to this position. Csortos was a first-rate actor, always authentic and true to life. He could do anything. He expressed his state of mind and the various degrees of gradual demoralization with few gestures, a flicker of an eyelid, a twitch of the mouth, a change of pace. But all his art could not save the film, for the director, Ákos Ráthonyi, was no more than an enthusiastic imitator.

The Way Back smacks of imitations from beginning to end. Its American model was dressed in French camera-angles and echoes of other films that Ráthonyi obviously admired—Machaty's *Extase* and Sternberg's *Blue Angel,* to add a few more Jannings gestures to Csortos's role.

The series of stories woven around the figure of Katalin Karády are veritable clinical variants of a slimy artificial type of film: *Never Ask about the Past* (Ne kérdezd, ki voltam; Béla Balogh); *Temptation* (Kísértés; Zoltán Farkas); *Disillusion* (Csalódás; Frigyes Bán); *Opportunity* (Alkalom; Endre Rodriguez); *The Fatal Kiss* (Halálos csók; László Kalmár); *Machita* (Machita; Endre Rodriguez); *Opium Waltz* (Ópiumkeringő; Béla Balogh); *Happy Times* (Boldog idők; Endre Rodriguez); *A Heart Stops* (Egy szív megáll).

When this phenomenon—which was far more unhealthy than the common comedy-dumping of the 'thirties—is studied as a curiosity of film history, the first stories of the young, developing Hungarian film can easily be recognized. Terrified by a new war, Hungarian film production, refusing to obey the need of self-examination, took refuge in the remotest past of film history in its search for stories and inspiration. In that remote period a high professional training at least helped directors to discriminate clearly between notions of good and evil, and thus to dispense at least some primitive moral justice, but the majority of the wartime directors who made the films mentioned above were ignorant of the very primary rules of the profession, and, easily confused by any intricate story, were unable to show even that primitive moral truth.

The films of József Daróczy, *Why* (Miért?), *Fidelitely,* and *Too Late,* represented a higher standard in the sentimental drama. A former staff officer, Daróczy appeared on the scene as a cinema owner in the 'twenties; in the 'thirties he was a successful producer. Having considered and studied every aspect and trick of directing with utmost care, he began to direct his first film at the age of fifty-six. He knew his public well, and was fully aware of what film-goers wished to see amidst the aimlessness and uncertainty of the war years. His films did not float in an imaginary reality of anywhere at any time, but endeavoured to reflect a semblance of the reality as it was seen in Hungary in those days. His pictures and their presentation are note-worthy: Hungarian provincial towns, familiar offices, shops, factories, turns of speech, customs; a lively and very typical Hungarian railway station; a florist's shop, a tram stop. However, the story, in the form of a sterile con-versation piece, is again about the dramatic love story of a touchingly decent man who is liable to err—men of forty are said to have wept in the cinema!—which has nothing whatever to do with the superficial problems of life at the time. It was only due to the exceptional abilities of Antal Páger, Elma Bulla and Klári Tolnay and to the whole well-chosen cast that the average cinema-goer could be made to believe that he had received more than from other Hungarian films.

The most typical example of the standards approved by Hungarian film in the war years, and of conceptions concerning true and profound art, is the film *Light and Shadow* (Fény és árnyék) directed by Klára Tüdős, the wife of a state secretary. This film is the purest example of the official policy of the Horthy era. Light implies a good, beautiful life; shadow stands for plain, ugly living. Let us live a pure, noble, moral life. Adultery is reprehen-sible. Who represents light? Where is light? Light emanates from the Hun-garian upper classes. Shadow is cast by the proletarians. The honest head of the family deserts his wife and his children for an ill-willed, mercenary woman, a "proletarian", who corrupts the Hungarian father, and throws him out with a voluptuous laugh. Hungarian mothers! Do not tolerate such things! For lack of a better idea, the Hungarian lady tolerates her husband's spree and in a meek Christian spirit of forgiveness admits to her villa at Lake Balaton children of the same miserable, low caste. Finally, the father, full of contrition, returns to his noble lady.

These events are accompanied by light and shadow effects produced with great display and marked by a curious mixture of styles, imitating French avant-garde and contemporary German films alternately.

In his experiments, representing a much higher level and aspirations, Lajos Zilahy tried to make literary films under Pagnol's influence *(Regain, la Femme du boulanger, la Fille du puisatier)*. Zilahy was aware of the importance of film as a medium and also of its duty to hold up before the nation a mirror while representing its problems. Zilahy's weekly, the *Híd,* published film reviews by eminent writers, even screenplays and outlines of films *(la Femme du boulanger).* It was his conviction that only literature could raise a film to the height of true art. Though this principle is wrong theoretically, in the development of Hungarian films it played an important role in the periods when it was applied, namely at the time of the Republic of Councils and before. So Zilahy tried to revive a decent tradition. He founded a firm, which put on the screen his own plays as well as works by Zsigmond Móricz, Jenő J. Tersánszky, and other writers who were his friends.

Fatal Spring (Halálos tavasz), directed by László Kalmár with the cooperation of Zilahy, scored a success which is almost incomprehensible today. Students and undergraduates of today who have grown up in a socialist atmosphere shake their heads when they watch the meaningless situations and burst into uncontrollable laughter in the most dramatic moments of a film which shows to them little difference from other specimens of melodrama from the war years. Nevertheless, there can be no doubt that something new was initiated and tried in *Fatal Spring,* and its novel traits were appreciated not only by the public, but also by the most exacting reviews. It was in reality this film, made in 1939, that started the trend which finally led to *People on the Alps. Fatal Spring* was meant to give a serious and uncompromising portrait of society if only within its own chosen narrow field, but this intention was baffled by the censor. The story is as follows:

A young man, having come from his country estate to the capital to work in an office, falls in love with the beautiful and flirtatious daughter of a rich statesman. The girl, flirting with other men, loves the hero in her own way and fascinates him by her sex appeal. She stops short of giving herself to him, but, with calculating coquetry, she never ceases to hold out the promise of near fulfilment. Plans for their wedding are discussed. The hero surprises his fiancée with another man and breaks off their engagement. The man finds consolation in the love of a modest, intelligent, and attractive girl working in an office. Without any prudery or fuss, the girl yields to him spontaneously and they become lovers; she accepts the position of a mistress which, in a feudal atmosphere, involves humiliation for her, though it is a perfectly natural relationship between social equals, entailing no humiliation. They are on the point of getting married when the rich girl learns about her former fiancé having found happiness in love. Wounded in her vanity, and with an element of jealousy, she wants him back. The hero finds no way out of his dilemma. He blows out his brains.

The story, written in the early 'twenties, when the counter-revolution was still in control, is rather trite. The suicide is forced. The almost mythical attraction and power of the woman's sex appeal are improbable, and are reminiscent of the sirens and vamps of Hollywood. Under existing Hungarian conditions, however, this breeze that streamed into the stuffy atmosphere of the cinema brought something new and good. The office was a real Budapest office, an insignificant factory of documents, where everybody believes himself to be of central importance; the apartment of the modest young girl radiates calm, practical philosophy, a fit place for her uncle, a sergeant in the fire-brigade, and a cheerful journalist who often drops in for supper. This seems very little: a bourgeois consciousness that has vanished with the past, but at the time it was new in a film-world teeming with hussar officers. This is shown also by the fact that the censor would not let the father be a general, and the policeman had to be transformed into a sergeant of the fire-brigade.

The opening scenes of the Danube in the grey light of dawn are good: the river carries along scraps of paper and other litter... a discouraged, dejected picture of a city suggesting a lurking awareness of the war. From literary aspects, including the story and dramatic construction, the other films of Zilahy showed more value than did *Fatal Spring. Virgin with Lamb* (A szűz és a gödölye) was another unsuccessful attempt to star Gizi Bajor on the screen: her stage manner appeared stilted on the screen, while owing to lack of experience in directing, these films were over-elaborate, mediocre, and often dull. *The Outlaw* (Betyár) of Móricz in a version diluted to suit the taste of Gyula Wlassich, under the title *Lovely Star* (Szép csillag), a screenplay by Ferenc Jankovics, belongs to this series. Screen versions of Móricz's works produced by other firms, for instance *Judge Sarah* (directed by Tibor Hegedűs in 1943), were, however, better.

As has been pointed out before, the Hungarian tradition of literary films stagnated in the war years. Neither the spectacular version of Mikszáth's novel *The Talking Kaftan* (direction Géza Radványi) nor screen versions based on the works of contemporary authors, as *Magdalen* (Magdolna), came up to expectations. Apart from Zilahy's above-mentioned attempts, filmed novels were still poor adaptations for the screen, in the manner of the silent film industry.

The Mikszáth film of Ákos D. Hamza is a revealing example, placing, as it did, *The Half of a Boy* (Egy fiúnak a fele) in a contemporary background. This film, made by a Roman Catholic firm and intended both by producer and director to be a film of resistance, shows the awkward position of the

Hungarian artists with humanist intentions, but with a confused ideology accepting social progress with eternal anxiety and reservation. The film is based on the changed children idea: an infant is smuggled into the cradle of a newborn baby at the manor-house so cleverly that nobody can tell which of the two babies lying side by side is the landlord's own. Therefore both children are brought up in the style of the upper classes, while the parents never cease to brood over the question of how to identify true Hungarian blue blood. When the family secret is finally revealed, nobody cares to speak to the otherwise respectable family.

In this story shy anti-fascist hints alternate with scenes of the nobility's annoying condescension. "We have had enough of war, of purposeless bloodshed, of racial persecution," declares the priest, one of the protagonists, in fine, very sensible words. "I shall shut myself in and see nobody until this madness is over", says the father, and this attitude is typical of the lower middle-class mentality of the age. But when the lady acquaints the servants with her democratic feelings by threatening to box the ears of those who will dare to address her by her title, it is hard to say whether one feels inclined to laugh or to be vexed. Moreover, the direction is poor, showing lack of experience and knowledge. So the protest of the well-meaning Pax Studio came to nothing; it remained an intention, and the film cannot even be regarded as a modest work of art in its own sphere.

Due to the war, Géza Radványi left France and returned to Hungary. In his film, *No Answer from Europe,* he used a spy story to voice the reservatiosn of an artist to the war which had just broken out. "What is suffering for us will bring business to you", says a character in the film to the rich tycoon when he learns about the war. Point-blank, Radványi declares that war is foolish, senseless bloodshed to promote the crazy ambitions of a major power. The film is not without sentimental, sad Hungarian elements, such as the Hungarian immigrant in America who longs for his village and dies on the ship that is bringing him home, while speaking about his old thatched cottage.

Géza Radványi came home from his travels abroad for a brief period as a well-trained expert. He was the first in Hungary to apply modern cutting and a mobile camera. He often resorted to cutting on movement—regarded as heresy in Hungary—thus producing animated life even in a studio as small, narrow and primitive as the premises on the Könyves Kálmán Boulevard, converted from a public soup-kitchen. He often conveyed movement by moving the camera against the actors' movements, stimulating the audience to think where required, he used quick and expressive cutting.

Under existing studio conditions, limited space was exploited cleverly by providing the ship's deck with steps, air-holes, and deck-chairs, permitting motion in various directions. In directing actors, Radványi's ways differed from the usual methods: he inspired his actors to live their parts. His other films—*Hearing in Camera* and *A Woman Looks Back*—also bear witness to this cultured attitude. It is a pity that these films deal with tragic love stories of a society which may exist anywhere, with little relation to contemporary Hungarian reality.

Another series of films displays the influence exerted by the trend of populist writers. In their own time, these films had a profound impact. At first glance they seem to be of equal value in both their ideological and their artistic standards: *Stephen Bors* (Bors István); *Dr. Jur. Stephen Kovács* (Doktor Kovács István); *The Thirtieth* (A harmincadik); *Landslide* (Föld-indulás); *The Daughter of the Mountains*; *The Golden Peacock*; *And the Blind Can See* (És a vakok látnak). Upon closer inspection, they are found to include realistic works of honest, progressive intentions as well as films echoing popular fascist slogans. For instance Viktor Bánky, the pampered director of the system, used all his films to make inciting fascist propaganda.

And the Blind Can See is the only Hungarian talkie from the time before the Liberation to have chosen for its subject the life of the working class in the capital.

The film clearly shows that its director had profited from the films of Marcel Carné: the manner in which István Nagy—who plays the leading part—bends over the metal which he is welding in a basement workshop reminds one of Jean Gabin in *le Jour se lève*. It was exceedingly rare in Hungarian films to show mechanics working, welding, talking in a workshop. The script was written by Dénes Barsi, and was directed by Imre Jeney, his first work. A plumber courts a young servant girl from the country. When she becomes pregnant, they go to a woman in an outlying district who is known to procure abortions; the workman pays the woman but the girl decides to keep her baby. The plumber loves the girl, but in his great anger at being driven into a corner without money or a home, he breaks with her and joins the army. What he dreaded before now serves to postpone a decision. The servant girl is dismissed and goes home with her shame to her village. Her parents want her to give up her baby to the bailiff's childless wife who would like to adopt it. But the young mother will not hear of it though she is in a hard and hopeless plight. Then the plumber comes home from the war; he has been wounded and has lost his sight at the front. Now that he is blind he becomes reconciled to the girl, the mother of his child.

What is great and moving in the film is the relatively decent representation of working-class life, considering that it had to satisfy the upper-class demands of Wlassich and his associates. The sequences of walks in the park, and of the servants' promenade in Baross Square are fine examples of *cinéma vérité* as are the sad, suburban streets, the world of tenements, troubles, taverns and kitchens rarely shown on our screen, the startling, newsreel-like shots of troop-trains going to the front, of farewells and tears, of men going out to meet senseless death. The world of the needy peasantry in the village, the surroundings of the village well, sly curiosity peering out from behind shutters are also good. However, the military heroism of the scenes at the front is shameful and ludicrous: "Well, boys, who is going to show Hungarian bravado!"; shameful, even if the hero gently gives some food to a frightened and starved Russian woman crouching on the threshold of her plundered house. The arrogant figure as acted by István Nagy is phoney and so is the "low" world of workmen loitering about in taverns. The simpering sweetness shown by the bailiff and his wife to the unmarried mother in her trouble is equally phoney; the film is nevertheless a noteworthy effort.

Both in execution and in its after-effects, due to the political opportunism of the producer, the irreconcilable contradictions of the period are shown most clearly in *The Thirtieth* directed by László Cserépy.

Its background is the administrative premises of a mine; the staff lives in an atmosphere of petty intrigue. The hunchback chemist's wife favours one engineer after another, and the chief engineer also takes his turn. A sort of leader of the miners—played by Somlay—does not surrender to this atmosphere of intrigue and strives to establish certain primitive social reforms. Among other things, he organizes a school, and the new schoolmaster soon arrives. However, the ruling classes and their representative, the chief engineer, are against miners' children going to school; in their opinion miners' children should not be educated because if they acquire knowledge, they may become dangerous. On some trumped-up pretext he requisitions the building previously allotted to the school, throws out the desks, drives away the children and, to make matters worse, actuated by a misunderstanding due to the report of a stupid clerk, he spreads the slanderous gossip that the school-teacher, who is known to court the young daughter of the miners' leader, is having a love affair with the hunchback chemist's wife. With the support of the miners, the school-teacher finds the thirtieth child and in a dramatic scene he thrashes the chief engineer because he had remarked, when a miner's child died under tragic conditions "...what difference does one miner's brat make?"

Social irritation, sympathy for the predicament of oppressed people, and romantic anti-capitalism are pervaded by the loud colours of Hungarian "national" demagogy. The director feels that something is wrong and that it ought to be corrected, but he doesn't know how; he knows little or nothing about social classes or social movements, living as he did under the magic spell of lofty slogans. The reason why it is so difficult to see the well-intended social criticism of the film clearly may be explained by the difference between the author and the director.

The author, Márton Kerecsendi, was a favourite of the fascists; the director, on the other hand, was a sober bourgeois expert who did not like immoderate extremes. He nevertheless wanted to represent reality, and to hold a mirror before his audience. The film gives a good picture of the difficult situation of Hungarian cinema in the war years. A politically untrained director who undertook to convey a social message was more easily confused by the intricate tangle of fascist ideology that obscured real problems with a thousand threads, than the well-versed craftsman who, from the very first, deliberately abhorred every kind of reality, and directed his own sentimental-melodramatic films with a shrug of his shoulders. László Cserépy tackled an acute problem, the problem of schools in mining communities, and immediately found himself up against cares and troubles never encountered, never realized before in a film, stumbling amidst the distorting-glasses of fascist ideology, which falsified these troubles in the enchanted castle of war-time Hungary. This ideological confusion is typical of other, less significant films of the period, too.

The artistic execution of the film is significant, first of all owing to the actuality of scenes taken near a real mine. The figures are animated and life-like; shaded and complicated. In Hungarian films this was rare, for at the time the most primitive kinds of black or white characterizations were in vogue. The situation was rendered increasingly complicated by the circumstance that the fascist press broke into exaggerated praise when a film treated a social problem even slightly according to the fascist taste.

Owing to the inciting articles of the contemporary extreme rightist press and to the arbitrary alterations made later by the producer or the distributors, partly also to the ideology of the script, this film has fallen into oblivion; however, to many people it is a dark memory as an anti-Semitic film. The Hungarian fascist press declared that the film was not against capitalists, but lashed out against the character of the "Jewish chief engineer". In point of fact, the chief engineer has a typically gentry appearance, with monocle, moustache, boots, and a Tyrolean hat.

Pressed by the censor and rightist circles, the producer agreed to insert an anti-Semitic phrase in the completely finished film delivered by the director. In the standard copy preserved in the Film Archive there is no such phrase.

Even so, the film cannot be excused. Solutions of a high artistic standard—which deserve a place in the archive of Hungarian film achievements—are mingled with false, demagogic clichés, reflecting the intellectual life of the period. And the cause of the people is represented not by the people, but by some representative of the ruling classes, in this instance by the school-master. The passive, suffering people only endure the kindness and favours conferred on them, and wait helplessly to be redeemed by those "qualified" for such leadership.

People on the Alps

"Hungary's achievement of *People on the Alps,* shot by a young director little over twenty, is of great importance. It proves that young people have a new message to convey by means of the cinema. They want to, and do, create and flight in the spirit of art, because they reject all mercenary claims. Let us leave the serious task of criticism to others, but without forgetting the lesson to be learnt from the Hungarian director István Szőts; the fresh instincts brought by Hungarian films into Europe's superannuated film production... The time has come to try ourselves. Hungary has shown the way. If the old men of cinema who piece together film products have nothing more to say, if the kind of film production they represent is exhausted, if their knowledge as directors is clumsy and false, well then, let us work without them: the money they have thought about so long will permit them to enjoy a calm old age. Let the song of the Alps, the song sounded for the first time by István Szőts, finally penetrate our own studios, and chase away the senile notables, the traders and profiteers—and from the Venice festival, too. We believe in the young who will fight and win their own cinema battles."

This is quoted from the September 25, 1942 issue of the Italian journal *Cinema.*

Szőts started in 1940 as a director's assistant. In 1941 he made a short film in the studio of the well-known sculptor, Zsigmond Kisfaludi Strobl. Then he directed *People on the Alps.*

The script was written by himself based on the short stories of József Nyírő, *Wooden Headboards* (Kopjafák). The cameraman was Ferenc Fekete, the music was composed by Ferenc Farkas. The leading parts were played by Alice Szellay, János Görbe, József Bihari, none of them fashionable film stars. It was Alice Szellay's first appearance on the screen; János Görbe was a young actor of Kolozsvár. József Bihari was an experienced actor, but at the time unknown to film-goers.

The story of the film:

In the Transylvanian mountains a woodcutter lives happily with his young wife. A boy is born to them; the woodcutter introduces his son to the forest, to the plants, to the wild animals, and dedicates to him a tree of life. The woodcutter and his wife know little of civilization. Old shepherds help the young couple with gifts, one brings a lamb, another a calf. One day some townsmen come to the place; they have bought the forest and from that day it belongs to a timber company. Those who live in the forest will now have to pay rent.

Since the poor woodcutter has no money and the chief forester of the company finds the young woman very attractive, the young people are offered jobs compelling them to move down to the settlement. Here the woman serves drinks in the bar, while the man, being familiar with the forest, becomes a guide for woodcutters. The chief forester soon sends him off to a distant region of the Alps that he might in the meantime approach the defenceless woman. He does so; but the beautiful young woman wrestles with him; in the scuffle the lamp is upset and the house burns down. When the man gets home he finds the smouldering ruins and a sick wife who has been exposed to the cold winter night.

The woman suffers and does not get better. They set out to the fair of Csíksomlyó in the hope that the Holy Virgin there will work a miracle. After a laborious trip they reach the place, but their pilgrimage does not bring the woman relief. A friar advises the desperate woodcutter to take his wife to a learned doctor in Kolozsvár from whom alone he may expect help. The disappointed couple go to Kolozsvár. Here the professor pockets his fee but cannot help; the exhausted wife dies.

Burial being a costly affair, and the woman having wished to rest in the soil of the Alps, the man has a bold idea: he dresses his dead wife and puts her on the train. During the journey he speaks tenderly to her and explains to the others in the compartment that she is ill. Gradually all the passengers guess the truth; they understand the situation, but no one betrays the man's secret, not even the railway guard. So the poor woodcutter brings his wife home and he buries her. Now his anger turns against the chief forester who caused his wife's death. He speaks to his fellow woodcutters and other men living in the forest. As the chief forester is a vicious man, the woodcutter decides to kill him in the name of the community. He kills him and is convicted. All the shepherds crowd to the place of the trial to speak as witnesses, but on the wrong day. Up in the mountains there was a mistake in the calendar, and they arrive too late, when the woodcutter, having confessed his deed, has been sentenced to long imprisonment. The shepherds declare their willingness to share his punishment, and one old shepherd is ready to go to prison instead of the young woodcutter, because he has few years ahead of him; it is no use, they are driven out of the building.

On Christmas day the young woodcutter suddenly appears; he has escaped from prison, to see his little son. The gendarmes in pursuit have wounded him. He is dying in silent agony in the old shepherd's hut. The old man cannot understand why he left the warm shelter of the prison where he had a blanket in the winter and some bread to eat. The dying woodcutter asks his old friend to go down to the village, to report to the authorities that he has caught the fugitive, to get the money promised as a reward for his capture, and spend it on his little son. The old shepherd does as he is told. The man dies.

The old shepherd trudges through the snow, carrying the child towards the hut. Since no priest will come into the Alps in such a blizzard, the mountain people arrange the scene of Bethlehem. They stand around a mother suckling her baby who personifies the Holy Virgin with the Child, and bring in their animals as it is written in the Gospel. They sing, these herdsmen...

It is easy to spot the weakness of the film: Rousseau's philosophy seeking an anodyne in nature against civilization. There can be no doubt that this philosophy, mixed with pantheism, showing little respect for urban civilization, and even rejecting the town as a dwelling-place for capitalists and the ruling class, i.e. as the embodiment of Evil, is naive and backward. How good it is to live in nature, amidst trees, birds, flowers and fawns; how good it is not to know what is happening in the world of gentlemen. Up here in the mountains there is no private property, no rent, perhaps not even money: here everybody lives purely and plainly. The opening shots of the film suggest such a spirit of modern pantheism. The bleak misery of the timber yard, the cold heartlessness of the town, from physician to landlady, point to the director's romantic anti-capitalism.

However, this romantic anti-capitalism was a positive element in the Hungary of the Second World War, when fascism was at its height. Affirmation of the humanist desire for a peaceful life was equally positive, while the candidly angry representation of the Hungarian peasantry's inhuman misery was still more so. In this respect there is not one false note in this film, or any dissonant grimace, both unfortunately characteristic of earlier attempts in a similar milieu, as in *Stephen Bors*.

The film is as excellent in the direction as in its message. Particularly striking today is the last third of the film in which the woodcutter kills the chief forester, is convicted, and the shepherds offer to take turns in serving his sentence. This series of pictures is modern, even in a 1974 sense, but in 1942 it was too unusual and too far ahead of its time. First of all, the wood-cutter is not seen killing the chief forester. The director lets the spectator imply what has happened. Secondly we do not see the court scene of the woodcutter being sentenced. We only see the scared shepherds loitering around the court building. Here is all that we see: the hero resolutely takes up his axe and reaches the house of the chief forester: cut to the court-house where the shepherds have just heard that they are too late for the trial, for it took place the day before. From this the audience learns what has happened in the meantime. The rather objective words of the shepherds amount to a severe indictment against the ruling class. This is also a novelty and a great artistic achievement. The director does not exploit the shepherds' consternation at having arrived too late, he takes as little notice of this fact as do the shepherds themselves. However, this draws attention to the shepherds' plight, their humiliation and misery. The film-goer looks on in dismay; though his emotions are not yet involved at this point, he has begun to think.

The director is helped by modern methods of acting. His actors play their parts with unsophisticated simplicity. Some of them do not seem to be actors at all. The pictures representing the Fair of Csíksomlyó create a similar impression: the Fair itself is seen on the screen, with a *real* procession of pilgrims, peasants praying in true ecstasy, trying to resolve all the desperation of their lives in the glimmer of hope promised by devout prayer. This sequence may be regarded as a notable use of the concealed camera.

Another case in point is the scene of the wounded woodcutter dying in the hut of his old friend. The old man has no idea what to do with his unexpected guest. He thinks of branding the wound when it is too late, when the man has nearly bled to death. Here, too, the apparent indifference of the dialogue, instead of the usual appealing text of the period, moving the audience to tears, is an entirely new feature and gives voice to social discontent. These two men regard the hero's wounds by the pursuing gendarmes with almost as listless an indifference as is shown by the wild animals of the forest, deer or stags, which, when wounded, drag themselves to a thicket where no one can witness their agony. These two men discuss the most natural steps to be taken, most natural for they are the most reasonable under the circumstances. The old man is to go and fetch the boy and take the blood-money, since by the time he gets back the woodcutter is sure to be dead.

What does this attitude reveal? It shows not only the wise resignation to death of people living in nature, but it says much more: the helping hand of society is nowhere to be found. One cannot count on anybody or anything —not on the priest or the shrine of Csíksomlyó, on the Kolozsvár physician, or on the chief forester offering money and prosperity, who is really a symbol of the whole ruling class, not even on the village notary who is scandalized when the old shepherd takes the blood-money.

Poor people can count only on one another, as when the woodcutter takes his dead wife home on the train. Here, too, the director avoids display. The dead woman is almost unseen, what is emphasized is the gentle care of the husband who speaks affectionately to his dead wife, for he still loves her. The guard, after a tense moment of bewildered hesitation, punches in a close-up the second ticket, that of the woman, giving the husband and the whole third class compartment to understand that he knows everything, but he is on their side... It is this simplicity without pathos, this treatment of the poor without condescension, and their representation with pure human sympathy which Szőts learnt and adopted from Soviet films. This style, this profound understanding of the underprivileged is reminiscent of *Road to Life*—or of the trilogy on Gorky's childhood.

The well-balanced camerawork, avoiding any conventional film-like approach, is also noteworthy. Szőts avoided the display of the camera and spectacular shots; he worked with extreme simplicity and directness. This was the Soviet style of the 'thirties, contrary to the earlier extensive use of montage and the highly developed American camerawork of the period. As a matter of fact the duality of the message of the film—and of the young, inexperienced director—is seen also in the camerawork. Where the social message is grave, the film gives uncompromising, pure realism; where pantheistic, romantic love of nature prevails, the camera presents beautiful, touchingly emotional, exceedingly effective, but slightly artificial scenes, such as the walk in the woods on the snowy peak, the scenes on the way to the Fair of Csíksomlyó, calling to mind the wandering of the Holy Family. At the woman's funeral the shot taken from the bottom of the grave is powerful: the coffin is lowered, as it were, on the spectators themselves, and for a few moments the screen is engulfed in seemingly everlasting darkness.

This duality appears also in the performance of the actors. His old mountain shepherd is perhaps the finest achievement of József Bihari in his whole career. He personifies the oppressed Hungarian people. The simple, ignorant woodcutter of János Görbe is also realistic. One can understand and believe his passionate, sometimes savage faith, his boundless love, and his simpleminded confidence in his master which, after his disappointment, can lead only to murder. The charm and mildly sentimental, sometimes affected acting of beautiful, madonna-faced Alice Szellay expresses more the romantic longing of an educated person to get away to virgin Nature, rather than the adamant purity of a peasant girl hardened by work and by life on a snow-capped mountain. The repulsive, stupid and sinister figure of the chief forester is reminiscent of the bailiffs seen in silent films; a monotonous part, almost a failure.

The men of the snow-capped mountains take retaliation for the innocent woman's death into their own hands by revenge on the chief forester, the symbol of the ruling classes. Though the gendarmes' bullets kill the avenger, and apparently order is restored, the men's stubborn looks make one feel that nothing will be forgotten. This mode of formulating a romantic revolt against oppression was the maximum that Hungarian films were capable of before the year of the Liberation, 1945.

Szőts himself was unable to carry on the revolt as he had intended to. He was not allowed to shoot the version written by Ranódy or Móra's novel; quite incredibly, not even a script written in collaboration with Ferenc Herczeg. "I have been informed," he stated bitterly in 1943, "that *People on the Alps* wouldn't be an acceptable film these days. I have also been warned to keep away from a Mikszáth and a Ferenc Herczeg script."[13]

From these facts it clearly emerges that *People on the Alps* was not a fruit of war-time film production; it came rather as a defiance. In fact, until the Liberation, István Szőts could put on the screen only one effectively photographed, romantic popular ballad of peculiar atmosphere, *Kata Kádár*. This short film was made to the music of Zoltán Kodály.

People on the Alps is the most outstanding Hungarian film made before the Liberation.

*Somewhere
in Europe
1945—1947*

Liberation was a milestone in Hungarian film history. Cinemas were flooded with new films. The first Soviet films showed the life of a previously unknown, unfamiliar society, in a new and interesting form; such masters as Eisenstein, Donskoy, Kozintsev and Pudovkin addressed a new public.

Liberated Hungary and the Last Private Film Productions

Béla Balázs came home, founded a journal, gave lectures, and began to teach the new public how to look at films, and new creative teams how to make films, training the first students of film production after 1945, who were to direct their first films in the 'fifties. He wrote and published a summing up of his views on film aesthetics, his first Hungarian book on film art, entitled *Film Culture* (Filmkultúra).

The effect of all this became apparent, first, in the more exacting criticism of reviews and in a better informed public. Progressive films reached Hungary. Untalented craftsmen who had been active during the war years disappeared, yet there was no structural change. From the Liberation to 1948, Hungarian film production was carried on by private enterprise: capitalists could produce films at the state studios.

The brief period of three years before nationalization in 1948 clearly falls into two parts. The first comprised the half-hearted attempts of private enterprise; four films from autumn, 1945 to spring, 1946. In the second, the four parties of the coalition government produced five films from autumn, 1947 to spring, 1948.

In liberated Hungary, between 1945 and 1946, there were altogether 280 cinemas[1] which played over one hundred American films, as well as a few dozen Soviet, French and English films. American film capital, concentrated in the firm MOPEX, launched a campaign to recapture the Hungarian market. It hired the Erkel Theatre and played cowboy films in the big auditorium.

The film studios had been hard hit by the war; their reconstruction took several months but this was accompanied by reorganization. Viktor Gertler became the director of Hunnia, Ákos D. Hamza of MAFIRT. Both men did their best to start production, but this required the co-operation of a businessman; the businessman needed capital, raw film, and, above all, a market. Did 280 cinemas promise a market? To make matters worse, there was inflation; it is a wonder that films were made at all.

The first Hungarian feature film to be produced after the war was a screen version of Sándor Bródy's play, *The School-Mistress* (A tanítónő), directed by Márton Keleti. The leads were played by Éva Szörényi and Pál Jávor. The second was a film version of a play by Ernő Szép, *The Gold Watch* (Aranyóra), directed by Ákos Ráthonyi, with Éva Szörényi and Gyula Gózon in the lead. Both films were made in the autumn of 1945.

Both titles are revealing. Both directors put on the screen valuable works of Hungarian literature. Thus the tradition of Hungarian film production to rely on literature was revived. However, when we realize that Sándor Bródy's novels had been made into silent films; that *The School-Mistress* had been filmed in 1917; that Ernő Szép's delicate lyrical poetry had failed on the screen in 1934, it becomes clear that these were belated efforts. In 1917 *The School-Mistress* was a modern story, indeed, a very topical one, in 1945 it was a classic of Hungarian literature. Where is the sweeping impetus of wanting something new, of wanting something different? Where are the problems which engrossed so many people after 1945, and were taken up one after the other, for instance, by Italian neo-realist films? Where is the really revolutionary confrontation with the past? The review published in *Szabad Nép,* March 24, 1946, was justified in pointing out this inadequacy. "These two Hungarian feature films produced since Liberation, *The School-Mistress* and *The Gold Watch*... cannot represent the new Hungary in this important medium of art... They view this hideous period of life in Hungary under Horthy from the forgiving perspective of a café table."

In the life-work of Márton Keleti, who had directed altogether a few ordinary comedies before Liberation, *The School-Mistress* was nevertheless an important step. The beginning of the film is encouraging: a well-established atmosphere, modern, quick cutting with a good eye for essential points and realistic acting, avoiding irrelevant distractions. Keleti directed the camera cleverly: with a few shots he put before the audience a village of 1905; its stupid and sly society, with the paltry squire, who, though powerful and important in his own village, creates the impression of a clown when he comes to town. The school scenes are excellent, and so are Éva Szörényi and her clumsy, fumbling colleague, Zoltán Várkonyi, looking as if he had stepped on the screen straight from a novel of Dostoevsky. In the last third of the film the magic vanishes: Jávor is again the old Jávor, no woman can resist him; the parents smile at each other; Lily Berky waves back to the public from an old Hungarian comedy; there is a fly with a splendid horse and there is a handsome young couple; the peasants give up the idea of emigration, for their landlord has changed for the better: the style of acting as well as that of the directing falls into the old groove with a heavy bump. Happy ending. Music.

The Gold Watch of Ákos Ráthonyi reflects the zeal of the ambitious pupil, as did all his "serious and profound" works, for instance *The Way Back* discussed in another chapter of this book. It is a film in the French style of the 'thirties which was justly admired in its own time. We are shown the scene from behind the police officer's sabre hung on the coat-rack or from the angle of a very low camera; at such moments it seems as if the director had nudged your elbow to prepare you for the overwhelming novelty of his shooting technique. And who is the victim to be sorry for? A poor little watchmaker, for who else but a watchmaker could be a workman in 1945? So the situation was again viewed from above, from the aspect of the ruling class: from that height the figures of workman and artisan seemed to merge. This attitude ought to have been fully abandoned by 1945.

The same attitude was revealed by Szilárd Darvas in his review of the film *Without Lies* (Hazugság nélkül) published in the journal edited by Béla Balázs, a film known in several versions.[2] The circumstances under which *Without Lies*, the third Hungarian film after Liberation, came to be produced, bore the mark of the old heritage. The film was financed by a hosiery manufacturer of Temesvár, named Pollák, on the condition that his daughter would play the lead. Well, she did play the lead under the name of Ági Polly, dancing, singing and chattering from beginning to end. In the film the spirit of the banal comedies of the 'thirties is blended in an astonishing manner with the style of "proletkult" ballet: at the end of the film Lajos Básti dances a labour-ballet among huge machines and dynamos, indicating that he is a hero of labour.

This whole, thinly trickling film production by private enterprise was brought to a Laurel and Hardy conclusion by the disastrous interruption of the shooting of *René der XIV. oder der König streikt* (René XIV, or the King on Strike), a film in German made in Budapest by Hungarian businessmen. The production of this film, directed by Ákos Ráthonyi, with Franciska Gaál, Theo Lingen and Hans Moser in the leads, was undertaken in the hope that the German-speaking market would show a demand for the Budapest comedy of an old type prohibited in the nazi era. As there was no more money, and the little that remained was soon spent, in spring, 1946, the producer went abroad to get money and raw film. He never came back; he remained in Vienna. Then Ákos Ráthonyi, the director, went off to try to raise capital. He, too, failed and stayed abroad.

This was the end of private enterprise in Hungarian film production. In 1947 a new method was introduced to revive film production: only the leading parties of the coalition government were given permits to produce films. This move had an economic basis in so far as the largest cinemas had been distributed among the parties.

Sarló Studio, the firm of the Peasant Party—with László Ranódy as manager—began to shoot *Prophet of the Fields* (Mezei próféta) in 1947 in Transylvania. Based on the work of Áron Tamási, the film was directed by Frigyes Bán, with Éva Szőke—known abroad as Éva Bartók—Gyula Benkő, József Bihari and Árpád Lehotay in the leads. The writer's name, the story, the Transylvanian background, the excellent actors promised another *People on the Alps*. Instead, the flattest, the most insipid, poorly directed and poorly acted film of Hungarian film history, with the most confused philosophy, was produced.

The Smallholders' Party produced a musical comedy, *The Light Muse* (Könnyű Múzsa), from the script of István Békeffy, under the direction of Zoltán Kerényi. The cast included Mária Mezey, Ida Turay, Éva Szörényi, János Sárdy, Gábor Rajnai and Kálmán Latabár, so all was for the best... In the film, Latabár's old gags were depressingly poor and clumsy. The tight-fitting garments on Ida Turay, inspired by the Hollywood muse, were far from thrilling; they were rather embarrassing, prompting the spectator to look elsewhere. The story is an imitation of American films, especially the dance film with Rita Hayworth, *Down to Earth*, in which the muse alights on earth, as in this Hungarian variant. The style of *The Light Muse* is that of Géza Bolváry in the early 'thirties: *Ein Lied, ein Kuss, ein Mädel...* In the latter half of the time the scene is laid in a gramophone record shop for the sake of the music; yes, but it was Tibor Halmay who made the jokes and it was Franciska Gaál who sang.

The Social Democratic Party put on the screen a film version of Kálmán Mikszáth's novel, *The Siege of Beszterce* (Beszterce ostroma). Márton Keleti directed, the script was written by István Békeffy and László Hárs. The film was shot in the months from December 1947 to the spring of 1948. This was the last Hungarian film to be finished before nationalization.

With this film, his second after Liberation, Márton Keleti remained faithful to the conception he had built up for himself, which he had followed also in *The School-Mistress*: a story about the past, addressed to the present as a modern version of a recognized work by a classical author. In this instance Keleti, very rightly, selected Mikszáth who had been so often and so grossly falsified in the Horthy era; after the adulterated versions of his work in *Old Rogue* and *Love and Money* put on the screen in the 'thirties, at last there came an opportunity for representing Mikszáth truthfully. On the whole, Keleti accomplished the task he set himself, although his work did not reach the level of later films based on Mikszáth. As a matter of fact, he concentrated on features of feudal Hungary which lent themselves readily to caricature; moreover, he shifted social exposure to several decades before the age of *The School-Mistress*. Acting was still stagey and conventional, but the style of direction was much more modern.

In these three years only István Szőts and Géza Radványi created work of lasting merit, work that was in inner harmony with the post-liberation period. None of these films could have been produced earlier. The film of Szőts had been prohibited in 1943. In his version of Móra's novel Szőts continued to weave the threads of thought taken up in *People on the Alps*, namely romantic anti-capitalism, swerving this time in the direction of anti-war attitudes and anti-clericalism. The film of MAFIRT, *Song of the Cornfields* (Ének a búzamezőkről)—like *People on the Alps*—chose for its theme the miserable lot of the peasantry. In this instance the abject poverty of peasants is shown not as the consequence of exploitation by the feudal landlord or directly by the ruling class, nor is it caused by depraved morals; it is due to the war and to superstition. Whereas *People on the Alps* only touched lightly on the disappointment of the hero and heroine after the fair of Csíksomlyó—no miracle has come to pass, the woman has not been cured—here, in addition to the peasants' fanatic belief and their expectation of a miracle, it is shown how wonders are brought about at the well by people who, exploiting the naive, childish faith of the superstitious peasants, become rich by collecting presents from these indigenous people hoping for a miracle. This is a noteworthy advance, and a positive achievement.

From Marxist view, *Song of the Cornfields* is undoubtedly based on faulty philosophy. Had the film been released, its faults would have been obvious; by expressing his thoughts and emotions stifled in 1942–43, Szőts would have progressed; he might have profited from debates and criticism. Yet as it is, *Song of the Cornfields* belongs to the outstanding pieces of Hungarian film history. The delineation of the world of peasants in the spirit of Ferenc Móra and István Tömörkény is very good, evoking as it does the pious misery of tenant-farmers and cotters. There is not a rustle in the air, charged with electricity under an overcast sky, and a calmly menacing line of poplars stand rigid as do soldiers under a command of attention in the tense moments of expectation, while despair gives way to ecstasy in an atmosphere vibrating with electricity.

Béla Balázs helped with advice when this new version of *Song of the Corn-fields* was written after Liberation, and it was he who wrote the script of *Somewhere in Europe* (Valahol Európában). The virtues of two Hungarian films of permanent value are bound up with his name. His early death is an irreparable loss, and the unjust criticism, applied to him as to Eisenstein, isolated him when his activities would have been the most beneficial.

In Szőts's film, Béla Balázs acted only as an adviser, but in Radványi's film he may be regarded as a collaborator. His influence is shown by the use of methods developed by Soviet films, applied in practice for the first time in Hungary. *Somewhere in Europe*—produced by the firm of the Hungarian Communist Party—is an epic on bringing back into society homeless children who have become vagrants, as in the film *Road to Life*. It was this masterpiece of Nikolai Ekk, produced in 1931, that inspired Béla Balázs to write the script. The pictures, scenes and characters correspond to those of *Road to Life*. As stated by Guido Aristarco: "This film shows the unmistakable influence of the Russians, to whose achievements Béla Balázs had contributed at the time by this theoretical work."[3]

The opening scenes of the film are based on the classical principle of conflictive montage: war, bombing, battles, deportation; from under a crumbling wall, from behind the palings of a reformatory school reduced to ruins by bombs, from the cracks in the floor of a death train children emerge. They move along the roads looking for food, they steal and keep themselves alive as they can. All this is seen without any dialogue or explanatory words, like the introductory scenes of a silent film.

Then these children form a gang; the strong ones rule the rest and they become a danger to society. They steal and plunder because they want to live. They find refuge in a partly ruined, partly intact ancient castle at a time when the authorities of the district are about to take severe measures. Here they get to know an eccentric musician who has come to live in this old castle to escape the horrors of war. The misanthropical musician leads them to the path of a sensible life, with love and patience. However, it turns out that society does not want them even when they are organized to live decently; but now they fight a veritable battle like creatures of a future new world, against the old, backward social order doomed to destruction. They conquer the old order, and their shouts of joy are harbingers of a better world as predicted by the great Hungarian poet Attila József.

This society of children is the most authentic, the truest creative element of the film. The way these children share their food, devise a wicked prank, and accept the stronger among them as leaders, acting instinctively after the ancient law of gangs and recognizing the advantages of such a choice in the interest of all; the way in which they realize the presence of some deeper and more serious civilization as they roam about the rooms of the old castle, unlike anything they had seen before in their wanderings; the way they try to overcome, with varying success, their ever recurring instinct to destroy, all these scenes show the power of observation. Géza Radványi made an excellent selection of children, collecting a crowd which included a number of types; he showed his best abilities in making these scenes.

The world of adults is more remote, strange and incomprehensible, particularly the character played by Artúr Somlay, that of the musician. Where has he come from? Why? Who is he really? Nobody knows. The world of the children who have become vagrants is truly international; but upon the arrival of adults on the scene the cinema-goer wants to know where he is to imagine the action to take place. This exaggerated generalization—"somewhere" in Europe—pumps the air out of the pictures, also out of the musician's figure, which was filled with pulsating life only by the sincerity and warmth of Somlay. *Somewhere in Europe* has entered into cinema history: it has been mentioned in French, Italian, German and English books on the art and technique of film making.

When the eventful years following 1945 are taken into consideration, this was no insignificant matter. Starting from scratch, Hungarian film production had got somewhere. The noise and battle-cries of the children defending their castle could be heard all over Europe. A message was addressed to mankind. The best men of Hungarian films in the time before Liberation took up work again: István Szőts, who after a single success had been persecuted by Horthyist power and the envious industry; Géza Radványi, who after a stay of two years at home, in 1942 signed a contract which took him to Italy, because he was not allowed to realize his favourite plans (one was a film on Madách), but he was forced to return to Hungary when the Germans occupied Italy. Besides these two, other experienced and talented experts resumed the work of shooting films, with more or less satisfactory results: Frigyes Bán, Viktor Gertler and Márton Keleti.

Liberated Hungarian cinema had taken its first steps.

*Cinema of the
Hungarian People:
The First Ten Years
1948—1958*

The nationalization of film production for the first time in history
was decreed in March 1919. That
new structure lasted only a few
months.

An Answer
to the Past
1948—1949

What the Republic of Councils
could achieve only temporarily was
accomplished in March 1948. On
the twenty-first of March, 1948,
Hungarian film production was
nationalized[1] (yet Czechoslovakian film production was nationalized by the
bourgeois-democratic government immediately after Liberation, in August
1945).

Organized work, planning, and financial investments larger than previously known in Hungarian film production became possible. The principal
demand was to ensure the social function and artistic level of films.

The films themselves could at last treat the real and acute problems of the
Hungarian people, and revive themes that had been shelved earlier for commercial or political reasons. The first fruit of nationalized Hungarian film
production was *The Soil Under Your Feet* (Talpalatnyi föld). What *People
on the Alps* only hinted at became the central theme of this film, namely the
dire poverty of the peasantry in the time before Liberation.

After so many well-intentioned failures, after so many films that contained flashes of art but added up to little more than provincial efforts, *The
Soil Under Your Feet* can still be enjoyed from a perspective of nearly twenty
years. The cinema of the Hungarian people had become a reality.

Its theme was drawn from literature. This time the novel which formed
the source of the film had been written by a contemporary, Pál Szabó: it
was published in 1941–1942 as a trilogy under the titles of *Wedding, Baptism,
Cradle* (Lakodalom, keresztelő, bölcső).

The film was directed by Frigyes Bán; soon after his completion
of *Prophet of the Fields* this assignment was a mark of special confidence in
him.[2] The cameraman, Árpád Makai, had been active since 1940; he could
do everything, applying his brilliant technique without boasting—or much
critical attention. Félix Máriássy acted as cutter, playing the most important
role when it came to setting the rhythm of the film. To look back at the
assistants in this film is interesting today. The camera assistant was György
Illés, the director's assistants were Sándor Zákonyi (at present a cutter),
Károly Makk, György Hintsch and Mária Luttor.

There is a wedding in the village. Dark, silent houses, only here and there can a flicker of light be seen. It is night; from a general shot of the whole village the camera descends, to stop at a clean, spacious courtyard. The thrumming of a double-bass is heard, the time of noisy revelry is yet to come, the wedding guests are finishing supper. For a moment the slowly moving camera stops by the hard horizontal surface of the long table covered by a white table-cloth; it stops again by the beautiful bride sitting with painfully stiff carriage among the guests. In vain does the young man who provides for the guests offer one dish after another (the first appearance of Imre Soós on the screen), in vain does he quote appropriate rhymes with a boyish smile; ominous events are approaching. Then, quick cuts: we see the bridegroom's self-assertive drunkenness (István Egri), his rich peasant father smiles with satisfaction at his good bargain of getting the cheap labour of the penniless bride; the bride's poor parents, half-dead with terror and respect; the solemnity of the village notabilities, aping town ways out of place on this occasion; their joviality to conceal their inhibitions, as they possess not one quarter of this peasant's wealth; then the bridegroom absorbed in drinking, as he raises his glass—then a cut to Jóska Góz, seen sitting over his wine alone, dark and morose, an empty inn around him.

The bride is the sweetheart of Jóska Góz, a poor peasant owning two acres of land. With the spilt wine he writes a capital M on the wooden table, and in that instant we are back again looking at the girl's face. Brief montage follows: the wedding feast is in full swing. The bride's dance begins. The bridegroom snarls at the bride. In the courtyard, swept clean for the day, masked revellers arrive, dressed as horseherds, to entertain the wedding party. Jóska Góz is among them and, wearing his mask, he asks the bride for a dance. And now a quick, hard cut: "Where is the bride?" She has disappeared. There is no scene of Marika eloping with Jóska, we only know that it has happened. There is no bride. There is a scandal. The terrified old couple are driven out of paradise; Zsíros Tóth, the rich farmer, vents his rage on them.

This first sequence of the films is as terse as a ballad, and it is sustained with a ballad tone. It revives old customs, the dance of masked, joking horseherds, the bride's dance at the wedding, elopement. The jilted lover grieving over his loss at the inn. Imre Soós recites rhymed sayings and verses before each new course. The film is near to the old sentimental melodrama. The danger is nevertheless avoided. First of all, what would be the end of a film—a triumphant elopement at the height of a noisy wedding feast—is only a tersely outlined beginning. The real trouble and the real story of

14. THE BEST FILM MADE IN HUNGARY IN THE 'THIRTIES WAS THAT OF GEORG
HÖLLERING, BASED ON THE SCRIPT OF ZSIGMOND MÓRICZ: HORTOBÁGY 1934–35

18. ZOLTÁN VÁRKONYI:
    THE BIRTH OF MENYHÉRT SIMON,
    1954. SCRIPT BY TIBOR DÉRY

19–20. ZOLTÁN FÁBRI:
    MERRY-GO-ROUND
    1955

the film are still to come. Marika has been married, by law she is the wedded wife of another man.

The lyrical awakening in the home of the Góz's acts as a transition from an ethnographic and ballad-like terseness to an everyday reality. This sequence takes no more than a few minutes; the members of the Góz family realize that trouble has moved in with them. Marika and Jóska live together without being married.

And then we are plunged into the life of poor peasants in the 'thirties. A new colour on the screen. After the ballad-like atmosphere, the lyrical delineation of happy love, scenes from the Horthy era are presented as in a newsreel. It is here that Árpád Makai, the cameraman, really excels. These scenes have an admirable documentary character. Marika hurrying through the market place of the small town to sell sour cream and other dairy products, Jóska carrying sacks of grain in the snow, the guard leaning out of the door of the village railway station store-house: scenes showing everyday life of a whole people before the Liberation. Moreover, this hard work, carrying sacks and going to the market at daybreak, is felt to make these people happy, because it brings results and joy of life, because there is work to do.

Soon a baby is expected. It will have a name, so its parents will have to be married. Jóska goes to the Zsíros's to discuss the divorce. There are no heroics, nor is there any fighting or other pseudo-dramatic excitement. Young Zsíros puts down the costs of the wedding with the accuracy of a grocer, from the wine and the calf to the day's wages of the cleaning women, altogether nine hundred and forty pengős.

Now the film shows every detailed account, of the smallest expenditure and earnings, and the slow process of fillérs and pengős being tied up in the corners of handkerchiefs.

But the money is not enough. The house of Marika's parents is auctioned, and it is here that we see the first threatening movement by the gendarme to quiet the man who dares to revolt for the first time in his life. The documentary character of the auction suggests the influence of *Ditte Menneskebarn* made by Henning-Jensen, 1947 (from the novel of M. A. Nexö).

And now a brief period of happiness: the two acres that Jóska made into a garden yield their first crop; shopkeepers of the town buy cabbages and tomatoes. The intrigue of the jealous Zsíros Tóth does not do much harm; he induces one of his friends to ruin the well and the crop, but this plot is forced and primitive.

There is no need for the childish intrigue of the Zsíros Tóth clan. A much worse danger threatens when the drought comes. The well dries up.

The action now proceeds rapidly towards a tragic end. A channel that feeds the landlord's fish-pond might be tapped to obtain water.

It is here that the trio of Ádám Szirtes, Tibor Molnár and Zoltán Makláry appeared for the first time as a group of revolutionaries from the people. However, what often appears today as mannerism, proving the far-reaching effect of *The Soil Under Your Feet,* was then a revolutionary novelty. The indigenous peasantry rebels, resorts to violence against violence, not for liberty, but for sheer life. After the steward's refusal they lead the population of the village to the dam; they cut through it and the life-giving water streams through the opening. Peasant heads. Gendarmes. Jóska wrestles with the steward who has galloped to the dam. He throws the steward over the dam and the man dies. The gendarmes fire a volley. Jóska's best friend dies and Jóska is led away in chains by the gendarmes. The marching off of Jóska Góz by the gendarmes is elevated to a heroic motif: the triumphant steps of Jóska are photographed from a low angle. The hero of the film is Jóska Góz, triumphant in his defeat, and the dreary circle of gendarmes, these sinister torturers, only underline the importance of the hero. "To be freed in 1945", says the title at the end of the film.

In the choice of its story, too, *The Soil Under Your Feet* came to be a model. The first two years of nationalized film production was a time for reckoning. The old films made during the Horthy regime with so much care—so as to be fashioned into the ideal of beauty and life—were looked upon with criticism. Out of the eleven films produced in the years 1948 and 1949, seven dealt with themes from the period preceding Liberation or from history, and only four chose contemporary subjects: *Fire* (Tűz), *Johnny* (Janika), *Anna Szabó* (Szabóné) and *Young Pioneers* (Úttörők).

The film versions of two Zsigmond Móricz novels stand nearest to the world of *The Soil Under Your Feet. Burning Meadows* (Forró mezők), screenplay by Zoltán Várkonyi, was shot in the summer of 1948, at the same time as *The Soil Under Your Feet.* The film was directed by Imre Apáthi. Though its execution is of a high standard and the film is good notwithstanding some discrepancies—much better than the films made of Móricz novels before Liberation—it cannot be compared to *The Soil Under Your Feet.* The film emphasizes the criminal aspects of Móricz's novel; the social drama is shrunk into a murder motivated by love. The compromise of the cast—Katalin Karády puts on her affected airs in a luxuriously furnished manor-house—reminds one of the worst traditions of the Horthy era. Even so, when the camera glides over the tired figures of the sleeping reapers with calm attention to details, and two galloping horsemen break into this dazed equanimity with a throbbing urgency as the only "true" life, or in the concluding scenes of the funeral and the tragi-comic scene of the notary, one may welcome a modern and valuable trend.

The screen version of *Gentry Skylarking* (Úri muri), the next film directed by Frigyes Bán after *The Soil Under Your Feet,* is better. In *Gentry Skylarking* a thousand traits of Móricz's world are scattered richly before us: the camera moves about with animated enjoyment, rushing and winding in and out in the scenes of revelry as if released from all the limitations of the stage. The drama is faithful to the writer and consistent in its exposure of society. It nevertheless lacks the montage technique of *The Soil Under Your Feet,* as well as its atmosphere and impact. The screen version is a highly cultured, thoroughly elaborated stage performance expanded into a film. Consequently the film excels in the episodes where the situation created for the theatre can be deepened, for instance in the scene of revelry conducted by Csuli Csörgheő, as in that at the inn showing the bagman stuffing himself with scrambled eggs; these scenes have been called sensational. However, there can be no doubt that social exposure was extended, for *Gentry Skylarking* represents a world into which the awful steward of *The Soil Under Your Feet* might have ventured only as far as the entry.

The first Hungarian colour film was a folk tale, *Mattie the Goose Boy* (Lúdas Matyi), adapted for the screen from the work of Mihály Fazekas. In this film a still more conscious effort is made to present the regions and meadows discovered in *The Soil Under Your Feet,* to make use of new opportunities for working on location. Kálmán Nádasdy and László Ranódy acted as directors, while the art of Barna Hegyi as cameraman conjured up the world of nobility at the threshold of the Biedermeier period in the early 19th century, without depending on sets, which are usually exceedingly important to indicate that a new style is being ushered in. He found typical features and characteristic elements in pastures, meadows, woods and the village fair, while the atmosphere preserved in contemporary engravings has been rendered by liveried attendants riding along in their richly braided coats, and by the disguises of *Mattie the Goose Boy.* This film abounds in newly discovered talent: Imre Soós and Teri Horváth, who played minor roles in *The Soil Under Your Feet,* headed the cast, as well as Éva Ruttkai, the star of so many subsequent films.

This distorted world of the nobility, the hotbed of innumerable tragedies, was exposed through ridicule in the film version of an old operetta, *Mickey Magnate* (Mágnás Miska), by Károly Bakonyi and Albert Szirmai, modernized by István Békeffy and directed by Márton Keleti. Now Keleti could profit from his experiences of the 'thirties: what appeared to be a serenely imperturbable through amusing world, in *The Bride of Torockó, You Just Smoke, Ladányi* (Te csak pipálj, Ladányi) and in *Vicki* (Viki), was now shown as ridiculous. In this distorting-glass servants were promoted to leaders, and have-nots became landowning peasants who bade a laughing farewell to their bitter past; so did the director to the world of his earlier films. Miklós Gábor, who as a youngster played a vagrant in Géza Radványi's film, here appeared as a handsome young man; Marika Németh joined Ági Mészáros as a promising talent. The real star of the film was Kálmán Latabár. His buffoonery brought something ancient on the screen from the sane humour of László Vitéz's puppet show; indeed, film-goers still roar with delight over the stumbling of Latabár.

Viktor Gertler also made a happy farewell to the past in his film comedy *Dress-Suit* (Díszmagyar) which gives a witty fillip to the memory of His Excellency the Regent. Among the films taking leave of the past, *Dress-Suit*—the artistic standards and achievement of which are incomparably higher than those of *Mickey Magnate*—is the only one based on an original script and not on a novel or operetta. The old film craftsmen were replaced by new ones: another sign of change. The script of *Dress-Suit* was written by László Hárs and Miklós Gyárfás from a short story by Tibor Nyíri and Lajos Pásztor.

It is the story of a Budapest student's gay adventure. Having pawned his clothes, the young man is compelled to go out one day in the dress-suit of his landlady's husband, never dreaming that there would be crowds of other men bustling about in the streets also in dress-suits, going to a reception in honour of the Italian king's arrival. The ingenious and modern exploitation of this basic situation of "clothes make the man" affords opportunities for poking fun at the ruling class mouthing its slogans and for ridiculing their confused schemes. Humour flows not from slapstick, but from the characters, for instance at the brilliant reception in Buda Castle, where everybody vies for the student's favour, because he had been singled out for conversation by the Italian king who was glad to find somebody at last with whom he could speak Italian.

Imre Jeney's film, *A Woman Makes a New Start* (Egy asszony elindul), based on a short story of Judit Beczássy, a noteworthy example of reckoning with the past, has been forgotten, strangely. The lead is played by Klári Tolnay opposite Ferenc Ladányi who brings new, vivid colours to the screen as the husband in this first film of his; Teri Horváth appears as the former servant.

The story is about a woman waiting for her husband, an engineer, to come back from the war. She has no idea that at his office he is now suspected of fascist crimes. Having no money the woman begins to work. She bakes cakes and with the help of a friend (Zsuzsa Bánki) she sells them. However, the friend decides to take the easy way and accepts the support of elderly gentlemen from the circle of her former friends. This leads to a break between the two women. With the help of her former servant the heroine gets work in the kitchen of the Orion factory, where she is later sent to a class to be trained. That is how she makes a new start and works until her husband comes home.

This first part of the film has considerable value. Imre Jeney, whose knack for filming everyday city life had been demonstrated in his *And the Blind Can See,* revealed a previously unknown world, the post-war life of so-called middle-class ladies. This was an important step, even if it was strongly influenced by Italian neo-realism. However, this influence was not so strong as to justify an accusation of imitation, on the contrary: it was heartening that this new Italian trend initiated around 1945 should have stimulated the imagination of Hungarian directors. Klári Tolnay, who had shed all her pre-liberation poses, became the director's excellent collaborator, she portrayed the many-faceted character of the woman looking round in this new world without compromise or make-up.

The shots of badly damaged streets in the Castle District are first-rate, and so are the black-marketeers selling round cakes, molasses, and flour; the practical lady of high rank who converts her apartment into an espresso; office intrigues and idle, gossiping old officials, who attribute every trouble to the coalition government; the film shows Budapest in the years of 1945-46. Thanks to Klári Tolnay's infinitely simple, fine performance, the woman's start at the factory is real, believable and natural. It was a good idea of the director to have the former servant address her former mistress by her former title when they meet in the canteen. Teri Horváth brings to the screen a thousand new colours. There is beauty in the workshop meeting where it is brought home to the woman that she does not know more than her fellow-workers, unless she can play the piano. These pictures breathe life. That is why these scenes of the workshop are so movingly beautiful, the first pictures inside a factory in a Hungarian film: the poster in the courtyard of the factory with the words "Land, Bread, Freedom"; the gate being opened to the lady who comes looking for work; snatches of music coming from the radio-repair workshop. Instead of the later, stereotyped phrases, how infallibly certain it sounds when in reply to reproaches for having employed a lady though jobs may become fewer at any moment, the party secretary replies, "Unemployment? In this country?" Twenty years have vindicated the truth of these words.

However, the end of the film and the complications following the husband's return are forced as though the conception of the film had been altered while shooting was in progress. The first few sentences suggest that, after his arrival, the husband will have to answer for his conduct in 1944 (no matter whether the accusations are true or only aspersions of his jealous colleagues), and he will have to fight his own battle alongside his wife. Instead we are plunged into a silly and unsavoury spy story: the engineer has invented some welding machine which he wants to smuggle out of the country for a goodly sum, and he wants to get out himself, leaving his family behind. If that is so, why did he come home? And can it be seriously believed that a welding patent is bought abroad at a price as exorbitant as he requires? An attitude ascribing every fault to "external" enemies, whipping up morbid suspicion on the plea of vigilance, begins to take shape. From this point cheap solutions follow one another in quick succession, in which the party secretary—Sándor Pécsi—and the woman fight for the invention. However, *A Woman Makes a New Start* is an interesting achievement.

The film *Fire* was directed by Imre Apáthi. Here a group of ministry officials are exposed who take money from the enemy for sabotage to hinder the development of factories. Instead of depicting the existing problem of the fight against those of the ruling class who refuse to give up their positions, the film shows insignificant officials of the old type, who believe themselves to be heroes when telling a reactionary anecdote, as spies bribed by the enemy, as men who have their pockets full of dollars and carry pistols while setting fire to Hungarian factories. The magnificent performance of Gábor Rajnai who plays a cunning, double-dyed official giving a caricature of his earlier roles—is a memorable feature of the film.

In addition to *Johnny* (Janika)—a sort of *Hyppolit the Butler*—by Stella, Békeffy and Keleti, based mostly on gags, and to *Young Pioneers*—never released—in which the whole young generation: Károly Makk, Tamás Banovich, Péter Bacsó, and Imre Fehér collaborated under the leadership of Ferenc Hont, the first work of Félix Máriássy as a director, *Anna Szabó* (Szabóné), deserves special attention.

The script was written by György Szinetár, Péter Bacsó and Tamás Banovich from a short story by the Transylvanian writer István Nagy. This was the first Hungarian film about workers; one in which their lives are part of the action.

The story is about a young widow, Anna Szabó, who asks to be transferred to a workshop where there are only women in order to help to improve the poor standard of work. In its first moments it seems to be a typical story of the period: work competition, heroic achievements in work shown with official pathos. But no. The story of István Nagy and the work of Máriássy as a director are strong enough to raise fundamental moral issues instead of pressing on us the events of daily political life as became the general practice later: namely the attitude of hundreds of thousands of women to their work, who for lack of an alternative living work in a factory, but have no interest in the factory. In Máriássy's film these are not slogans from an editorial.

The question arises, what to expect of these women who were good enough for a passing flirtation, but are unused to regular work, who quarrel in the opening scenes and come to blows? The poorly ventilated, neglected workshop, the skilled workmen condescending only on rare occasion to set foot into such primitive premises, the old workman who reads to these irritated women an editorial from the *Szabad Nép* instead of helping them to make order: these were realities. This was the situation directly after nationalization, particularly in the years 1948–1949.

Anna Szabó goes to work with enthusiasm, but very stiffly, with the awkward pride of a woman newly awakened to consciousness. Today it makes one smile how frequently she quotes slogans heard at the meetings of the work committee; but that was also a reality. In those days rhythmic applause was induced by sincere enthusiasm. And the mistakes which Anna Szabó tries to correct flow from human nature. Anna Szabó wants to bring about a change, and this is a serious task.

Máriássy's introductory scenes are beautiful: a factory fence running along the railway-line, crowds of men streaming to work, the camera's diagonal journey of disclosure, proceeding in a direction opposite to the moving crane, creates a world previously unknown to Hungarian films. Some early signs of Máriássy's individual style may also be discerned: delineation of character by lingering over small, apparently insignificant details. In this respect the dialogue of the lovers, Ádám Szirtes and Éva Ruttkai, at the staircase, and their awkward declaration of love deserve special notice. Notwithstanding the naive directness of the dialogue a pleasant and winning freshness radiates both from the acting and the direction; again and again one is reminded of the contemporary spirit of *Ladri di biciclette*.

Unfortunately Kornélia Sallay, who plays Anna Szabó, is an inadequate actress. Stiff and lifeless, one feels she is only following the director's instructions. Therefore we are not on her side, we do not share her cares or her enthusiasms. She seems a sour party worker; this hurts the whole film.

The first two years of nationalized Hungarian film production brought considerable results. Without any exaggeration this change may be denoted as revolutionary: out of eleven films one masterpiece and several works of lasting value—this was an achievement which Hungarian film production of the'thirties failed to bring about. And all this was accomplished by directors who had worked also in the Horthy era, but had been denied the chance of using their talents and of finding stimulating sources of inspiration: Frigyes Bán, Viktor Gertler, Imre Jeney, Kálmán Nádasdy, Imre Apáthi and Márton Keleti. Yet the new and the young, for instance those who were to introduce Italian neo-realism into Hungarian cinema, exponents of the best pre-liberation films—particularly István Szőts—were still absent. Ten years later this absence was to be one cause of the crisis. László Ranódy alone was allowed to resume activity—as assistant director — and Félix Máriássy was promoted from the group of trained assistants who had matured into directors at the very threshold of Liberation...

The many new actors and actresses were also an exceedingly refreshing element; after almost twenty years' monotony, it was good to see Ádám Szirtes, Imre Soós, Teri Horváth, Éva Ruttkai, Tibor Molnár, Miklós Gábor, new faces and personalities.

"Singing Makes Life Beautiful" Propaganda as Chief Aim 1950—1952

Never before had so many films been made in Hungary on modern themes in a working-class milieu as in these three years: 14 out of 18 films. Therefore one is tempted to say that, having reckoned with the past, Hungarian film production turned its attention to the present. However, this would not be altogether accurate, for these films did not give a true picture either of the present or of the future. They much rather gave a picture representing the future as imagined by people of a sectarian mind, or of a present they would like to live in.

The films of 1950 all dealt with contemporary subjects; *Stars* (Csilla-gosok) was a story of a farmers' co-operative; *Liberated Land* (Felszabadult föld) an optimistic sequel to *The Soil Under Your Feet; Catherine's Marriage* (Kis Katalin házassága) a "gay story about work-competition"; *Singing Makes Life Beautiful* (Dalolva szép az élet) a workshop comedy.

The series was continued in 1951 with *Underground Colony* (Gyarmat a föld alatt), on the nationalization of the oil-wells of Lispe; *West Zone* (Nyugati övezet); *Full Steam Ahead* (Teljes gőzzel) about the fight of rail-waymen for the success of a hundred-thousand-ton project; *Honesty and Glory* (Becsület és dicsőség) about "a married couple reformed by work-ing in shifts in honour of Stalin"; *Battle in Peace* (Ütközet békében): the Hungarian People's Army stands guard over the peace front; *Baptism by Fire* (Tűzkeresztség) on sabotage by rich peasants in a farmers' co-operative; *Try and Win* (Civil a pályán): join the movement "Ready for Work and Battle!"

In 1952 *The First Swallows* (Az első fecskék): the porcelain factory of Zsolnay at Pécs produces insulators instead of bourgeois china. *Department Store* (Állami Áruház) and *The Storm* (Vihar) are perhaps the only excep-tions in this series.

In the years 1951 and 1952 only four films were made on themes drawn from the past: *Erkel, Semmelweis, Madame Déry* (Déryné), and *A Strange Marriage* (Különös házasság).

Direct, daily political propaganda was the task of cinema; films were to show the problems discussed in the daily press. Incidentally, by the time such a film was finished its subject was no longer topical. In the case of an active film industry and politically well-trained artists the task would not have presented unsurmountable difficulties; for instance, Italian neo-realism produced a number of excellent films without a previously written script, the theme being suggested by some news item. Having read that women workers had thrashed a black-marketeering baker, turned his shop upside down and founded a party, Luigi Zampa quickly rushed to the spot and began to shoot his film *Angelina,* partly with the women who had been in the riot, with Anna Magnani to lead them. That is how Rossellini's film, *Paisà,* was made, and even *Roma ore undici* by De Santis, but after more thorough preparations.

The problem was not so much that of propaganda being too closely related to our day than the lack of reality, a beautified version of which had to be put on the screen. The mirroring function of the film—and of art in general—was relegated to the background, and the task of the people's education was made to prevail in a wrongly interpreted sense of the term. The screen was to represent what life *ought* to be. Piryev, the director of the Soviet film *Siberian Rhapsody,* prided himself with great satisfaction on having presented parking lots for motor-cars, the like of which had never existed in Siberia before this film, but came to be established in considerable numbers after the release of his picture. It was the future that was to be shown! "Let us dream!" However, without knowing the present, one can have no idea of the future; the future is built from the present. But Hungarian films took little notice of the present as it was in those days.

As a matter of fact attention was concentrated increasingly on embellishing both future and present. The unsteadiness of the government was aggravated by political mistakes, and this unsteadiness tolerated no criticism. Moreover, the Rajk affair and the consequent arrests created an atmosphere of suspicion and distrust. In the sphere of cinema it followed that directors with an inadequate political education avoided raising real problems; they confined themselves to directing the film demanded by the script. That is how a Soviet marching song became the principal musical motif of *Singing Makes Life Beautiful,* the rhythm of which was drummed by Kálmán Latabár happily on the window-sill of an office window.

After two triumphant years at the start, this turn of events did much harm. Although Pudovkin critized the schematism of Hungarian films as early as August 1951, on his second visit to Hungary as an adviser, upon closer analysis of the essential difference between schematism and true realism not much improvement is found to have resulted until the June 1953 decision of the Central Committee. "As though one saw the world through a telescope at a distance of many kilometres"; such a beneficial distance dims mistakes, Pudovkin remarked with a touch of irony when he discussed *Catherine's Marriage* in an address delivered at the House of Art Associations.[3] In an article published in *Szabad Nép* in May 1956, András Kovács emphasized that schematism was an almost inevitable infantile disease, and pointed out the inadequate training of Hungarian directors: "as well as present political relationships... there were few directors; moreover, they failed to show any imagination. We did not know the new Italian films, while in Soviet films we saw only the traditions that were not of permanent value. The mercenary traditions of old Hungarian films were also allowed to assert themselves, since they were often compatible with schematic demands, while a stiffer critical attitude precluded the appropriate espousal of the cause of such films as *People on the Alps, Somewhere in Europe,* or even *The Soil Under Your Feet,* works of a high standard even though their contents may be debatable at some points... All these factors nevertheless fail to furnish a satisfactory explanation of schematism... When the social and political preconditions for a straightforward representation of the conflicts of reality are lacking, the strongest call for a full portrayal of life is futile. The contradictions due to the personality cult, to the formal interpretation of democracy, of criticism and self-criticism having become formal and to the violation of legality which created deep social tensions and intrigued the film-makers even more intensively, could not be put on the screen truthfully, because any artist who exposed these contradictions in their full depth would in many fields have found himself up against the mistakes of political origin dominating public life. There remained nothing else but to gloss matters over and to tell half-truths."[4]

In the meantime Soviet films had also reached a stage of stagnation for similar reasons. The great Soviet silent films did not reach Hungary, and furthermore, Eisenstein was branded a formalist. (In the early 'fifties Soviet films rarely touched modern, contemporary subjects.) Apart from the few films on contemporary subjects, for instance *Cavalier of the Golden Star* (Кавалер золотой звезды), *The Fall of Berlin* (Падение Берлина), the majority were pictures like Pudovkin's *Zhukovsky*. In 1952, for example, altogether twenty-two films were made in the Soviet Union, of which thirteen were merely records of theatre productions. Not screen adaptations of plays, but the staging of some important theatre was photographed, with the curtain going down after each act.[5]

Of course, ingenuity of the enterprise did not always imply success. In Hungary, for instance, true success was scored by the four films which drew their themes from the past, and not by the films on modern Hungarian topics. However, they supplied opportunities for a lesson.

Only one of the four, Mikszáth's novel directed by Márton Keleti, *A Strange Marriage*, had the power of social exposure, by virtue of its artistic efforts to dispel the myth of a feudal Hungary shining and radiant. After the falsifications of the years preceding Liberation—and after the attempt of the firm Orient, *The Siege of Beszterce*—at last here was a film version of Mikszáth's which may be said to represent this Hungarian classic worthily. In the script of Gyula Háy the novel is cleverly concentrated around the core of Mikszáth's message, namely exposure of the clergy, the members of which are ready to do anything in their own interest. The outdoor scenes taken amidst the flower-beds of well-kept gardens recall the successful methods applied in *Mattie the Goose Boy*. It is only the overelaborate Hungarian braided garments which tend to belie the age.

The effect and significance of the other three period films are entirely different. All three were based on original scripts (by István Békeffy, Sándor Dallos and Gábor Thurzó with István Békeffy, respectively). All three take their audiences back to the national movements of Hungary in the Reform Age: *Madame Déry* shows us the lives of actors, referred to as the country's day labourers; *Semmelweis* commemorates the tragic fate of the physician who discovered the prevention of puerperal fever; *Erkel* is about the life of the great Hungarian composer, a contemporary of Verdi. Thus these three films revived progressive Hungarian traditions; can a period film have a nobler task? Yet on a closer analysis, concessions to nationalism are encountered at every step.

The superficial atmosphere of its period, the inappropriate music and false portrayal of society are such concessions in *Madame Déry*. In *Semmelweis* and in *Erkel* the more exacting standards of direction and execution on a grander scale deserve notice, because their romantic nationalist ardour is at least justified by history. When Márton Keleti's *Erkel* is compared to the Soviet film on Erkel's contemporary, *Composer Glinka* (1952), or to the Italian film about Verdi, its direction is by no means inferior, on the contrary: the portrayal of social conditions is truer, more effective and more graphic than in the other two. Frigyes Bán's biography of *Semmelweis* is a work which abounds in powerful, dramatic scenes, drama that matches the tragic turn in that great scientist's life, and is a worthy counterpart of both the old Hungarian Semmelweis film and the DEFA version (made in 1950 by Georg C. Klaren).

As regards directors, an increasing want of a younger generation is felt. Eight years after Liberation it was still only the experts from the 'thirties who were active; Máriássy, who began to direct in 1949, was joined only by two stage directors, Zoltán Fábri and Zoltán Várkonyi. In his lecture mentioned before, Pudovkin strongly emphasized: "New forces should be enlisted to work in film production. No effort should be spared to prepare the young and set them to work."

The special interpretation of the task of a director took shape in these years. It may have been due to the atmosphere of general distrust, but at the time it was the script that was regarded as the real work of art. Therefore the film's author was the writer of the script. Every word of the script could be checked in advance; the director was only the executive who conducted the script like the conductor of an orchestra playing a Beethoven symphony. Traces of this theory, denoted as "script-centred", may be found in Béla Balázs's *Filmkultúra* of 1948: "Today's script is not a half-finished product, an outline or a design, it is not a means towards a work of art, but a complete work of art in itself... Musical notes are also only symbols of music which are realized by instruments. Yet no one would dream of regarding the music of a Beethoven sonata as a half-finished product or an outline... soon scripts will be more popular reading than drama, which is more abstract."[6]

In another place in *Filmkultúra* of 1948 he actually speaks of the projection of a film as a stage performance produced by means of special technical instruments: "Most film-goers are unaware of looking at the performance of a script, as they look at the performance of a drama in a theatre."[7]

This unusual statement, particularly from the pen of Béla Balázs, not only represented a stage in a still open theoretical debate but also a trend which became noticeable about 1950. This can be proved by an irritated statement by Béla Balázs himself in the No 3, 1945 issue of the illustrated journal *Fényszóró*, in which he voiced a sharp and strong protest against making a fetish of scripts in general: "The scenario is no nearer to being literature than the architect's design is to being a painting or a work of graphic art; in fact it is the preparatory work for a building. A script is not literature, but, if I may choose a work corresponding to design, a written plan."

This opinion of Béla Balázs is diametrically opposed to his view expressed in *Filmkultúra* of 1948. In the last year of life Béla Balázs found himself compelled to comply with the sectarian trend which had been gathering strength from the year 1947; this sectarian trend recognized on the screen no virtues but those that could be checked and demonstrated in literature, and regarded the script as the real work of art.[8]

A Soviet publication declared: "It is classical literature... that has helped directors to get rid of the remnants of formalism. The means of formalist art were inadequate to render literary works on the screen."[9]

In the same publication the films of Eisenstein, for instance *Old and New*, the films of Dovzhenko, for example *Earth*, as well as Pudovkin's films were branded as formalist works imbued with bourgeois ideology, because too much attention was devoted to "camerawork and similar problems" instead of stressing literary values.

Other publications also popularized this "script-centred" attitude of the early 'fifties.[10]

In these years when the script became so important, almost a fetish, when literary work was regarded as the exclusive value, it is remarkable that, apart from a single Mikszáth film, neither the classical nor contemporary literature of Hungary was represented in our films. Scripts—valued equally as a drama or novel, as explained above—were written by first-rate craftsmen such as István Békeffy and György Szinetár whose film activity had begun in the 'thirties; nearly all the truly eminent and highly appreciated writers of the age held aloof from the screen. At present almost every important Hungarian author has a contract with the film studios, whereas in the years 1950–1952, except for two scripts by Ernő Urbán, the *Semmelweis* of Sándor Dallos and one operetta, literature was represented by István Örkény *(Honesty and Glory)* and by Miklós Gyárfás *(The First Swallows)*.

Under such conditions the director could not develop; he endeavoured to "execute" the approved script with minute care, to direct it with a good cast. In the case of any special ideas, unusual sets or cutting, he might have incurred the accusation of formalism. In a review of the *Underground Colony* published by *Szabad Nép*, an idea of Zoltán Fábri, the director, is referred to as a bold break-away from the script, a brave and original ingenious invention: "The lighting of a cigarette by Forrai and pressing it out in his embarrassment is, for instance, *not included in the script.*"[11]

Even under such unfavourable conditions success was achieved: *Madame Déry* was exhibited in twenty-one countries, *Erkel* in eighteen, *Mattie the Goose Boy, Try and Win,* and *Semmelweis* in fourteen; in the years of the cold war these figures meant appreciation. Since exhibition costs money it cannot be regarded as a mere polite gesture. Besides the socialist countries, *Mattie the Goose Boy, Madame Déry* and *Erkel* reached France. In Great Britain these three were shown in addition to *Semmelweis*. Moreover, the Netherlands, Greece, Italy, the USA, Canada and Finland also bought Hungarian films made in these years. These facts are rarely mentioned in reviews or by the public, though they confirm Hungarian cinema successes.

The number of cinemas and of film-goers also increased at the same rate. Never before had so many people seen Hungarian films in the country. In the year 1952 there were 2446 cinemas in Hungary, six times more than before Liberation. In these cinemas one million and fifty-four thousand spectators saw a film in 1952; the number of film-goers per film was six times higher than in France.[12]

Even if there were no other motives, these greatly increased audiences should have induced nationalized film production to create better works of a less ephemeral value.

Zoltán Fábri's film *Fourteen Lives Saved* (Életjel) was awarded the Prize of Labour at the 1954 Karlovy Vary Film Festival. Since the distinction of *The Soil Under Your Feet* in 1949 at Mariánské Lázně this was the first prize brought back to Hungary from a festival.

Nearer to Life 1953—1954

The film created a great sensation. Mark Donskoy congratulated the director personally; when shown to film-makers in Moscow, the projection of the film was interrupted eight or ten times by loud applause. The Brazilian director Alberto Cavalcanti, one of those who created the French avant-garde of the 'twenties and later worked in Great Britain, called the film excellent and praised its merits of direction with enthusiasm.

Actually *Fourteen Lives Saved* was another film in the series of heroic achievements in factories or elsewhere. The script by Tibor Tardos, though showing more inspiration and suggesting more personal experience, than did the scripts of *The Storm* or *Honesty and Glory*, its literary standards did not differ much from the others. It did, however, differ in its highly ingenious direction.

This was the turning point.

Zoltán Fábri, who in *The Storm* had shown how much human passion could be expressed in a normal account of a farmers' co-operative by the director's ingenuity, broke away from the earlier approach and directed his own film in *Fourteen Lives Saved*. In this instance life presented an event that was a nation-wide sensation, namely a mine disaster, the exceptionally fortunate outcome of which made the usual optimism unnecessary, for everybody knew that the miners finally escaped.

The tragic predicament of men confined deep in the mine provided opportunities for the director to apply profounder psychology and insight than usual. Fábri boldly availed himself of the possibilities afforded by light and shadow—forgotten since *The Soil Under Your Feet*; he also employed cutting, even montage. However, it was by no means accidental that Cavalcanti, in his above-mentioned favourable comment, criticized the schematic treatment of personal aspects in the action. The director's attention did not, perhaps could not, extend so far. Instead of God it is a cabinet minister who frees the miners with his fervent supplications and omniscience, and also gives advice to the helpless engineers.

In this more encouragingly creative atmosphere we came nearer to life in that period, and real troubles and real joys could be shown on the screen. Eight out of the fourteen films produced in two years were contemporary subjects. But what a difference between Keleti's two films, *Singing Makes Life Beautiful* and *Penny* (Kiskrajcár)! Based on a script by András Sándor, Boris Palotai and Gábor Thurzó, the latter gives an account of the hard years of building Sztálinváros (now Dunaújváros) and of the development of a working girl released from the narrow-minded atmosphere of her peasant family. Although this film is also full of the sort of pathos that is apt to provoke smiles now, it represents also less serene aspects of life, hooligans streaming in, attracted by rumours of an easy living, the dishonest acts of a lonely female clerk hungering for love who cloaks her misdemeanours by the use of slogans; finally, it shows a real event in the history of the country, an event known to everybody, the building of a real town.

Of the films on themes from the past the screen version of Zsigmond Móricz's novel *Relatives* (Rokonok), directed by Félix Máriássy, was the best, although the greatest success was scored by the Biedermeier comedy *Liliomfi*, the first film directed by Károly Makk. In *Relatives* a class which had been neglected for a long time on the screen, that of the more progressive elements of the provincial middle classes in the Horthy era, was put under the magnifying glass. What Máriássy—with the help of Gábor Thurzó's script—has added to this world is the opinion of an artist today about the past world of Móricz. That is why the detailed representations of the provincial party with the guests dancing the shimmy is an integral part of the film, that is why the social relationships of the county attorney general's failure are more clearly discernible than may have been intended in the novel, that is why the apparently innocent selfishness of his wife, rooted deeply in her own class and family, is more petty and less moving, although it is one of the causes which precipitate the final tragedy. The intense life of the couple, with rare happiness in love, their days varied by modest amusements and beset by paltry cares, is excellent, and so are their quarrels and bickering, and their preparations for the party (Mr and Mrs Kopjáss are played by László Ungvári and Klári Tolnay). The world of the town-hall gentlemen, known from *Gentry Skylarking*, is less colourful, but nevertheless accurate. *Relatives* is a valuable film, rich in delicate observation. The other literary script was a film version of Ede Szigligeti's play, *Liliomfi*. This fresh film, flinging all cares to the wind, the first work of a prepossessing young director, owes its greatest power to its heretical though not falsifying deviation from the "sacred" literary source; what is

35–36. ANDRÁS KOVÁCS:
SUMMER RAIN
1960
37. KÁROLY MAKK:
THE FANATICS
1961

more, the director's original zeal sheds a more revealing light on the social conditions of the period—without pomposity—than the good Szigligeti could have ever dreamed. A newly discovered actress, Mariann Krencsey, and Iván Darvas, given the lead after many minor parts, make a delightful comedy team. Sándor Pécsi, their worthy partner, appears to proclaim his joy over his escape from the confinement of his stereotyped roles.

Chin Up! (Fel a fejjel!) shows the tragedies of fascist times and the subsequent joyful events of Liberation through the life of a circus clown. In this film, interspersed with banal scenes, a new characteristic is seen, the use of tragi-comedy. Márton Keleti's direction, the script of Margit Gáspár, Károly Nóti and Péter Szász, and Kálmán Latabár's acting try to revive and apply the forgotten elements of slapstick. Instead of an edifying story, instead of the official humour of a school festival, at last there was a glimmer of genuine humour in this film.

Notwithstanding repeated defeats, Hungarian historical films refused to abandon their sham optimism and perpetual glory. These films are strange manifestations of a great inner uncertainty. For example, *Rákóczi's Lieutenant* (Rákóczi hadnagya) abounds in treachery, defeat and scenes showing the infinite misery of serfs to become finally the triumphant march of Rákóczi's revolt ending in wretched exile in Asia. What is more, the memories of the tragic failure of the Republic of Councils after several months of magnificent constructive work are rounded off with a big victorious scuffle learnt from American films: *The Day of Wrath* (A harag napja). After *Brigade No. 39* (A harminckilences dandár), which dared to present a tragedy with artistic means, it is a strange experience to see *The Day of Wrath* again, openly falsifying history as well as the original drama. Optimism streams from Bessenyei, playing a communist leader; with a white bandage round his head and other minor wounds he steps out towards a better future in a rhythm copied from schematic Soviet films. It is sad to remember that this version was produced as a result of official, superior intervention. Of the contemporary reviews only that of Endre Vészi published in the June 2, 1955, issue of *Szabad Nép* contained a hint: "...a few errors of the first version of the film have been corrected in the work now released for presentation." The more tragic, that is to say the truthful first version (that followed the drama as staged in the Theatre of the Hungarian People's Army) was scrapped. The film, based on the drama of Kálmán Sándor, was directed by Zoltán Várkonyi.

Although history has also been simplified and embellished in *The Sea Has Risen* (Feltámadott a tenger), the direction of László Ranódy and

Mihály Szemes (based on Gyula Illyés's script entitled *Two Men*—Két férfi—and supported by the shooting script of Kálmán Nádasdy) has discharged a noble and urgent task in raising a monument to the revolution and the War of Independence of 1848 in a series of vivid sequences. Compared to similar great national enterprises of film history, *The Sea Has Risen* is not worse than the others, in many respects it may even be said to be better and more thorough. *Viva Italia,* made by Rossellini in 1960 to celebrate the hundredth anniversary of Italy's national unity, is more superficial, more rambling, and it was made seven years later. It contains no delineation of character, Rossellini never thought of going into such details; he simply presented famous events as in a picture-book. In *The Sea Has Risen* Zoltán Makláry's fine portrait of Bem is rich in detailed psychological observations. Yet upon analysing the still discernible deeper values of the spectacular picture, we find that these have faded, as have the colours of the film.

When comparing the unsuccessful, dull products following the magnificent start of 1948, the superficially political, monotonously directed films of the early 'fifties with the success of *Fourteen Lives Saved* at the festival of Karlovy Vary, a few noteworthy works of a higher level and a few amusing comedies in the years of 1953–1954, these may be registered as an achievement.

Finally, several young directors made their first films in these years: László Ranódy, who made *Love Travels by Coach* (Hintón járó szerelem), as well as János Herskó, Károly Makk and György Révész (*Under the City*—A város alatt; *Liliomfi*; *Twice Two Is Sometimes Five*—Kétszer kettő néha öt).

A few new faces emerge also among the actors: Mária Medgyesi *(Love Travels by Coach)*; Ferenc Zenthe, Tibor Bitskey, Éva Vass *(Rákóczi's Lieutenant)*; Zsuzsa Gyurkovics, Ferenc Kállai *(Twice Two Is Sometimes Five)*; Mariann Krencsey, Iván Darvas *(Liliomfi)*; Ferenc Bessenyei, Juci Komlós *(The Day of Wrath)*; Hédi Váradi (*Young at Heart*—Ifjú szívvel).

Yet when we look at the surrounding world of that time, the picture is not so exhilarating. At the time of nationalization, in 1948, Hungarian films reached the level of world standards in every respect. The style of the films directed by Szőts, Radványi, Bán, Jeney, Nádasdy and Ranódy, their methods of making contact with the audience were perfectly modern. But inventiveness diminished for fear of being accused of formalism, and unimaginative, stiff photography was equated with realism. Nor did the rising generation bring replacements. The best fruits of Soviet film art, the works of Eisenstein, Donskoy, Dovzhenko, were barred from presentation in Hungary. Italian neo-realism was superseded by another trend (Fellini) before its achievements could reach Hungary. A few films did, but the trend itself was not discussed.

Only one film can be called a contemporary one, taking an honourable place not only among our best works of these two years, but also among the best Hungarian films made after Liberation. However, neither the public nor the critics paid any special attention to it at the time; because of its apparently modest theme, it was overshadowed by the optimistic tragedy of the fourteen miners.

This film, *The Birth of Menyhért Simon* (Simon Menyhért születése), was made by Zoltán Várkonyi from a script by Tibor Déry. Almost symbolically, the leading parts were played by Ádám Szirtes and Ági Mészáros, the hero and heroine of *The Soil Under Your Feet*; symbolically, because it seems as if the camera sought to represent the life of this couple as it continued in liberated Hungary, in socialism, after their hard suffering and ordeals of the 'thirties. The same serene and happy love, gestures which indicate mutual understanding without the need for lengthy dialogues, the same conjugal harmony where a crisis is caused not by the unexpected appearance of a third, but by the complication of ordinary workaday life. In this case the complication is due not to drought, as in *The Soil Under Your Feet,* but to a snowstorm nearly preventing the doctor from reaching the forester's wife who is having a baby somewhere high in the Bükk Hills. It is admirable how this simple story could be made into a film of lasting value by good dialogue and modern direction with attention to details and psychological insight.

The same camera ideas may be observed here as in *Une aussi longue absence*, made almost ten years later, and in other new-wave films: penetrating into the microcosm of the human soul, so far unrevealed on the Hungarian screen, following each gesture, interrupting phrases with a casual epithet, a smile vibrating across the lips being answered by a flicker of an eyelid. With apparently casual words the dialogue shows us a real world, over which the bombastic phrases referring to feats of work-competition roar past impatiently.

The dialogue between the woman, preparing herself for her confinement, and her loose-limbed husband, the way the woman encourages her husband, who is more frightened than herself, and the marks of tenderness were unusually novel, even bold touches of direction in 1954. It must be emphasized that this idyll that could easily be pushed into schematism, always stays on the side of true art. It depends not on Rousseau's romantic return to nature, but on existing social reality, what we are shown at the beginning of the film with the objectivity of a documentary. At last the party secretary, as played by Sándor Pécsi, fights for people, educates and lives among the people; he does not sit in his office, suspicious and supercilious, casting stealthy glances at the world, as in many earlier roles.

The daily ritual of the forester's evening ablutions, the routine, workaday gestures of holding the soap and handling the towel are transformed into an affectionate dialogue between the forester and his wife. The minute observation of the midwife putting on her stockings when she is getting ready for the long drive in the sledge is of a similar nature, and so is her trudging through the deep snow and the men gloating indifferently over her efforts to extricate herself.

When one thinks of the scenes in which Ádám Szirtes, as the forester, tries to comfort his wife with funny songs though he needs comforting himself, of the way he stops again and again in mumbling these queer little tunes while thinking of the incomprehensible phrases in the medical book he bought weeks ago and peeping with half an eye at his wife—one feels inclined to share the view of the contemporary critic who declared *The Birth of Menyhért Simon* to be the best Hungarian film since *The Soil Under Your Feet*. One of its remarkable features is the appearance of real wood-cutters and foresters of the Bükk Hills. It is a pity that there has been no sequel to this film, ahead of its time by several years.

Fuller Development 1955—1958

In the early 'fifties good and poor films alternated in the work of every director, without exhibiting any special individual characteristics. If a director was lucky he was given a good script, and if he was talented he produced a good film. But if a man was either unlucky or ungifted, the result was a filmed ideological lecture, or a film obviously brought forth in torment and sweat. This state of affairs began to change slowly and gradually in the two years discussed in the preceding chapters. The director had some say in the script and could collaborate with the writer, and, what is still more important, the studio became a place for his creative work instead of being the place where the script was "photographed". The script ceased to be a fetish. On April 12, 1954, *Szabad Nép* published an article entitled "The Film Is an Art Medium", encouraging directors to greater independence and criticizing the mistaken methods of earlier years. The best directors began to watch themselves, evaluating their former successes and failures; they started to select themes that stood nearest to their hearts, to their spheres of interest and to their abilities. Gradually certain differences could be discerned between the individual directors, if not in themes, but first in style, method and conception. This was an important step in cinematic development, because film craftsmen became artists, artists with an opinion of the world, of our world, which they loved and wanted to show to us.

No doubt, the best director of these years was Zoltán Fábri who had shot his first film in 1952. His third film—after the success of *Fourteen Lives Saved* at Karlovy Vary Festival—*Merry-Go-Round* (Körhinta, 1955), is still one of the finest works in the history of Hungarian cinema. In his next film, *Professor Hannibal* (Hannibál tanár úr, 1956), Fábri continued to broaden his depiction of social conditions through the portrayal of characters.

The script of *Merry-Go-Round* was written by the director in collaboration with László Nádasdy from a short story by Imre Sarkadi.

In the hands of Fábri the love between a young man in a farmers' co-operative and the daughter of parents obstinately pursuing private farming, a theme beset by innumerable stereotype pitfalls, was rendered convincing by profound psychology and a realistic presentation of the milieu. The action develops through the girl's consciousness; the audience is on the girl's side and perceives events through her eyes. From the first moment we learn about the emotions of the scared daughter of sullen, hostile parents; the positive hero, the young man from the farmers' co-operative, appears only later in the crowd of the kermis, at a time when we are shown him through the eyes of the girl, and conceive a liking for his virtues from her angle. Cheerful multitudes swarm about the fair, the merry-go-round turns, the hands and smiles of the girl and of the boy drift together in selfless joy. The motion of the rocking seats controlled by physical laws can only now and then be changed by the young man with the aid of a gentle push or swing. However, as the merry-go-round slows down, the ominous black Sunday best of the girl's father standing there stiff as a post assumes an ever grimmer shape, then his face reminds her painfully of the face of another, of the man whom she does not love but whom she must marry.

Without dialogue this poetical sequence clearly shows the situation and outlines the contours of a potentially tragic conflict.

Now comes the characterization of the father. Dry, rational speech; his words sound flat and toneless over the table of the outdoor restaurant of the fair. They talk about the girl's future, but her thoughts are elsewhere; she watches a lady-bug.

At the farm the father and the prospective bridegroom are shown bargaining. They have to join forces because they are the last two peasants who have remained outside the co-operative and insist on farming their own land. That is what makes the marriage necessary. While they are bargaining over wine, mother and daughter are sighing. They dare not say what they are thinking; the clock ticks and the shelled corn falls harshly.

A guest arrives: the smiling swain of the merry-go-round. He has come to woo the girl. A silence of pleasant excitement reigns for a moment. The advances of the young man who has come to pay his courtship are rejected with lashes of contemptuous words. He is given to understand that his presence is undesired. The young man greets and goes away.

As in Tchekhov, apparently indifferent words conceal tense impulses and decisions, threats and promises. The film-goer understands at once without being pushed. Though forbidden by her parents, the girl meets the young man. The co-operative is having difficulties. These pictures are still fraught with the memory of former schematism: hot-tempered, didactic words in the office, arguments copied from the daily press, explanations. The two lines of the drama tangle. The two lovers will not surrender; in the rain, along the muddy farm roads by the ploughed fields, but not inside the office among the posters, their revolt and dogged steadfastness is felt to assume a social character: with her love the girl votes for the future, and against submission to the myth of the land, like her mother; that she might choose the way of life she prefers.

And then the wedding. A splendidly directed wedding it is, a worthy counterpart of, and improvement on, the wedding in *The Soil Under Your Feet*. Frantic dancing is seen in a close room emptied for the purpose. It was a marvellous idea to let this wild, boisterous revelry take place in a relatively narrow, closed room with a low ceiling. In a spacious hall or out-of-doors, passions might have evaporated, but here...

The lovers dance. In a side room the father drinks, clinking glasses with his friends, with his prospective son-in-law. The dancing lovers give way on the screen to brief, swift flashes of restless rhythm: faces, legs, piccolos, violins, faces, feet, and sweeping skirts flit across the screen. This change from an orderly narrative manner to a classical montage construction is good, because for the dancing lovers the surrounding world begins to vanish; they are aware not of the whole, but only of parts of it.

However, reality roughly intrudes, exactly as at their first meeting on the merry-go-round. As a result of brilliant camerawork—seemingly an endless circle—the dark, menacing figure of the father comes into view. We follow the camera—and the girl's eyes; the commanding gloomy black clothes check the ecstatic motion by their very presence. The dance is over. There is a scandal.

After this scandal the film shows fatigue. Emotionally the wedding scene has provided a perfectly clear and final picture. The father is compelled to accept his daughter's decision; the director cannot, or will not, represent this mental process, so painful to the father, with the same intensity as in the treatment of the preceding events. He cannot do so because we have lived the film not through the father but through his daughter. An axe is hurled through the air at a gatepost. This quasi-murder, his fright and mental crisis after his impetuosity, break down the father's resistance; he resigns himself to the inevitable, a victim of forces beyond his control. He loves his daughter; this love leads him through his daughter's marriage to join the co-operative. Possible; yet this end is more arbitrary than the rest of the film.

As has been shown, Fábri possesses a store of professional knowledge which he can use in the service of his message without having to resort to forced and empty formalist bravura. He has displayed and applied the methods of expression congenial to film art; he has proved that monotonous, unimaginative direction is not realism, and still less socialist realism, but only want of talent, a tradesman's job where twelve always make a dozen. Fábri channeled this brilliance of direction to convey a topical and important message. He presented a highly significant moment in the reorganization of rural life, a moment that had made a number of previous films stumble and fall. The story of Dovzhenko's *Earth*, if told in a few words, could also sound appallingly schematic and standard—wealthy landowner peasants kill a young peasant, a party secretary, who organizes farmers' co-operatives; however, his death unites rather than divides the people of the village—yet Dovzhenko made of this an immortal cinema masterpiece. In the same way, the story of *Merry-Go-Round*, based on a simple variation of the Romeo and Juliet conflict, and dealing with the problems of joining the farmers' co-operative, has been made a work of art by the director's individual style and power of artistic expression—as the original short story was elevated by the literary merits of Imre Sarkadi.

All this applies also to the actors, to the fresh, natural talent of Mari Törőcsik, a newly discovered young actress, to the simplicity and open-hearted smile of Imre Soós, avoiding the slightest touch of pathos, to the rich young peasant played by Ádám Szirtes ingeniously, with close observation of innumerable details, to Manyi Kiss's portrayal of the peasant woman who reconciles herself to her lot and puts up with everything, finding comfort in the thought of submitting to the will of God. All these characters are full of life, colour, and variety, like the people we meet every day.

Merry-Go-Round (though a much better film than *Fourteen Lives Saved*) has never been awarded a prize at any festival; it is nevertheless mentioned in many accounts of international film history as a proof of Hungarian socialist films being capable of superb achievement; in fact, it has become the symbol of the modern Hungarian cinema. A French manual has entitled its chapter dealing with Hungarian films: "Un charmant 'Carrousel' hongrois."13

Professor Hannibal goes back into history. Its period was the least glorious era of modern Hungarian history: the white terror of the 'twenties. Hungarian film production, which still insisted on presenting triumphant struggles, needed the strength to look directly into the face of the recent past. The challenge was taken up by Zoltán Fábri when he put on the screen the tragi-comic fate of the schoolmaster Béla Nyúl (Nyúl means Rabbit in Hungarian) nicknamed Professor Hannibal by his pupils. The miserable life of Mr Nyúl, the schoolmaster, was told by Ferenc Móra in one of his most disillusioned novels (that in its time could not be published); it was from this novel that Fábri drew his script. Mr Nyúl wrote an essay on Hannibal, the Carthaginian general, the formidable enemy of the Roman Empire, and this fatal essay decided his future.

One fine day his wife sent this modest essay to her husband's former school-friend, Mr Murai, a Member of Parliament, hoping that he would help them. Instead of reaching Murai, the essay fell into the hands of nationalists wearing crane-feathered hats who read into the study mockery of their extremist political creed. The essay came at the most opportune time for exploiting it as "the enemy's work"; at a mass-meeting the author was accused, together with other similar wretched intellectuals. Of course, this accusation was directed not so much against the person of the insignificant Béla Nyúl; it was a pretext for using extreme rightist slogans in order to stir up the members of a fascist student organization. Professor Hannibal became the victim of this "mass-meeting"; though he had promised him help and a better post, Mr Murai also betrayed him. In his alarm Béla Nyúl

—in the manner of Jeanne d'Arc—retracted his "tenets". However, he cannot escape disaster; backing from the crowd now coming to exalt him, he falls down from the wall of the Óbuda amphitheatre, the people cover his body with a sheet of newspaper advertising the rumba.

This film of Fábri, denouncing perverted nationalism, is perhaps more mature as art and more unified in style than *Merry-Go-Round*. Take, for example, the scene at the Gellért swimming pool. Mr Murai is not a cruel man, he does not drive away Béla Nyúl who has contrived to get a word with him by hiding in the boot of his motor-car. Mr Murai takes him to the swimming pool and they bathe together. But he is not above ducking poor Nyúl—not seriously, just for fun—and enjoys the spectacle of the man gasping and kicking. This fun nearly ends in tragedy, because Mr Nyúl cannot swim and he sinks to the bottom. A baleful prelude to subsequent events. The swirling water of the pool, teeming with people enjoying themselves, and Professor Hannibal losing his foothold again and again, is also a symbol; the symbol of life in that period. This symbol is certainly present and has an effect on the film-goer whether or not he is conscious of the film's chief aim.

This tragi-comedy is repeated at the big rally. The arena becomes silent when Mr Nyúl comes in. Then loud yelling fills the air, and a deserted, helpless little man stands alone in the awful space. The square is empty. Then stones begin to rain on him. "Down with Nyúl!" And Nyúl delivers an address; he apologizes and retracts his statements. In this recantation the words flattering the ruling classes are the most arrant nonsense ever uttered by man in a terrified, feverish effort to save his life: "And Hannibal, clinging to these roots in the soil, wrote on the sky with flaming letters that the God of the Hungarians is still alive." As disaster approaches, the film seems to be coming to a solution and drifting towards a happy end: Béla Nyúl is given frenzied applause. Mr Murai is glad that Nyúl has come to his senses; after all, Mr Murai did not mean any harm, he only wanted to use Nyúl "a little" to push his own interests. Here Fábri applies the change of rhythm observed in *Merry-Go-Round*: calm scenes are replaced by a hectic montage. Béla Nyúl steps back—and is dead.

The title role was played by Ernő Szabó with remarkable power, able to portray a genuine hero or an insignificant average man, scared to death.

The fame of *Professor Hannibal* reached every part of the world; in the early summer of 1957 it won the Grand Prix at Karlovy Vary. In their excellent international film history, Ulrich Gregor and Enno Patalas, the progressive West German film historians, give a detailed account of the film.[14]

Beside Zoltán Fábri, it was Félix Máriássy, working in the profession from the early 'forties and directing since 1949 *(Anna Szabó)*, who developed into one of the most important directors with the most individual style. After a few schematic films he showed his abilities in *Relatives*. In his next two films he took subjects not treated before and probed into the problems of Hungarian reality of the time in a strong spirit of criticism.

Spring Comes to Budapest (Budapesti tavasz), made for the tenth anniversary of Hungary's liberation, screenplay by Gábor Thurzó, based on Ferenc Karinthy's novel, gave an effective, tight account of the events and problems in the capital during and before the siege. With the sober realism characteristic of his concept, Máriássy fortunately managed to avoid the cheap effects which might have been inspired by the solemn anniversary. To put it more simply, Máriássy has the virtue of carefully avoiding clap-trap. Even such episodes as the journey of the two nuns at the beginning of the film with deserters, the nuns' embarrassed smiles and the guns left in their charge relax the atmosphere. A similar intentionally relieving scene comes at the end when the disbanded groups of soldiers who were hiding in cellars emerge and in the moment of liberation greet the Russian soldiers with music in the courtyard of the block of flats; they do not play the national anthem which begins with "God", or the Internationale which they do not know, but the Hunyadi March.

The sequence of the executions on the Danube embankment—showing only the discarded shoes and the deserted embankment—scenes that have become classic in Hungarian film history and the montage of the air-raid shelter deserve particular mention. A clever portrait is given of various classes of society thrown together casually, the mistress of an estate having her supper in a special armchair, her coachman, and the caretaker, an arrow-cross man (a Hungarian nazi), who is the first to throw out his chest and declare himself loudly a communist. The scenes presenting a cross-section of society, for instance those in which the arrow-cross district leader, played by Samu Szabó, dictates from a small notebook with the patience of a demented exegetist, have proved to be more lasting from the perspective of seven years than the original love story, the chief subject of Ferenc Karinthy's novel.

Félix Máriássy's other film represented the world of working people as it really was in the 'fifties, and not its beautified version as had been the practice before. This film, *A Glass of Beer* (Egy pikoló világos), attracted attention not only at home but also in the socialist countries, as the first work which portrayed socialist reality with the means of neo-realism. The film was bought by nine countries, in a relatively brief period of time it was seen by audiences numbering nearly three and a half million people, and at Karlovy Vary it was awarded the Grand Prix of 1956 jointly with *Abyss* (Szakadék).

Reference has here been made to this remarkable success at the very outset because it showed the profound interest of the wider public for its own problems, for its own life; people were not curious about what life would or might be, they wanted to see what it was really like. *A Glass of Beer* gave an answer. The script of Judit Máriássy presents the apparently dull events in the life of a working-class family living in the sixth district of Budapest: the soldier son, the pleasure-loving daughter, the mother, the neighbours; the staircase badly in need of a new coat of paint, the doorway shedding its plaster, this time without any festive crinkled-paper decoration which benevolently covers the peeling walls of the side-street tenement house. A good many turns of the story are rather melodramatic, and today the influence of Zavattini can be detected, to say nothing of older effects, even commonplaces, such as the scene of the desperate girl leaning over the steam of the engine on the bridge. The magic of the first portrayal of everyday Budapest is nevertheless of significance; the Danube bank above the city, the district beyond Dózsa György Street and the Budapest Museum of Fine Arts, the giggling bevies of young girls sitting with their glasses of beer and longing for adventures perhaps only for a dancing partner, the soldier son for whom everybody is sorry (because he will lose so much weight), but of whom secretly the whole family is very proud—all these scenes have the charm of a never to be repeated first experience.

At the time all this created the impression of bold sincerity; since then it has been imitated innumerable times and been surpassed by life so definitely that it is gradually becoming a document of film history and one thinks of it less as the living masterpiece which it was felt to be—with justification. However, the short scene remains a minor masterpiece in which film people visit the factory, disturbing the quiet rhythm of productive work, while a parade of prospective stars transforms the scene into an excited bustle; everybody wants to appear more beautiful and better than he or she actually is. This engaging grimace implied a farewell to the sugar-coating methods of film studios and opened the way for a more truthful and realistic tone to assert itself.

The film version of József Darvas's *Abyss* in 1956 was finished fourteen years after its director, László Ranódy, conceived his first plan. (During the war Wlassich's supreme film office prohibited the scheme.) It was now carried out not as planned, with real peasants, but with new actors, such as Margit Bara, fresh from Transylvania.

Abyss presents the serf-like misery of have-not peasants in Hungarian villages under Horthy's regime as mirrored by the cares, enthusiasms and disappointments of a young village school-teacher on the Great Plain, a son of the people. The film is noteworthy for its genre, because its literary source was a drama: *Abyss* is the first manifestation of Ranódy's peculiar epic style on the screen. In a ten-to-fifteen minute sequence of genre shots he conjures up a typical Hungarian village of the 'thirties, and he links these scenes, almost reluctantly, with the teacher's doings, his courtship and with the crisis of his love affair. The actual tragedy, the death of a tenant farmer's gifted son who is compelled to work as a swineherd instead of going to school, remains only an episode. Some critics reproached the director for his episodic treatment, but it was this unforced epic flow, in an anecdotal mood yet in a sharp critical spirit, that brought fresh colours into Hungarian cinema and showed the promise of a definitely new and individual style. *Abyss* marked an important stage in the history of Hungarian film art.

Károly Makk who had worked as an assistant since *Somewhere in Europe*, and made his *début* as a director with *Liliomfi* in 1954, now came out with a film on social problems, *Ward No. 9* (A kilences kórterem) and with a contemporary light comedy of the Liliomfi-type, *Tale of the Twelve Points* (Mese a tizenkét találatról).

In its time *Ward No. 9* had an unusual effect. The best proof of how much truth the film revealed was furnished by the offended statement of the Union of Hungarian Medical Workers. In fact, the conceited doctor chattering about the unusually wide range of Yma Sumac's voice while pressing his palm on the belly of a patient with peptic ulcer was a familiar scene to many members of the audience, whether the physicians of the Trade Union Social Insurance Centre liked it or not. On the other hand, this overcritical exposure, this publicistic tone "telling the doctors a few home truths" did much harm to the unity of the film and detracted from its lasting value.

The makers of the film added so much to the personal history of Gáspár Tóth, who insists on finding out the truth about his gastric operation, that with the passage of years the film has fallen to pieces and into separate sequences. The repulsive physician is punished not for refusing to see a patient when he was on night duty, but because he deserted the nurse he had seduced and caused her suicide. For the film Gáspár Tóth's peptic ulcer is only a pretext for showing the hospital as a symbol of society and for exposing numerous faults made in the period of the personality cult. Since the author of the script, Tibor Méray, is not a literary man, the dialogue remains on a journalistic level. Therefore the sinister ballet of white-coated physicians fussing around Gáspár Tóth who has come for a post-operative examination, their eager but menacing attitudes add up to something comical rather than critical. Thus only a few scenes still have a value in film history, though often imitated since, such as rush hour on the trams, excited visitors waiting at the hospital door in ward No. 9 with its various types of patients. Some scenes which may have created a deep impression at the time, the nurse shelling peas before committing suicide, or the conversation about the fighting in Korea during the operation, are now seen as unnatural and mannered.

In connection with this film the outmoded manner of its acting must also be mentioned. The movements of the actors, the rhythm of their gestures, the tempo of speech, the technique of modulation, even their appearance all seems outdated. It is perhaps Tibor Molnár alone, as Gáspár Tóth, who with glowing eyes fights for a true cause in the spirit of a modern Michael Kohlhaas, and Andor Ajtay as the impassively nasty physician who give memorable performances on the screen; as for the rest, the affected cheerfulness of Imre Soós, the unsophisticated helplessness of Mariann Krencsey, even Miklós Gábor as a selfish doctor, are no more than figures moving in and out of sets.

Apparently, *Tale of the Twelve Points* is the work of an artist exactly of the opposite temperament. But only apparently. Because it would be wrong to believe that the criticizing artist is not fond of the criticized society. Makk criticizes on a basis of love, as evidenced by *Tale of the Twelve Points*. The script of the old, well-proven team, Békeffy, Jeney, Bacsó and Szász, shows Budapest households agitated by news of the football pool—it seems incredible that the film was made before the lottery was started!—presenting a middle-aged couple who endure the hardships of having no proper home with wry humour, a pair of impecunious young people, an arrogant football player, with the environment of the People's Stadium in the background.

The stages in the career of Zoltán Várkonyi, always searching—perhaps a little nervously—for new paths, are marked by experiments of many kinds: the screen adaptation of a play by Molière, *Georges Dandin*, a serious and beautiful film on the labour movement, *Strange Mark of Identity* (Különös ismertetőjel); and a passionate reckoning with the mistakes of the personality cult, the impetuosity of which, however, sweeps away what is right together with what is wrong: *The Bitter Truth* (A keserű igazság).

Strange Mark of Identity is an important film: it presents the fight led by the communists in a complex period of the war years, and pays tribute to the memory of Zoltán Schönherz who died a martyr's death. It shows the most important stages in the struggle against the war, against fascism and for the future of the Hungarian people, with convincing power and a truly noble pathos. The representation of the famous demonstration of March 15, 1942, is fine; the long shot of the preparations for the execution in the courtyard of the military prison on Margit Boulevard, while unsuspecting, cheerful crowds pursue their everyday life as usual, is an extraordinary experience.

Of the young generation of directors, György Révész shot his second film, *Gala Dinner* (Ünnepi vacsora), based on a scenario by Boris Palotai. It is a drama of conflicts between the new and the old intelligentsia; the film is a distinguished work in which the action proceeds in a somewhat leisurely rhythm.

Three young directors appeared with their first films: Tamás Banovich, *The Empire Gone with a Sneeze* (Az eltüsszentett birodalom), a tale drawn from Tamás Török's play for juveniles; Frigyes Mamcserov lengthened his excellent short film of Karinthy's novel, *Please Sir* (Tanár úr kérem), into an indifferent feature film; Imre Fehér directed a new version of *Sunday Romance* (Bakaruhában), a short story by Sándor Hunyady (filmed in Hollywood as *The Girl Downstairs*, 1938, directed by Norman Taurog, with Franciska Gaál and Franchot Tone). Two of these three, Banovich and Fehér, together with Makk, had been in the profession from the start in 1948; it was time to present their own works.

Imre Fehér's film, *Sunday Romance*, is the most valuable of these works, as well as one of the finest chapters in Hungarian film history. The script was written by Miklós Hubay, the leading parts were played by Margit Bara and Iván Darvas. A journalist serving as an infantryman, thanks to the goodwill of his commanders, is allowed to wear civilian clothes when off duty. One day strolling about in uniform in an amusement park he meets a beautiful servant girl. He begins to court her; he is attracted by the simple devotion and loyalty of the girl. As a matter of fact, the girl is a servant in the family where the journalist often goes for supper and to court the ladies. On such an evening their relationship, which can hardly be concealed any longer, is revealed; the brunt of the scandal has to be borne by the girl rather than by the journalist. The servant girl leaves the provincial town after having been disappointed not only in love and in a man, but in her whole world.

Sunday Romance is a modern and honest film because it consciously and carefully avoids over-vivid material and presents its story in a straight-forward way. From the very beginning it is a relief that the director refrains from over-emphasizing the atmosphere of the Monarchy, saying: what a queer, ludicrous world with its bowlers, hobble-skirts, cabs, monocles and walking-sticks... He takes this Imperial and Royal world seriously, treats its figures as equals and he does not regard them as half-witted idiots; after all, they built up Budapest in barely two decades. He actually takes these people seriously in order to judge them severely, pointing out the laws of their very wise, well-calculated and purposefully arranged world and of their conduct, leading inevitably to contradictions, and last in the analysis dem-onstrating their own futility.

Our hero's walk in the town, where life runs its regular and sensible course, shows us people drinking beer, and in the garden of the café the delightfully stupid local primadonna singing her recruiting song in tight hussar breeches. The source of trouble is not the deliberate wickedness of some character of the film or some professional capitalist. The mentality of these people is determined by their social environment; and the hero paying court in his infantry uniform is well aware of it. He would like to get out of this trap; he is even prepared to marry the girl servant whom he loves; but this does not depend on his own will: such a love or marriage is made utterly impossible by society, and he has neither the strength nor the means to revolt. At least that is how he feels. But he only feels so; he knows that what he is doing is immoral. All the more so as the servant girl loved him as her equal. When he is on the point of telling her the truth the girl silences him by saying that she had guessed he was lying and he had really no land and was poor, but it did not matter.

Margit Bara's enchanting interpretation and Iván Darvas's conception of the figure balancing upper-class cynicism and real emotion belong to the best performances in the history of Hungarian films. Margit Bara is simple, ignorant, but very beautiful; moreover, she radiates intelligence, in the orig-inal sense of the term, beyond objective knowledge. It is therefore a terrible humilitation to the man when he sees her profound contempt and wordless departure which are more tragic than suicide with cyanide; a deep humilia-tion, because she makes the man feel that she fully recognizes the infamy of his conduct, that it was not with a silly love-sick chambermaid that he had had a passing love affair. These merits are a credit to the director; it is worth while to look attentively at the splendid scene when the young gentle-man is exposed at supper: the servant girl's dignity, her silent reaction to the blow. Her conduct is of a much higher order than the forced, off-handed cynicism and awkward insolence of the journalist who steals love under false pretences in an infantry uniform.

The shooting of *Sunday Romance* was started in the summer of 1956 but finished only in the spring of 1957. The events of 1956 interrupted the work on this film as well as on others.

The third film of young György Révész, *At Midnight* (Éjfélkor), from the script of Iván Boldizsár, deserves special notice, as a good use of improvisation. The question is whether to remain at home, or set out in the hope of adventure, of a better life, of variety beyond the open border. We are in November 1956. This question was an acute problem; György Révész gives a prompt answer flavoured with delicate irony, and without lies.

The *Geschichte des Films* of Ulrich Gregor and Enno Patalas (Gütersloh, 1962) rates it as the most interesting Hungarian film of this period.[15]

In 1957 many new directors became active. This increase in the number of directors was promoted by a significant government order: the Newsreel and Documentary Film Studio under the name of Budapest Film Studio was made available again to directors for the shooting of feature films. In the 'thirties, large numbers of films were produced at this studio: almost every new director shot his first film here. Now that it was made possible to produce feature films under another management, new tastes could assert themselves, which contributed to the development of a healthy competition. So from 1957 to 1963 there were two feature film studios, Hunnia Film Studios, and the Budapest Film Studio.

The depiction of everyday reality in a sincere manner yet not in the spirit of an editorial is also a new phenomenon of the period. After *At Midnight* of Révész, *Spiral Staircase* [Csigalépcső] (Bán); *Dani* (Szemes), and *Danse Macabre* (Ranódy) were also such dramas on topical issues, endeavouring to satisfy an interest spontaneously shown by the public. At the same time there was an unconcealed demand for simple comedy, and the studios began to produce films with the avowed aim to entertain, regrettably of not very exacting standards in most instances: *A Quiet Home* [Csendes otthon] (Bán); *An Adventure in Gerolstein* [Gerolsteini kaland] (Farkas).

Classical literature was represented by a new Móricz film, *Bird of Heaven* (Égi madár), directed by Imre Fehér, as adapted by Tibor Cseres.

The Iron Flower (A vasvirág), a script by Miklós Köllő, based on a short story of Andor Endre Gelléri, was put on the screen by János Herskó.

Some literary figures, who had turned away from film making, began to appear here and there in the studios. New actors, new faces became known.

In 1959 seventeen Hungarian feature films were made by fourteen directors. Three of these, Keleti, Máriássy and Fehér, shot two films within this year, and only two made their first films: József Kis (*A Window onto Heaven*—Égre nyíló ablak) and Gyula Mészáros (*From Saturday to Monday*—Szombattól hétfőig).

Decade of Directors

It became obvious that exaggerated caution in admitting the young to the studios and the veritable monopoly of the "great" who had made their names would lead to a crisis. And this crisis did come. In the other film-producing countries dozens of young directors appeared with their first films. Quantitatively, such an extensive conquest had not been encountered in film history since the silent films. These young directors introduced a new tone, new approach and a new idiom trampling on old authority. With aggressive ruthlessness (like the directors of the French New Wave), guided by the older generation (as were the young Soviet directors, Chukhrai, for instance), looking back in anger (like Tony Richardson and his companions in Britain), fascinated by the brutally frank reality of newsreels (like the Americans who make films away from Hollywood), they all contributed to changing, with astounding rapidity, the picture of film festivals, the review columns of international journals and, finally, the cinema programmes.

In the meantime in Hungary there was silence: old, well-proven tricks were applied again and again with the persistence of good craftsmen. This does not mean much, for what created a sensation in 1955 has become obsolete since. The government noticed this dangerous stagnation and issued several fortunate orders: study was reformed at the Academy for Dramatic and Film Art, young lecturers were appointed to share in the work of technical training, a circle of students with creative aspirations formed the "Balázs Béla Studio" and were given support; and its members were granted opportunities for directing short films to prove their talent and try their strength. This considerably widened the access of new young directors to the studios, gradually decentralized the uniform central artistic control by setting up first two, then four creative studios, so that from the first of January, 1963, the varying tastes of young directors were allowed a wider scope.

At the same time a growing number of Hungarian films were presented in other countries and at international festivals and were awarded prizes. Czechoslovak and Egyptian co-productions were followed by an American–Hungarian collaboration, Richard Thorpe's *The Golden Head* (Az aranyfej).

Personal contacts with Soviet, Polish, Czechoslovak directors became more frequent. Thus by 1966, the situation became radically different from what it was in 1959: instead of the ten or so directors who were active in the 'fifties, no fewer than forty directors worked in 1966, thirty of them steadily. In the years from 1960 to 1965 Hungarian cinemas presented the first films of nineteen young directors.

It is worth while to inquire into the qualitative changes brought about by this numerical, statistical advance.

The most important change is that the production of individual—good or poor—films has been superseded by creative works in which the directors express their views of the world where they live and work.

In the 'thirties and 'forties directors were accustomed to directing ready-made scripts after their own taste and to the best of their abilities. Although various differences of taste became evident in the finished films, examples of which have been pointed out in earlier chapters, the basic idea of the script rarely came from the director. Some significant or successful work of Hungarian literature was selected at the central office, a short story, a novel, or a play, which the film studio found suitable for reflecting the historical and political situation of the moment, and for presenting the tasks to be achieved.

However, from the early 'sixties, a much greater responsibility has devolved on the director; the public has demanded more initiative—naturally in films with an artistic message. Scripts have still been prepared after the usual international method by various professional and non-professional writers, but the initiative has passed into the hands of the director. It is he who has planned the message, a personal message, to be conveyed to the world about the world, expressed sometimes in a whole series of films.

It so came about that some members of the generation which had had so much success in the early 'fifties, whose names had been known for their high achievements on the screen—like Bán and Gertler—were superseded. Márton Keleti was, however, noted for his exacting, expert work as a director and for his flair for good stories. His comedy, *The Corporal and the Others* (A tizedes meg a többiek), the first film since *Chin Up* to treat the war in a satirical tone, had an enormous success. Viewed by world standards the story is far from original: Keleti imitated Comencini's film, *Tutti a casa,* casting Imre Sinkovits in the role of Alberto Sordi. His film had the merit of presenting a topical subject in Hungarian environment. Keleti's reliable methods invariably bring pleasant surprises. The fate of the generation that started to work in the years following 1945–1948 is of peculiar interest. The members of this generation represented the first "new wave" of post-liberation Hungarian cinema in the mid-fifties. What is it that Fábri, the director of *Merry-Go-Round*, Máriássy, the director of *Spring Comes to Budapest*, Ranódy, the director of *Abyss*, have to tell the audience of the mid-sixties?

Zoltán Fábri is still an eminent director of international reputation. The others now make screen adaptations of literary works, sometimes rewarded with considerable success, as László Ranódy's *Skylark* (Pacsirta). For his acting in this film Antal Páger was awarded the prize of best performance together with Saro Urzi at Cannes in 1964. Others, like Zoltán Várkonyi, have made films based on great events in Hungarian history, producing extremely popular screen versions of works by Mór Jókai—the Hungarian Dickens—*Men and Banners* (A kőszívű ember fiai), and providing proof that in execution and colour technique Hungary can satisfy the world market. Others have endeavoured to show the everyday life of the Hungarian man-in-the-street in a style drawing on formerly deservedly successful, now however, outdated Italian neo-realism. In these efforts pathos sounds ever more insincere, as in Félix Máriássy's *Every Day Sunday* (Pirosbetűs hétköznapok) and *Goliath* (Karambol).

Both Fábri and Máriássy insist on the well-proven medium of literary adaptation. Scripts derived from novels which have stood the test of the book market and have received favourable reviews afford reassuring support. However, Fábri is clearly capable of giving these adaptations a suggestive power that reflects his own personal experiences.

In the early 'sixties Fábri directed three films, two of which were versions of literary works: *Darkness in Daytime* (Nappali sötétség), based on a novel of Boris Palotai, *Birds Become Silent* (A madarak elhallgatnak), and *Twenty Hours* (Húsz óra), adapted from the story of Ferenc Sánta. In his third film, *Two Half-Times in Hell*, in Great Britain *The Last Goal* (Két félidő a pokolban), Fábri again followed the well-trodden path, drawing his story from the years of fascism. In Fábri's life the war was a decisive experience in 1941, when Hungary entered the war, Fábri was twenty-four years old: when he fails to find a topical theme, he can always fall back on war stories which invariably bring success and, it must be added, deservedly. Though lacking unity, it is a fine film with several perfect sequences.

The story is based on a real incident: a football team of German soldiers and one of Hungarian labour-camp inmates play a match on the Führer's birthday which Hungarians are obliged to lose; instead, the labour-camp team revolts and wins the match, whereupon they are mercilessly murdered. The plot is so suitable for the screen that a second version has been made in the Soviet Union. Very cleverly, Fábri kept the decisive match for the end of the film. This gave him opportunities for showing essential features of the war: the human relationships and conflicts of helpless prisoners who were at the mercy of their guards, of the sergeant acting like a hospitable innkeeper and his superior beaming paternal amiability. The most memorable scenes are those representing life in the camp: the banging in the evening on empty tin boxes, distribution of the mail, when inmates of the camp are handed out leaves of trees instead of the letters from their relatives. One of them, when ordered by the paternal sergeant to read from the leaf, recites a poem by Attila József; the fencing ace who used to be admitted to the presence of the regent refuses the—perhaps—life-saving favour (of being selected to play in the team), because even here, in his humiliation, he feels he belongs to the ruling class and tragically fails to realize his position as a victim. In his next film Fábri turned to the same theme; to the period of fascism and the years of racial persecution, but this time he only tried to repeat what he had conveyed more convincingly earlier. Only a few brilliantly shot scenes have saved *Darkness in Daytime* (Nappali sötétség) from oblivion (the excellent camerawork was by János Tóth).

Then Fábri proceeded to direct *Twenty Hours*. Ferenc Sánta's outspoken book, which tackled touchy problems and showed numerous difficulties in the countryside, created an immense sensation and was widely read. The notes of a journalist in search of good stories at a farmers' co-operative have become symbols of the twenty years' path following 1945, beset with deviations and stumbling-blocks but nevertheless bringing progress.

The social and economic reconstruction of the Hungarian countryside offered fine opportunities to Fábri so fond of tense dramatic situations. It therefore flowed from Fábri's personality that his delineation of the most extreme characters was the most successful, while the figure of the journalist is colourless, vague, even static. In fact Fábri pushes the journalist into the background to appear on the screen as a narrator, permitting the director to reveal the real sources of the tragic tension.

No classical structure could cope with this task, therefore Fábri, for the first time in his career as a director, abandoned the representation of regular drama and, breaking up the normal chronology, showed only the events which he found to be the most interesting. Since Fábri's attention was invariably held by the dramatic climaxes, the film gives no development of character or psychological motivation; the heroes are always seen to clash at the height of passion.

The most consistently elaborated figure is that of the chairman of the farmers' co-operative, played by Antal Páger. On the screen nearly the whole time, he is perhaps the truest mouthpiece of the director. Here Páger has been cast in a role worthy of his talent: after the depressed, introverted petty bourgeois of *Skylark* (who might have stepped out of a Pagnol film) awarded a prize at Cannes, here he plays an extroverted peasant, full of zest for creative work, who finds joy and satisfaction even in martyrdom.

The directors of the third type came from the generation that received a socialist education after 1945, at the Film College headed by Ferenc Hont, Béla Balázs and Géza Radványi, and became active in the 'fifties. These directors have grappled with numerous crises, followed devious paths and found it hard to attain balance. They are the permanently young, though all of them are around forty; many of them are still mentioned as promising, encouraging talents, though some produced a few failures after a good start.

The most important of these men, with the most typical personality as regards his career, is Károly Makk. Born in 1925, Makk, as mentioned before, started in 1954 with a Biedermeier comedy, *Liliomfi*, and made his best film *The House Under the Rocks* (Ház a sziklák alatt) in 1958 (awarded the Grand Prize at San Francisco Festival). Later he directed a historical drama on the struggles of the Red Army during the Republic of Councils in 1919, then turned his attention again to the present to direct, in quick succession, four films dealing with problems of the intelligentsia of our days. As a matter of fact his deep interest in reality has made Makk's career a consistent one.

Although *The House Under the Rocks* takes place in the time directly following the Liberation, the story of the film is topical. Based on a scenario by Sándor Tatay, Makk put on the screen a rural tragedy with extraordinarily thorough, almost exhaustively elaborate, psychological details, breaking away from the monotony of a black-and-white representation. In this drama everybody is right from his or her individual point of view, first of all perhaps the vine-dresser cotter, driven to murder though he is a quiet, decent man with pure impulses. The importunate affection of the hunchback woman inspired by her avid longing for happiness is equally plausible, and so is the beautiful wife's union with the forester in her effort to create a quiet family home.

At the time reviews did not voice general enthusiasm for the film, on the contrary: since the drama takes place in the first year following the Liberation, its director was reproached for having disregarded social reality and treated his material in the attitude of art for its own sake, although there are several passionate disputes in the film between the young man (Ádám Szirtes) who represents progress, his hunchback sister-in-law (Irén Psota), and the cotter (János Görbe) who, having grown cautious and hesitant as the result of a serious illness after captivity and a depressing environment, stubbornly resists change. It is certainly not by the will of the director that the poor peasant becomes a murderer. This development is explained by reactionary forces, by his environment, and his clinging to the past. Had he listened to the advice of his wife and his fellow prisoner, he might have broken the spell and escaped from his sister-in-law, as well as from the service of the rich peasant. What is this if not the portrayal of social conditions and problems? The pictorial construction of this 1958 film, its technique of direction vie with our most modern works. The hunchback sister-in-law's cart on the lower road meeting the wedding procession; the tipsy conversation between the old man making brandy and the weak-willed hero in the cellar, virtually conjuring up the past; the contrast between the grim prison walls of the Badacsony rocks and the infinitely free, smooth surface of the lake are all splendid solutions of the director.

His next project was *Brigade No. 39*. It is difficult to say something new on this subject after *Chapayev* and *We from Kronstadt*. Makk has succeeded in doing so.

The two heroes of the film are true popular revolutionaries as well as two opposite types: one is the enthusiastic but inexperienced young workman with a tendency to anarchism (Ádám Szirtes), the other an old peasant, who has become a wise, level-headed, but firm cavalry commander (József Bihari). The film presents the cares and worries of these two popular heroes in a way that we feel the justice of their cause and understand that their faults flow from human nature, which faults, however, do not compromise the cause itself. It furthermore shows the brave battles fought by the brigade on the frontiers, against foreign intervention in support of Horthy, and the director is not afraid to give a truthful picture of the failure of the Republic of Councils, but in a manner to make everybody feel that real victory is only a matter of time.

In addition to a good script and excellent acting, this is all to the credit of Károly Makk's work. His direction and control of the camera are in the grand style.

After two such excellent films, one of which earned international recognition, Makk turned his attention to the problems of the intellectuals, first in a light and (by now) insignificant comedy—*Don't Keep off the Grass* (Fűre lépni szabad)—then in *The Fanatics* (Megszállottak). The latter was in every respect suitable for the modern and frank treatment of the present; the script was written by a young scenarist of the studio, Lajos Galambos, who has since become a successful author.

The film is about engineers who discover a vast sea beneath the waterless region between the Danube and Tisza rivers, and try to bring the underground water to the surface. The discoverer joins forces with the chairman of a farmers' co-operative and with a well-borer, and after a hard struggle, often necessitating the circumvention of laws and regulations, they finally build an irrigation system.

However, the central problem of the film is not the engineering difficulties, not the heroism of the act, but whether it is permissible to do good and to be useful by disregarding rules, acting without the support of the authorities or even with the certainty of their disapproval. (Later this problem was made internationally familiar through the Czech film by Kadar and Klos, *Obžalovany,* which won a prize at the Festival of Karlovy Vary in 1964.)

So, after some interval, Makk again took for his theme the enthusiastic zest of communists for performing feats of work and for construction. After the "positive heroes" of the period of the personality cult, who worked day and night, never slept, never loved, ever burned with zeal and knew the Marxist classics by heart, it was extremely difficult for Károly Makk and Lajos Galambos to represent this fanaticism authentically, convincingly, and without pomposity. The two heroes of the film, the engineer searching for water (György Pálos) and the chairman of the farmers' co-operative (Ádám Szirtes), fight boldly for a great cause in a noble alliance, committing faults when inevitable, in order to improve the water supply of the Great Plain. In the normal sense of the word they are absolutely wrong: they trespass, spend money without permission, drill wells instead of surveying the land, employing, moreover, a private well-digger, and are rude to their superiors. They take upon themselves a certain illegality for the sake of a great and true cause the success of which serves the interest of the working people.

Makk does not justify their transgressions; his is not the philosophy of "the end justifies the means". Emphasis is laid on the heroic nature of the sometimes apparently hopeless fight for a true cause. And this is beautiful. The struggles of the makers of the film—with themselves, against their own compromises—are also rare, even if they sometimes fail, for they *have* compromised, for instance in the closing scenes which are accurate and servile copies of the closing images in *The Soil Under Your Feet*: dozens of watering machines irrigate and spray the rich growth of green seedlings; or the *deus ex machina* who appears in the form of a Member of Parliament and unexpectedly puts everything to right, thereby jeopardizing the fundamental theme of the film, for what would have been the outcome if no Member of Parliament had happened to pass that very way just then?

A few words must be said about the friendship between the two protagonists. The films of our age over-saturated with sex seem to forget about friendship. Therefore a close relationship between two men has not been represented in western films without innuendo.

This alliance has been rendered magnificently by the actors and by lively and modern camerawork. For the direction of the film also runs along modern lines: in Hungary it was the first clear sign that the wind of the great "revolution" which involved the film art of the whole world had reached this country. Together with the cameraman, György Illés, Makk made conscious efforts to convey modern ideas in an up-to-date form.

If the film contains such values it makes one wonder why it failed.

The answer may be sought not only in the attitude of the public expecting the cinema to provide entertainment in the wrong sense of the term: "I go to the cinema to relax; that is enough for me," or in lack of understanding, but in the film itself, even in all the other films of its kind for which blame is assumed by *The Fanatics*. The subject itself, the script, the plot were too elaborately devised to prove a theory. Animated direction and the script-writer's sincere passion could not counterbalance this. Moreover, the story was not interesting enough, whereas most spectators expect to be thrilled by such a drama. So there arose an incongruity between the audience's "traditional" demands and a mode of representation on the screen which began to assert itself in the years around 1959–1960. The development of "authors' films" has followed a faltering course in Hungary, therefore directors often adopted, together with modern style, also the ideas of the men who applied the methods in question in their creative work, for instance Truffaut, Antonioni and Fellini. As a result, the director failed to win even the public on which he had counted, and this explains how *The Fanatics* came to be rewarded only by the Hungarian Critics' Prize—given for the first time that year.

The failure of *The Fanatics* made Makk uncertain: two of his films made in quick succession, *Paradise Lost* (Az elveszett paradicsom), a screen version of Imre Sarkadi's play, and *The Last But One* (Az utolsó előtti ember) failed to win either the favour of the public or the approval of the critics. Actually these films display a high professional efficiency and a good capacity for the modern direction of actors; however, their plots rest on contrived conflicts: a popular physician, having performed an illegal abortion in the case of his friend's wife and caused the woman's death, flees from justice, but his love for an innocent young girl whom he meets in his flight induces him to give himself up *(Paradise Lost);* a parachutist dies because he deliberately opens his parachute later in order to appear bolder than his rival *(The Last But One)*.

What could be more natural for the director than to take refuge from these failures in a period comedy in colour; all the more so as once before he had scored success with a comedy poking fun at the past. That is how *His Majesty's Dates* (Mit csinált Felséged háromtól ötig?) came to be made: a comedy full of ideas, a "Hungarian Boccaccio" mocking false national feeling pertly and gaily. Here we have to stop for a moment, in order to point out a new, interesting lesson. Makk had spiced his film with a number of delicate ideas, all of which he invented himself. Nevertheless, when his film was presented in Vienna at the comedy festival of 1965, all reviews censured him for having directed his film under the obvious influence of Richardson's *Tom Jones*.

In point of fact Makk could not have known *Tom Jones,* since he shot his film almost simultaneously with that of Richardson; however, *Tom Jones* having been first on the world market, Makk was unable to compete with the famous film. The films of small countries often experience such setbacks, which is one of the reasons why it is more difficult for Hungarian films to triumph—regardless of their merits.

Imre Fehér experienced similar treatment, in a still more ruthless form. After *Sunday Romance* none of his films made a hit. *The Truth Cannot Be Hidden* (Húsz évre egymástól) and *Woman at the Helm* (Asszony a telepen), produced in quick succession, were both failures, though the first was the adaptation of a highly successful play in the style of the "angry young men" of English literature, while the second was photographed by one of the best cameramen, Sándor Sára, with much ingenuity and skill.

György Révész is tossed about between deplorable melodramas and shatteringly profound tragedies. Sandwiched between two such poor and abortive attempts as *Hail Days* (Fagyosszentek), a peasant drama, and *Four Children in the Flood* (Négyen az árban), a film for juveniles, he made *Land of Angels* (Angyalok földje). This gloomy picture of life, based on the novel of Lajos Kassák, is a bitter story of the revolt of tired people, driven to work

from dawn to night, who refuse to pay rent. Notwithstanding its dark colours, the film radiates an optimistic yet deep and moving humanitarianism
which, coupled with the tender and affectionate representation of workmen
living in slums, may explain how it came to win two great prizes at the Mar
del Plata Film Festival. (In addition to the Grand Prix the film was awarded
the Jury's Special Prize.)

It is worthy of note that *Land of Angels* snatched the Grand Prix from
The Loneliness of the Long-Distance Runner. This extraordinary success was
not appreciated to the full, though it might have served as a lesson that our
virtues and achievements should not be taken for granted. What virtues
may be mentioned in this connection? In a director, knowledge derived
from ideological conviction, from adequate training, is a virtue; and so is the
right composition and cutting of sequences and lively expression of the
message in an age when technical mediocrity cannot be made good by the
best-intentioned message.

In this connection a remarkable method introduced by Hungarian directors has to be pointed out, namely the promotion of extras to minor
heroes. From the viewpoint of acting Hungarian films are composed on
two planes; there are leads who, one or two in number, dominate the screen,
and there are extras who move, as it were, like a living set, indicating the
period and the situation. Characters of minor significance present their
transiently important thoughts by stepping forward as protagonists and
occupying, briefly, the foreground of our attention. The method followed
in Italian and French films, permitting several characters, sometimes more
than a dozen, to move in an intricately composed space, is rarely applied
in Hungarian films. These figures move through the scenes in accordance
with such an accurately elaborated choreography—sometimes without uttering a word—and create the impression of such animation that one can guess
the story of their lives. A case in point is the scene-shifter in Fellini's film,
$8^1/_2$: whenever the director appears on the scene this scene-shifter performs
a belly dance to attract his attention; various members of the shooting group
encountered in the winding corridors of the summer resort hotel also function in this way. Révész has availed himself of this method: he did not place
such figures in succession, cutting one after the other, but made them crop
up in various scenes. The tenants of the house in *Land of Angels,* their
conduct upon the overseer's arrival, the people at the inn, the showmen
in the park, etc. are good examples of this.

The careers of Mihály Szemes and Tamás Fejér are also marked by many
failures and a few unexpected hits. Fejér, who had won a prize at an amateur

film festival of Paris in the 'fifties and who used to be an enthusiastic adherent of avant-garde films—started with a series of banal comedies, and even *Undisturbed Happiness* (Miért rosszak a magyar filmek), a satire in which he mercilessly criticized the faults of even his own methods, failed. Only *Love in the Suburbs* (Kertes házak utcája) aroused international interest; it was presented at the Film Festival of Cannes in 1963 and also in NewYork.

The subject of the film is the crisis of a superficial marriage; the husband, a one-time skilled worker, now a high-ranking official, gets alienated from his wife who started as a weaver and, in turn, despises her husband's social climbing.

Szemes's career has been more even than that of Fejér; he is more cautious in resorting to studio work and strives to be sure of eliciting response. The public has received his films favourably and his *Alba Regia* (shown in Great Britain as *Branded*) has been presented in more countries than has any other Hungarian film before. Reviews have been nevertheless reserved in their praise.

A Certain Major Benedek (Alázatosan jelentem), based on László Bóka's excellent novel, deals with a less common subject: the physical and moral ruin of a field officer serving in Horthy's army. Again the fine shades are noteworthy here: the officer played by Miklós Gábor is not the obtuse military swell seen in hundreds of films, but a thinking man with several prepossessing traits who cannot be exempted from awareness of responsibilities. *Alba Regia,* with Tatiana Samoilova, a story of general interest, has had greater success. Based on a real incident, the film evokes through the person of a humanitarian physician the days of the battles fought for the liberation of Székesfehérvár. The film—awarded a silver medal at a Film Festival in Moscow—has several good sequences, but is lowered to mediocrity by the psychological inconsistency of the love story.

The more marked success of this film, surpassing that of contemporary works, was obviously due to the subject. In the 'sixties, whenever Szemes dealt with the present, as in *Our Kid* (Kölyök) and *The New Gilgamesh* (Új Gilgames), the beauty of several brilliantly executed details was marred by sentimentality and the triviality of the love story.

This brings us to the next "type" or "group" of directors which, of course, does not correspond to the production teams of film studios. These directors presented their first films in the 'sixties. Without any arbitrary discrimination they fall into two classes. There are men who in age belong to the generation of Fábri and Makk, such as Miklós Jancsó and András Kovács, and there are some who are actually younger in years, such as Gaál and Szabó.

Many of those who belong to the generation of Fábri and Makk are tormented by problems in their creative work; the achievements of some of them, though very encouraging, elude evaluation. Their work may be characterized most aptly through the art of Miklós Jancsó and András Kovács.

Miklós Jancsó (born in 1921) is four years younger than Fábri and four years older than Makk. He directed his first feature film in 1958, *The Bells Have Gone to Rome* (A harangok Rómába mentek), the second followed, after a pause of four years, in the autumn of 1962, *Cantata* (Oldás és kötés). It was worth waiting so long, for in the meantime Jancsó earned wide appreciation as a director of newsreels and documentary films, acquired skill in every detail of the craft, learnt to make quick decisions, and to adjust himself to existing conditions and unexpected situations without giving up his principles and conception. His short film on the life and work of the Hungarian sculptor György Goldman was awarded a prize in San Francisco.

Cantata may be regarded as an overture to the renewed Hungarian film art of the 'sixties. Many critics had divided minds about the film, and there can be no doubt that, notwithstanding the gratifying award of the (shared) Prize of the Hungarian Critics, *Cantata* was given a cooler reception in Hungary than, for instance, in Italy. Ugo Casiraghi, the critic of *Unità*, wrote about *Cantata* as follows[2]: "What does the title (the exact translation of the Hungarian title is "To Unravel and to Tie") actually mean? Doubtless to unravel old knots and to tie new ones. It depicts the crisis of an intellectual, a surgeon, represented by Jancsó with such extraordinarily profound insight as to be comparable only to Mikhail Romm's *Nine Days of a Year*, about atomic scientists..."

The knot to be unravelled by this surgeon of thirty-two is of a very significant nature. Thanks to socialism, his life and his career have been easy. Though of peasant stock and therefore in a favourable position, the self-conceit inspired by this favourable position has made him assume an attitude of inhuman schematism. He has locked himself inside a circle which isolates him and deprives him of a deeper understanding of reality. As a scientist and a communist educated in the Stalin era he feels that he has learnt too little from others. It is a fine idea that this crisis, arising in conjunction with his own work, not only awakens his conscience, but also shakes his faith in his own skill as a surgeon... Jancsó guides him along the difficult path of rediscovering his own childhood: this is a critical journey.

Cantata was received in Italy with warm approval, and a similar welcome was given to Jancsó's next film, *My Way Home* (Így jöttem made), in 1964, in the Soviet Union. The film recalls moments of the Liberation without any pathos, purely and simply, without evading any problem. The hero of the film is a young student who knocks about in the spring of 1945 at the western frontier of Hungary and is taken prisoner several times by Soviet soldiers. After his second capture he is sent to help a severely wounded Soviet soldier of his own age who, being unfit for other service, has to mind the cows. Sometimes a military lorry comes that way to take the milk to the wounded at the field-hospital. Gradually the two boys learn to know each other and become friends. The film is the story of the slow disappearance of mutual distrust. Finally the Soviet soldier dies of his inadequately treated wound. The Hungarian student, after having brought a doctor who is unable to help, puts on his friend's Soviet uniform and sets out homewards. The film is marked by excedingly suggestive scenes, concise construction demanding tense attention and concentration, and incidental music woven from folk songs and Bartók's *Allegro Barbaro*. (Bartók's music was a decisive factor also in *Cantata*.) This terseness has been enhanced by Jancsó into a merciless vision of oppressive power in his film made in 1965, *The Round-Up* (Szegénylegények), his first to score a real success at home.

The Round-Up is a masterpiece; as Fábri put it "...perhaps the best Hungarian film which has ever been made." This spontaneous statement deserves special attention, because it was the first time that a Hungarian film not only "had success", "turned out well"; or received a prize at some festival, but film artists themselves, even the most eminent Hungarian director, who has given testimony of considerable self-restraint, appreciated the film and realized that a significant piece of work had been produced.

The Round-Up is a historical film. The action takes place in the 1860s, at a time when Garibaldi had finally achieved Italian independence from the Habsburgs and papal supremacy, when the Hungarian ruling classes entered on a compromise with the Austrian ruling classes. It is the period of Visconti's *Senso* and *Il Gattopardo*. This moment of history is interesting not only as a parallel of the Italian *Risorgimento* and as the beginning of the era remembered in general as "the good old days" (the Hungarian Victorian Age) but chiefly because it affords an opportunity to represent an appalling and unfamiliar historical truth which is the reverse of everything that has been said about these years.

The consolidating Hungarian government wished to establish general security in the first place by bringing under control the victims of the process of rapidly developing capitalism, peasants and gentry who had forfeited their land and many of whom had formed bands of highwaymen to rob and plunder. This was all the more important as active participants of the Hungarian revolution, put down in the autumn of 1849, also took refuge by joining these highwaymen, and these politically dangerous elements had to be eliminated. That is how it came about that the police of Count Gedeon Ráday, who applied in his work modern principles of prosecution and criminology, investigated the cases of ordinary felons and criminally neutral political refugees of the revolution simultaneously.

However interesting and astonishing a story this may be (the English reader will come nearest to grasping the situation if he thinks of the Irish movements of liberty at the close of the past century; Italians will find a parallel in the reorganization of the mafia in the opening years of the present century), it is an opportunity for a gripping historical film far above the average level. Jancsó has gone much deeper: having created a tense situation, he used the theme only as a means for rendering a peculiar psychological state. If such comparison is permissible at all in the case of this exceedingly original and typically Hungarian film, Jancsó's method is most apt to recall that of Ingmar Bergmann in his trilogy: circumscribed, closed scenes; laconic dialogue; the incentives of actions and men withheld from the audience to the point of mystification; careful composition; movements in space following perspectives lost in the infinite horizon. These are special touches, characteristic of modern methods of film direction, particularly of Bergmann's.

All these are, however, only external features; the atmosphere of the film, even its drama and its peculiar self-imposed logic are so absolutely Hungarian that the film demands an extraordinary effort from the foreign film-goer. The end of the film also bears the individual mark of Jancsó: as in *Cantata* and in *My Way Home*, the tragedy running its course at the height of emotional paroxysm, the unexpected, sudden, though predictable massacre of the revolutionaries, who are singing with childish joy, is left to the last minute; the quick and cruel cutting off of this scene leaving behind a feeling of frustration—while allowing the incidental music, the anthem of the Habsburg dynasty, to roll on in the dark, after the disappearance of the last image—are marks of the ingenious individuality of an artist.

It is encouraging that the splendidly constructed sequences of pictures of the light-footed, bat-wing-cloaked police in *The Round-Up*, as well as those of its white-clad peasants, their luminous white that suggests mourning, are having success all over the world.

The Round-Up brought world-wide fame to Jancsó and to Hungarian films. His next film, *The Red and the White* (Csillagosok, katonák) made in 1967, was a Soviet–Hungarian co-production; it was shot in the town of Kostroma in the Soviet Union.

Let us deal with this film at greater length than is usual. Not because it is regarded as Jancsó's best film, but because it reveals in the most exemplary way all the virtues, all the creative touches, which raised Jancsó to world fame. Moreover, this film is the first ever and perhaps only work in which the Soviet socialist revolution and its international effect—in 1919 Hungary was the only country where a Republic of Councils was established outside the Soviet Union—have been represented by the film company of a people's republic.

The Red and the White deals with the fight of Hungarian internationalists for Soviet power and secondarily for the victory of world revolution in 1918–19. At the end of the First World War tens of thousands of Hungarian officers and soldiers who were Russian prisoners of war, under the impact of the revolution of 1917, joined forces with the Soviet power which had superseded the czarist government, and in the civil war that followed they fought with the Red Army against the white officers who tried to restore czarist rule. Many of this astonishingly huge mass enlisted in the Red Army in the hope of being released from captivity and of returning home. They thought that any method was good enough to get out of their prison camps. Only a tiny minority recognized the revolutionary significance of their commitment.

The film begins with slow-motion pictures. The Red Army sweeps onward solemnly; heroes gallop with drawn swords and this mad, dashing gallop is reduced by the camera to a sublimely impressive pace. The director evokes a legend, that of Tshapayev and Stshors. It is by a similar method that Dovzhenko conjures up Ukrainian history at the beginning of *Zhvenigora;* in the distance of the remote past horsemen approach and pass in slowmotion. With Dovzhenko this also conveys the passage of time; however, with Jancsó, it is only meant to create the atmosphere of legend and myth.

The beginning of the action itself is all the more perplexing: the sound of gunfire is heard from several directions, a handful of Hungarians are retreating behind the protective walls of a convent which they still hold. Although they are obviously pursued by a superior force, the members of the small unit cannot agree even on questions of defence. Their arguments disclose the political, social and ideological diversity of opinions reigning among these Hungarian internationalists, ranging from self-confident but blindly passionate communists to the cautiously calculating peasants craving only to get home and inspired to enthusiasm solely by the looting of big estates and the re-allotment of land. Perhaps because they were divided in spirit or because of their military bewilderment in their position of evident disadvantage, the forces in the convent have been annihilated.

Troops of the victorious army swarm onto the scene, words of command are rapped out and the almost reassuring presence of regular military discipline is felt. The instinctive realization that anarchy is being replaced by order gives a frightening sensation. The director's ruthlessness is manifested here: when they appear, the staff of white officers are alarmingly more prepossessing than the disorderly, quarrelling internationalists in retreat. It is now that the oppressed, the humiliated, the dirty and the hungry rush into their wild and bitter war against the well-fed, the calm, and the organized.

The czarist officers offer a sham chance of escape to their victims in that they promise to shoot only those who are to be found in the town after the passage of another fifteen minutes. However, the roads leading to safety are blocked in every direction by wooden fences and the revolutionaries who attempt the hopeless feat of climbing over the fences are picked off by the officers who seem to take extraordinary pleasure in this form of hunting party for human game. The faces of the officers in charge are barely visible, indicating that it is not personal power which is forfeited, but the power of a whole class, as in *The Round-Up*. Faces are seen only in glints of light, but it is enough to permit insight: despite their immaculately clean black uniforms, these men glitter in white as they stand in their speeding motorcars; only their white teeth flash under their peaked caps while they cheer loudly, triumphantly.

The faces of the revolutionaries and their justified action are seen all the more distinctly.

Soldiers on horseback galloping in wide, open spaces and shots of active figures moving against a background of nature make it possible to express, solve or explode conflicts by motion and extraordinarily direct action, which in this film almost invariably implies death, physical and biological annihilation. However, the moment people find themselves in an enclosed space, when they are surrounded not by nature but by walls and barriers erected with their own hands, they are compelled to express themselves in a more complicated manner, hence their relationships also become more intricate.

In the final series of pictures in a powerful setting, without a single cut, the battle is fought with alternating success until the Kirghiz soldier, so near to our heart, is wounded; his death marks the beginning of his company's death march. This is not a routed, quarrelling group any more, but rather a unified revolutionary company.

It is an unforgettable scene where the white-shirted revolutionaries, after having vanished for a moment from before the spectator's eyes, are seen trudging into the water of a flat meadow, to march on again into the distance. After the arrival of the relieving troops of cavalry the soldiers water their tired horses at the banks of the Volga and when the hero, played by András Kozák—the only man to remain alive—salutes the corpses of the fallen revolutionaries with his sword, we know without being told that we shall see this man again before very long, as the commander of the Hungarian Red Army in the spring of 1919.

These remarkable scenes in *The Red and the White* present Jancsó's virtues as well as his future mannerism. Like an indelibly powerful vision, the picture is imprinted on the mind and consciousness of the audience; the image itself speaks, interprets, teaches, indeed, the spectacle conveys the artistic idea: words and action are only inseparable, secondary features of the image. Long series of shots taken with a brilliant technique virtually drag the viewer onto the screen, so that he feels as if he were there in space and action; he does not require any justification or explanation, he accepts and understands every event, be it ever so vague or obscure. Simultaneously this irresistible emotional identification with the visual experience the director releases emotional reserves of such intensity that in weaker, less closely composed scenes of the film natural and indispensable balance is on the point of being jeopardized. In some instances elements of form tend to dominate while movement on the screen and also of the camera leans towards the over-stylized; in others, where the minimum of essential information is withheld, the audience, kept in the dark, is compelled to guess what is happening.

In Jancsó's next films the balance is tilted now in one, now in the other direction: either full enjoyment of the film is marred by lack of information, *Silence and Cry* (Csend és kiáltás), or excessive use of dynamic elements leads to mannerism, transforming some sequences into a kind of pantomime, *Confrontation* (Fényes szelek). The latter is his most successful work, as evidenced also by the debate it roused. This was the first Hungarian film about the then young generation that stepped onto the political scene directly after the Liberation of 1945, their selfless enthusiasm knowing no bounds and seeking perfection, the frenzy of power born of this enthusiasm turning to violence, which subsequently brought its own revenge.

In some of Jancsó's recent films emphasis on sex and the bold representation of awkwardly intimate relationships seem to dominate in such an
arbitrary way that it is hard to draw the line between artistic achievement
and a flair for profit making through catering to the lowest instincts of audiences, *Sirocco*. Pro-Jancsó and anti-Jancsó groups have emerged; the
former praise the master without criticism, the latter refuse to recognize
any merit. The director, hearing nothing but the applause of his fans, turns
away from the public to create only for himself. That is how we get to the
enigmatic *Agnus Dei* (Égi bárány), the confused contents of which permit
audiences to interpret the film in any way they wish.

In his last Hungarian film, *Red Psalm* (Még kér a nép), anarchistic,
fermenting-whirling impulses seem to have cleared and settled in Jancsó.
In the film a strike of farm workers in the opening years of the century
is presented in the style of popular dance ensembles. Let us hope that
this highly gifted Hungarian director, the maker of so many films of lasting
value, will once more find his own voice, and rise to new peaks of creative
achievement.

András Kovács is another remarkable personality among the directors
who began their careers at the same time as Jancsó.

After having taken his degree at the Budapest Academy of Dramatic and
Film Art, Kovács became head of the Writers' Department of the nationalized Film Studio and helped to develop film production and art in the
early 'fifties, writing at the same time reviews and studies on the principles
governing film art. This man, considered an exclusively theoretical expert
with a tendency to speculative reasoning, after 1957 voluntarily started a new
career as a director from the bottom of the list of directors' assistants.
Working with unswerving perseverance and dogged patience he got so far
as to shoot his first film, *Summer Rain* (Zápor), in 1960.

Summer Rain is a remarkable film on the divorce of a peasant couple;
however, Kovács's next two films, *On the Roofs of Budapest* (Pesti háztetők), made in 1961 and *Autumn Star* (Isten őszi csillaga) in 1962, were less
successful. Then, after a pause of two years and a long tour of study in
Paris, stimulated by the *cinéma vérité* movement, he began to make his own
special kind of documentary film, *Difficult People* (Nehéz emberek) in 1964.

When it became known that the film was being shot, the attempt was
received by the public with reserve and suspicion. This is not surprising,
considering that this sort of documentary film now in vogue has little to add
to Soviet documentary films of the 'twenties and English films of the
'thirties, especially to those directed by Harry Watt and John Grierson.

One often hears that, in this type of documentary film, the director has no hand in shaping the photographed reality—a claim which is both untrue and impossible. András Kovács, fortunately, did not shrink from the task of shaping reality. The film shows its director interviewing several Hungarian inventors whose novel devices, though patented and praised, are not actually manufactured in Hungary for one reason or another. Redtape, lack of initiative and dread of responsibility is the clinical picture of the case, reflecting Parkinson's Law with flashes of terse humour. Indeed, the film is in a sense a cruel screen variation on Parkinson's serious satire. It reveals how effectively twenty years after the Liberation redtape and indolent officialdom connive with professional jealousy. A variety of characters appear before us for an hour and a half in an exceptionally direct manner. We see the director, microphone in hand, plying different types of individuals with questions. Two things distinguish this film from the usual television interview. First, the cruel logic of the director's questions suggests the thrill of a quiz; and second, the ingenious method of cutting, which reflects a study of the methods of Rogosin and Leacock.

The director pursues the riddles facing him with imperturbable logic. He begins by finding each inventor, presenting him and his ideas in his own environment. The inventor expounds his ideas at some length. The director puts brief questions to him, which the inventor answers or refuses to answer, thereby revealing his concealed thoughts and emotions. Then the director starts a tour of investigation to look up the persons named by the inventor as having helped or hindered him in his work. They also express their opinions, disclosing—at times with a single gesture—their malevolence and cowardice, or their noble humanitarianism. This method acquaints us with numerous types of intellectuals belonging to a technical intelligentsia which so many recent novels and newspaper articles have lauded as the true heroes of our age. It turns out that some of them are educated, intelligent people, while others, posing as heroes, are pitiful figures who, taking refuge behind their slide-rules, peep out from behind the protective shields of Einstein and Fermi. The director never takes sides in words, although, naturally, there is much talk in the film, without professional skill, haltingly and at times stammeringly. Nevertheless, due to this method of interrogation and the very composition of the film, the director does, in fact, take sides, revealing his antipathies or sympathies. This is what makes him a true artist.

In using this creative method the director also needs luck. Take the engineer who is refused payment for his important invention because of the cost of the blueprints, though the money is legally due to him. We have already had the opportunity of seeing three cases in which the director talks with the inventors. This fourth conversation would become boring except that the personality of the engineer turns out to be of the kind that forbids a long, coherent conversation. So the director now uses an inverted method and shocks the spectator by showing him the trifles on which the inventor is wasting his time because he has been slighted. At the same time, the director helps to disclose his great solitude—which in this case is an innate feeling of loneliness and has nothing to do with society—and simultaneously shows us the erudition of the man. How could all this be achieved without putting the words into his mouth? The director looks up his hero in the TV studio where he happens to be participating in a musical quiz. This is an unexpected bit of luck on the director's part, for the quiz was not pre-arranged. So we now see before us the television quiz programme and, half laughing, half crossing our fingers, watch our hero, the talented inventor, coming in second with a perspiring forehead and blurting out at long last the title, date and composer of the composition which has just been played. He accepts the book prize with the transfixed smile of a schoolboy praised by his headmaster, and the expression on his face shows that universal order has been restored in his mind and there is meaning to his life, after all. It is at this moment that the director intercepts him with his microphone. As the audience of the quiz show slowly disperses and the stagehands and cleaners take over, the inventor, without being able to enjoy his success for even a minute, now begins to tell the director in an irritated voice about the cross he has to bear. This is reminiscent of Leacock in whose film *The Chair* the director catches his victims at the most unexpected moments, e.g., when the executioner strokes the electric chair, explains with expert enthusiasm how it is operated and expresses his anxiety over the possibility that the condemned person—with whom he had become acquainted in the first scenes—may be acquitted, thus depriving the executioner of this opportunity to show off his professional skill. This creative principle is soundly applied by András Kovács as is the method of not even trying to disguise his microphone. He wholly discards the method of the "hidden camera". Instead of spying on people he questions them and thereby—like Leacock— raises this genre from the level of natural history films on animal life to a human level. Yet he does not copy this method like certain Hungarian or Polish directors when trying to follow in the footsteps of Antonioni or Truffaut.

Kovács's next film, made in 1966, represents the massacre of Újvidék (Novi Sad) committed during the war, a shameful crime of Hungarian fascism.

Three arrested officers and a sergeant remember the *Cold Days* (Hideg napok, 1966) of 1946 in their cells, before they hear their verdicts. The film has several excellent episodes, such as the desperate dilemma of the railway station employee who has to point out those she knows; when she realizes that her honest and frank information may send some people to their death while saving others, she pretends to know everybody, uttering the words with increasing emphasis until she screams in panic. This sequence gives a magnificent picture of the mental crisis of a simple woman in revolt against the senselessness of war and the evil of fascism.

In his next two films Kovács strove to merge reality, as represented in his documentary film *Difficult People* and the traditional elements of screenplays—acting and dialogue; in 1967 in *Walls* (Falak) with success, but *Relay Race* (Staféta) proved to be a disappointment. *Walls* is an important film delving, as it does, into the sore spots of Hungarian society, giving food for thought and also incentive to action. (That is why Kovács has referred to these works as "activating films".) In *Walls* the heroes are leading Hungarian intellectuals who are often faced with the decision whether to compromise or, remaining true to their principles, shoulder complications and fight for their ideas, in the last analysis for the progress of socialist society. In his preface to the script of *Walls* Kovács put it as follows:

"What does being a revolutionary imply in a system ruled by revolutionary forces? That is the question. Theoretically the issue is simple: support the revolutionary system, defend it in case of danger, but criticize its mistakes... That is to say, act as one of the government party and also as one of the opposition."

How can this be realized? In the film one of the heroes says: "...it is much more decent to accept a compromise in order to attain maximum results than to do nothing with a clear conscience".

In connection with this phrase, Kovács adds the following remark: "Many people regard compromise as equivalent to cowardice, adaptation, opportunism; why this general confusion of ideas? Most probably the explanation lies in the absence of experience of real, wise, logical compromise from the life of our society, due to circumstances created by history. Under feudal conditions, where dependence is one-sided, there can be no compromise for the people. There can be concessions from the powers that be, there can be adaptation, submission or cunning on the part of the oppressed, but for mutual concessions the antagonists have to be on an equal footing, where both have elbow-room, where it is reason and not coercion which decides the issue. And publicity is also necessary, so that everybody can take stock of the aligned forces and judge for himself whether a compromise has been reached or principles have been set aside in order to come to terms. Finally, there have to be clearly defined aims... Thus we lack experience in recognizing that there may be several equally valid approaches to the truth. We only know extremes, heroes or traitors, all or nothing, regardless of circumstances, of the actual balance of forces."

These sagacious, useful words elucidate Kovács's aims, his persistently reiterated message; moreover, they furnish proof that his films—particularly his less successful works, for instance the *Relay Race*—are hardly more than accumulations of such sensible arguments, without convincing artistic power. Therefore the next film of Kovács, made in 1972, *Fallow Land* (A magyar ugaron) was a pleasant surprise. Quoting as his title that of a poem by Endre Ady, he has given a remarkable account of counter-revolutionary conditions in the autumn of 1919.

The younger generation is represented in Hungary by István Gaál and István Szabó. These young men are not hampered by the difficulties that had to be overcome by their predecessors. István Gaál enrolled in the Academy of Dramatic and Film Art as an electrotechnician, yet his diploma film attracted international notice. This short film, *Surfacemen* (Pályamunkások), a rhythmic study of the activities of railroad workers, was awarded a prize at the International Congress of Youth and Students in Vienna in 1958. The young director, having attracted the attention of the Ministry of Education, was sent to Italy to finish his studies at the Centro Sperimentale di Cinematografo in Rome.

Gaál spent two years in Rome, acted as assistant in the shooting of several films, working in Francesco Maselli's crew. After his return, to everybody's surprise, he did not strive to obtain a commission for a feature film, but decided to work in newsreels and documentary films. As a newsreelman he visited every part of the country, learning, observing, and collecting experiences. In due time he made several short films; *To and Fro* (Oda-vissza), on the building-trade workers who travel to the capital every week from remote farms; and *Tisza—Autumn in Sketches* (Tisza – őszi vázlatok), presenting the beloved river and riverside regions of his childhood, which incidentally served as a preliminary study and draft to *Current* (Sodrásban). Gaál has done his best to learn every trick of the trade: credit is due to him for the excellent camerawork of Sándor Sára's film, *Gipsies* (Cigányok). He has also worked as a cutter, and all his activities have been carried on systematically, in accordance with a carefully thought out plan. Against this background he began his first feature film in 1963.

38–39. ISTVÁN GAÁL:
CURRENT
1963

40. ZOLTÁN FÁBRI:
TWENTY HOURS
1964

41–42. ISTVÁN SZABÓ:
THE AGE OF DAYDREAMING
1964

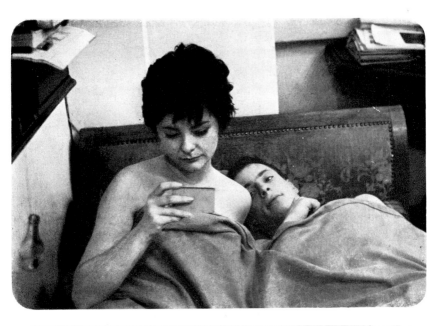

43. MÁRTON KELETI:
THE CORPORAL AND THE OTHERS
1965
44. RICHARD THORPE:
THE GOLDEN HEAD
1963. A HUNGARO–AMERICAN
CO-PRODUCTION

45–46. ZOLTÁN FÁBRI:
THE BOYS OF PAUL STREET
1968

51. GYÖRGY RÉVÉSZ:
    MARTIN CUCKOO
    1973
52. GYÖRGY RÉVÉSZ:
    A JOURNEY AROUND
    MY SKULL
    1969

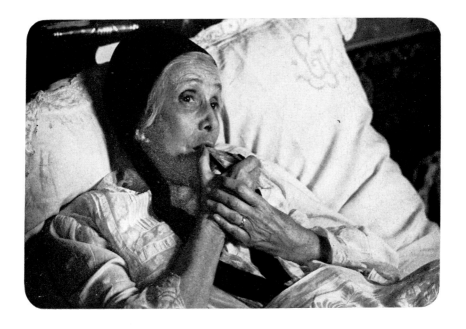

54. KÁROLY MAKK:
LOVE
1970

57. ISTVÁN GAÁL:
THE FALCONS
1970
58. PÁL GÁBOR:
JOURNEY WITH JACOB
1972

59. ISTVÁN SZABÓ:
LOVE FILM
1970

63–64. FERENC KARDOS:
PETŐFI '73
1972

65. MIKLÓS JANCSÓ:
CONFRONTATION
1968

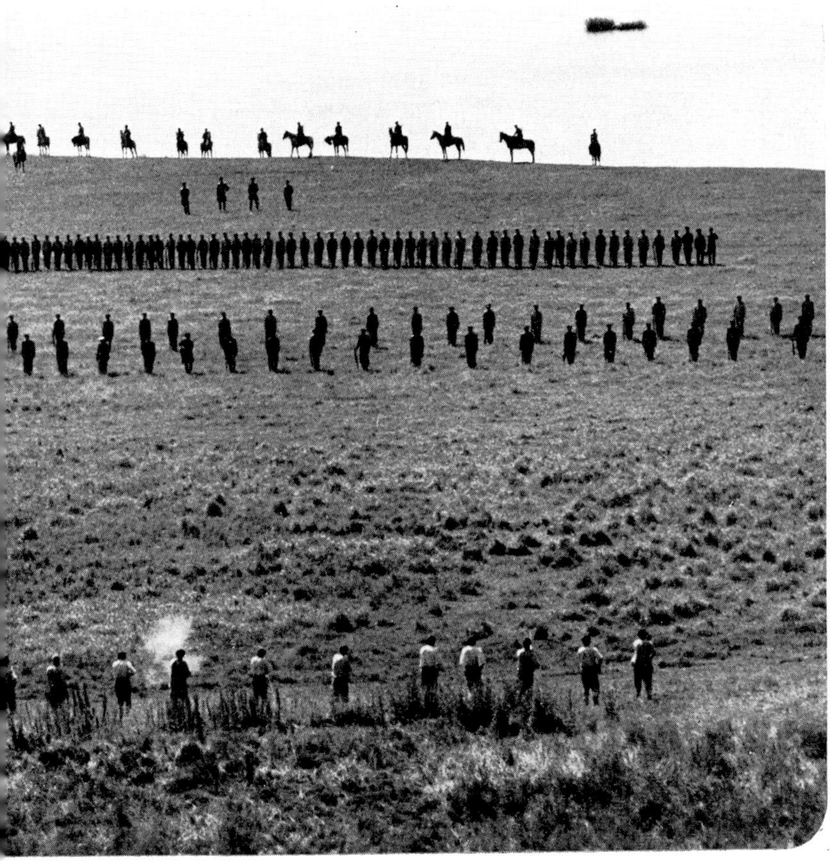

70. MIKLÓS JANCSÓ:
SILENCE AND CRY
1968

71. MIKLÓS JANCSÓ:
RED PSALM
1971

72. MIKLÓS JANCSÓ:
    RED PSALM
    1972

Current is about young people suddenly growing up after the accidental death of one of their companions. In typical Hungarian surroundings, on the banks of a river, we see young people playing football, and chasing one another. They are spending their vacation here, after finishing school. They are just half a dozen youngsters, but they are so painfully brimming with life and even more painfully, almost hostilely young, that every man of forty or more—in England no less than in Hungary—looks at them with the same nostalgic indignation. A bunch of boys and girls whose faces never form in our memory as individual faces, for all we remember is a teeming, impersonal conglomeration. We see only six or eight insolently happy boys and girls having fun on the banks of the Tisza. The director has succeeded in creating this impression so well that some critics and many spectators try hard to remember which of the boys was the one who drowned in the Tisza, and because they cannot recall his face, they blame the director. And yet, this fusion of faces was deliberate, for it is only after the unexpected death of one of the boys that the faces begin to take on individual features. This death has no criminal aspect; it is a simple case of someone having been drowned in the river because he overstrained himself or trusted too much in his abilities. His youthful self-confidence was no match for the current of the river—or of life, if you prefer. Nor is any crime mentioned further along in the story, which tries to tell us no more than that this merry band of youths, shocked by the sudden death of one of their group, begins to ponder on life, together and individually, on life's meaning, on death. Their ruminations end in exasperated clashes. They slowly disband in pairs: a couple having a superficial affair suddenly realize with dismay the shallowness of their relationship and begin to quarrel, as they attempt to find out whether or not they mean anything to each other. A boy who likes to draw is forced to face the fact that he may not be so gifted after all and that only the people of his native village admire his drawings. A shop-assistant who was the most agile member of the group is later seen enjoying the interest the customers take in him: between selling half-a-pound of salami and a pound of sugar, he finds himself, perhaps for the only moment in his life, the central hero, because he happened to be present at the accident.

Gaál presents this interesting psychological process with restraint. It is gratifying to the Hungarian spectator that this crisis, so characteristic of youth all over the world, is here presented in a Hungarian environment. That is, the background is present-day Hungary, set forth with such naturalness that anyone, say an English tourist, looking out from time to time from behind the wind-screen of his car between the frontier and Budapest, would find it just so. In reflecting on the present state of the country the director discards the broad gestures of a tourist guide and the false pathos that made so many of our earlier films conceited and unnatural.

Behind the two or three hundred year old houses of a small village, there loom the outlines of modern factories. During the search for the body we see sights that recall great Hungarian paintings, and we enter a modern artist's studio filled with half-finished sculptures. Unquestionably, the director is making every effort to mingle national tradition and social innovation, past and present, with evocative symbolism. Such efforts often run the risk of lapsing into superficial symbolism. Here, however, the director operates with such a sympathetic and cultured effort and so much sincerity that the result is identical with his innermost intentions. From his stay in Rome Gaál brought back with him Vivaldi's solemn music as a background to the landscape of the Tisza country, lending dignity and sincerity to the scene in which people are hunting for the drowned body. Freshly baked bread with a burning candle on top is placed in the water, and the loaf begins to turn around, apparently indicating the position of the corpse. Even in Mark Twain a similar scene represents a ridiculous turn in the story because of the superstition involved, when Tom Sawyer watches a similar excited search on the Mississippi. But in this film we are deeply moved by the scene, not only because of its extraordinary expressiveness, nor because the old woman in the scene is a peasant woman who does not realize that she is acting.

The film reveals the approach of a painter. In general, exaggerated attempts at pictorial composition rarely succeed because their affected originality makes them excessively conspicuous. In this connection, there is a scene in Gaál's picture which proves that our young director, despite having studied in Italy, was able to preserve a Hungarian outlook. Some of his critics regard his approach here as rather strained. I have in mind the moment when one of the boys, the son of a married couple who are both doctors, remains alone in his study and is overcome by solitude. We catch glimpses of modish objects, to the accompaniment of Renaissance music—a glass of water, an electric switch, a cactus, parts of a stringed instrument enlarged to improbable size, and so forth. This étude reminds one of the attempts of Moholy-Nagy in the 'twenties.

A lamentable drawback of the film is the imperfect acting and the often shallow dialogue, or even lack of dialogue. Modern English cinema has solved in a most interesting manner the ways and means of uniting dramatic, literary dialogue with the pictorial power of expression of the screen. The films of Karel Reisz, Tony Richardson, Lindsay Anderson and others are interesting proofs of how well the pithy, hard dialogue of a drama destined for the stage can be adapted, as if by magic, to the screen, without resort to the dubious tricks of veiling them with cinematic devices so much in vogue in the 'thirties, and still used today far too often.

For his second feature film, *Green Years* (Zöldár 1965), Gaál chose for his theme the undergraduates of the early 'fifties, that is to say the generation which represented the people for the first time at universities and colleges, which experienced every achievement of the new social order as well as all its mistakes. The hero of the film is a peasant boy who comes to the capital to study. Instead of being admitted to the medical faculty for which he had applied, he is enrolled in a French course and becomes a French teacher. He looks about him in this entirely new world with alternating joy and suspicion; he is disappointed in love; his friend, a zealous party man, is unexpectedly arrested on a trumped-up charge. Gradually he awakens to the realization that there are and there will continue to be struggles in life with which one has to cope with by oneself.

In *Baptism* (Keresztelő 1967), Gaál devoted his attention to the lives of two members of the intelligentsia originating from peasant stock, in slow, epic detail. As a director with a preference for closely knit, well-defined forms, he found himself again in *The Falcons* (Magasiskola 1970), a screen version of a short story by Miklós Mészöly.

Gaál preserved the short story's terse conciseness in his film and showed sympathy for Mészöly's desire to translate his themes into abstract terms, a method which he has favoured himself on other occasions. At the same time as he concretely placed his film, the story floats free of time or place, and is not even linked to any particular society. In Gaál's version, always bearing in mind the realism that is part of the nature of films, a nature reserve showing a peculiar, rigid asceticism and dangerous signs of budding fascism, is shown in the context of contemporary Hungarian society which operates rationally, knows and accepts its objectives, and which, not neglecting its problems, can nevertheless be described as stable and well-balanced. This strange, alienated nature reserve originally came into existence for rational purpose and without any preliminary mysticism. This reserve is a falconry designed to protect the large fish-breeding stations on agricultural estates that employ practical and rational methods. The idea is to destroy the waterfowl which eat the fish. But this is only a rationalization on the part of the man in charge of falcons. What he is really doing is practising falconry, an ancient manly sport that has no rational justification. Falconry was always a sport even in Central European feudal countries where certain mystic overtones had survived from the time when falcons were used for hunting. Thus a kind of falcon—the *turul*—was the totemic animal of one of the Hungarian tribes which migrated from the prairies of Eastern Europe.

Gaál sees the conflict in the circumstance that this little reserve is neither just a sports establishment, nor is it effective for the purposes for which it is supposed to function, as the extermination of rare waterfowl disrupts the ecological equilibrium. The fact is that the fanatic in charge of the falcons is living a lie to maintain his group which serves no real end except that of its own survival. An institution of this kind which is an end in itself, without social use or benefit, and dissociated from society, is easily perverted into rigidity and inhumanity. A young student, working on a dissertation on falconry, sent to do his practical training on the station, becomes aware and conscious of this. He leaves the farm, he almost escapes from it, to find his place in life among creative and constructive human beings living a rational existence; people who, in great contrast to the original short story, watch the military methods operating in the falconry station with open hostility.

The photography and the direction of the film, the relationship between landscape and human beings transmits these thoughts and ideas to the audience in the brilliantly original way that reminds of Gaál's earlier films. The very *puszta* which Jancsó, in *The Round-Up* (the location of the two films is identical), exploiting all the resources of black-and-white photography, used to depict a world that is bleak both inside and out, is now populated with the thousand-and-one colours and shades of human thought, and in harmony with them, those of nature. Everything is alive and moving in this bleak grassy plain and since it is alive, it fights, struggles and works. The colours suggest the nature and mood of the characters and of the landscape, and they almost intimate what is to follow. Few words are spoken. This terseness is not forced, it arises naturally from the situation. Not words but the practice of falconry indicates the situations whose sequence compels the young man to leave. And when, in the mists of dawn, accompanied by the drone of electric wires, the hero slowly starts on the way back to life and society, it is culture and civilization, as against a Rousseauian nostalgia, whose call determines the future of the hero.

The Falcons received favourable reviews in several countries. The Rome film magazine *Bianco e Nero* printed the whole script, and numerous French and English critics hailed it as a new trend in the "Hungarian school", quite different from the style of Jancsó. In his latest film, *Dead Landscape* (Holt vidék, 1971), Gaál treats the tragedy of a young married couple living in the solitude of a deserted village as an experiment in how to express the problems of a whole social layer with a cast of only two or three actors performing amidst scenery illustrative of the characters' state of mind.

In his film *The Age of Daydreaming* (Álmodozások kora), which has been particularly successful in France, István Szabó, a director even younger than Gaál, deals with the enthusiasm and disappointment of young intellectuals who have finished school and are about to face life, describing their naive dreams, hard struggles and unexpected setbacks. They view the world of successful adults with annoyance and embarrassment, because in discussions, instead of replying to arguments, the adults are all too ready to point out that it was they who built up this country for the young at the cost of immense sacrifice. This is something deserving respect, but no argument in a discussion. Szabó is keen to observe even the minutest reactions of his own age-group which would most probably escape the notice of other directors: the superficial nature of romantic love and attachments, virtually lighthearted enthusiasm for great causes and achievements concealed under a thin veneer of cynicism artificially constructed for defence, the desire to be guided and educated and the exasperation at being taught.

Szabó's most mature film is his second work—*Father* (Apa, 1967). The author, the director of all his screenplays depicts his own childhood, the path of life of a fatherless wartime generation, rather in their desires than in their deeds. The course of the hero's life and all his decisions are determined by the non-existent father who died at the end of the war. In all his thoughts, fears and loves, amidst moral crises and disappointments he takes refuge with this father-image. Gradually he comes to exempt himself from responsibility for his actions. Slowly and by degrees he raises his father to the pedestal of the ideal admired in the period. Now he is a heroic guerilla—which he never was—now an eminent physician, then a sympathetic friend. Szabó's scenes, composed with unparalleled lyrical delicacy and tender love, have added a new and original colour to Hungarian film art, unlike anything produced so far. In further films, adhering throughout to his own, self-evolved style, he has, moreover, shown a brilliant ability to avoid falling into the mannerisms of repetition, though certain situations, settings, and pictorial visions recur as dominant motives in all of his works.

Both in treatment and theme *Love Film* (Szerelmes film, 1970) is a sequel to *Father*. The hero of *Father*—the same actor—as an adult re-lives his childhood, this irretrievably lost paradise to be revisited only in memory, and goes through a conflict of love with a young girl who has made her home in France.

Szabó's new film, *25, Fire Brigade Street* (Tűzoltó utca 25, 1973), covers a period of thirty years in the lives of the citizens of Budapest through the inhabitants of a ramshackle house, which is due for demolition, in an old district. Here the story melts into a series of lyrical observations, as in so many other films all over the world produced in the late 'sixties and early 'seventies; obviously, the director has abandoned an epic or dramatic treatment. Szabó's films, which are hard to describe in words since they owe their effect to the visual spell of the motion picture, remind the spectator of Fellini's *Rome*; he, too, evokes pictures like visions, but these pictures are photographs not of an outer world, but of the artist's inner universe, projections of a world transformed by his state of mind and held fast with the help of inwardly turned eyes.

Besides those previously mentioned, works by a fair number of other young and not so young directors have been noted in reviews and in film histories of the 'sixties. The very fact that twenty films a year display such a wide scale of styles, colours, themes and messages, as well as a rich variety of personalities among directors, is perhaps the strongest evidence of the importance of Hungarian film art.

The art of Jancsó, Kovács, Gaál and Szabó has influenced their masters, the elder generation: after several failures the art of Károly Makk was, as it were, renewed. The film version of Tibor Déry's short story, *Love* (Szerelem, 1970), about the struggle for moral and spiritual integrity of the wife and mother of a man thrown into prison innocently in the early 'fifties, is a fine example of noble realism on the screen, reborn through the inspiration of Szabó's technique for "building up" sequences. In *Face to Face* (Szemtől szembe), based on the play by Imre Dobozy, Zoltán Várkonyi has represented through the predicament of the officers of a company the last days of the war with outspokenness and a readiness for controversy, as if continuing to thresh out the subject-matter of *Cold Days*.

Of Fábri's adaptions of novels and plays to the screen with their close attention to literary detail and elaborate photography, as in *The Tóth Family* (Isten hozta, őrnagy úr) and *Ant's Nest* (Hangyaboly), special merit is due to the film version of Ferenc Molnár's popular novel for juveniles, *The Boys of Paul Street* (A Pál utcai fiúk), with a cast of young English actors.

György Révész has directed a remarkable film version of Frigyes Karinthy's autobiographic novel written in the 'thirties under the title *A Journey Around My Skull* (Utazás a koponyám körül). The Swedish surgeon

Olivecrona performed a successful operation on Karinthy for a brain tumour; the novel and the film deal with the disease and the operation. Lately, in 1972 Révész directed a film musical on the hero of Józsi Jenő Tersánszky's picaresque novel, *Martin Cuckoo* (Kakuk Marci).

Kovács's passionate documentary style has been carried on by the popular script-writer of the 'fifties, Péter Bacsó, who depicts the unsolved social problems of our time with impassioned criticism: *Outbreak* (Kitörés), *Present Indicative* (Jelenidő), *The Last Chance* (Harmadik nekifutás). A grotesque comedy gives a caricature of the petty bourgeois who dreads violence and is therefore prone to feelings of aggression himself: *Bald Head for Bald Head* (Forró vizet a kopaszra). In *Outbreak* past and present struggles are represented from the angle of a young specialist in a big factory. He censures some of the older generation who concentrate on preserving their achievements and take only a casual interest in the problems of the young. *Present Indicative* shows the moral courage of a factory worker and the cares of the socialist brigade movement. In *The Last Chance* a communist managing director, a former workman, feels that he is no longer able to cope with the responsibilities of his office. Defiant and offended, he returns to work as a welder and finds himself faced by the troubles of the working class.

The generation of the age of Gaál and Szabó—most of whom attended the classes of Felix Máriássy at the Academy of Dramatic and Film Arts—work in different styles, and have different approaches; yet, in essence, they derive their themes from the subject-matter introduced by Gaál and Szabó. The joys and tragedies of building up socialism are shown in *The Thrown Up Stone* (Feldobott kő), the only film directed by the cameraman Sándor Sára, as seen by a peasant boy who has become an artist. Ferenc Kósa presents thirty years of Hungarian peasant life in *Ten Thousand Suns* (Tízezer nap), a film rich in beautiful, comprehensive, artistic composition. Ferenc Kardos tells the story of an old, retired workman from Csepel in *Red-letter Days* (Ünnepnapok) and in *Petőfi '73* draws a picture of Petőfi as seen through the eyes of the present young generation, directed in the style of *The Strawberry Statement*. The principal episodes in the life of Sándor Petőfi, the Hungarian poet and revolutionary, are played by secondary-school pupils in modern clothing and surroundings. Pál Gábor has delved into the lot of young workers in *Horizon* (Horizont) and *Journey with Jacob* (Utazás Jakabbal). In *Forbidden Ground* (Tiltott terület) he is concerned with individual reaction and conduct during a fire in a rubber works. From this brief survey of their films it is evident that the respective generations of Gaál and Szabó are truly interested in the real conflicts of socialist society.

There are many more noteworthy directors and films: Zsolt Kézdi Kovács, Zoltán Huszárik, Lívia Gyarmathy, Márta Mészáros, Judit Elek (as women, these three directors are naturally interested in the position of working women, the subject of many of their films); furthermore Pál Sándor, Gyula Gazdag and others have proved their talents more than once. However, the inclusion of a precise and detailed list is the task of an encyclopaedia rather than of a book intent on following closely correlations on a wider plane. Going into further detail here is unfeasible, all the more so as to give credit for good points calls for the equally unbiassed registration of mistakes and inadequacies. For instance, it is striking how numerous are remarkable, successful *first films*, and how few good films are found among the second and third films of the same directors. The number of directors harping on the same theme and the same message is alarmingly high, as if they lacked the ability to learn the trade in the true sense of the term and then to develop beyond that point: they have spoken out on what was rankling in their minds and—they have nothing more to say. If we do not shun generalization it may be stated that in Hungary in the 'sixties there were more good films than good directors. Except for the elderly generation, there is hardly any director who has made more than five films and those who have acquired perfect training in the craft are still fewer in number. Without our fortunately excellent cameramen, all experts in brilliant technique (Sándor Sára, György Illés, István Hildebrand, Ferenc Szécsényi, Tamás Somló, Elemér Ragályi, János Kende), many a memorable Hungarian film would not have been half so good. Oddly enough, good comedies are also few and far between. In the Hungarian film industry the notion has taken root that only a tragedy is of artistic value; comedy, as such, is conceived of as cheap entertainment, and, to make matters worse, directors are not equal to the job of producing even cheap entertainment. Of course, these shortcomings also derive from the relatively small number of films made yearly. Twenty films a year provide insufficient scope to cover all types of screenplay, even though, as I have shown, these twenty films offer a considerable diversity.

The Hungarian film industry is also restricted by the means available: the yearly budget allotted for the production of Hungarian films is very modest and the technical equipment of the studios rather out of date. On the other hand, the amounts spent by the Hungarian government on technical advancement and investment in order to promote film production are nevertheless significant when one considers the limited resources of such a small country as Hungary.

Under these conditions Hungarian film production could rise to its present level only as a result of the support of millions of cinema-goers and the allotment of still larger sums than before by the state. What is still more important is that directors following the various styles have been given the opportunity for the frank and often controversial representation of Hungarian social problems.

At all events it may be said without exaggeration that in its own, modest way, Hungarian film art has contributed to the achievements of international film art. It is noted with interest and is reviewed; critics and cinema-goers see Hungarian films in Italy, France, the United Kingdom and the United States as well as in the Soviet Union, the German Federal Republic (chiefly on television), Poland, Czechoslovakia and other socialist countries. Thus, an international history of films published these days is not complete without a chapter on Hungary.

Appendix

Hungarian Feature Films Made Between 1945 and 1974

1945

WITHOUT LIES (Hazugság nélkül)
Viktor Gertler, *Ági Polly, Lajos
Básti, Artúr Somlay, Kálmán Latabár*

THE SCHOOL-MISTRESS
(A tanítónő)
Márton Keleti, *Éva Szörényi, Pál Jávor*

THE GOLD WATCH (Az aranyóra)
Ákos Ráthonyi, *Éva Szörényi, Gyula
Gózon*

1946

RENÉ XIV (Unfinished)
Ákos Ráthonyi, *Franciska Gaál, Theo
Lingen, Hans Moser, Klári Tolnay*

1947

THE PROPHET OF THE FIELDS
(Mezei próféta)
Frigyes Bán, *Éva Szőke (Bartók),
Gyula Benkő, Árpád Lehotay*

THE LIGHT MUSE (Könnyű múzsa)
Zoltán Kerényi, *Ida Turay, János
Sárdy, Kálmán Latabár, Mária Mezei*

SOMEWHERE IN EUROPE
(Valahol Európában)
Géza Radványi, *Zsuzsa Bánki, Miklós
Gábor, Artúr Somlay*

SONG OF THE CORNFIELDS
(Ének a búzamezőkről)
István Szőts, *Alice Szellay, János
Görbe*

1948

BURNING MEADOWS
(Forró mezők)
Imre Apáthi, *Katalin Karády, Sándor
Szabó*

FIRE (Tűz)
Imre Apáthi, *Klári Tolnay, Lajos
Básti, Gábor Rajnai*

THE SOIL UNDER YOUR FEET
(Talpalatnyi föld)
Frigyes Bán, *Ági Mészáros, Ádám
Szirtes, Tibor Molnár, Imre Soós,
Teri Horváth*

THE SIEGE OF BESZTERCE
(Beszterce ostroma)
Márton Keleti, *Klári Tolnay, Andor
Ajtay, Éva Ruttkai*

MICKEY MAGNATE
(Mágnás Miska)
Márton Keleti, *Ági Mészáros,
Miklós Gábor, János Sárdy, Marika
Németh, Kálmán Latabár*

1949

GENTRY SKYLARKING (Úri muri)
Frigyes Bán, *Sándor Deák, Ági
Mészáros, Sándor Tompa*

DRESS-SUIT (Díszmagyar)
Viktor Gertler, *Gyula Benkő, Mária
Lázár, Iván Darvas*

YOUNG PIONEERS (Úttörők)
Ferenc Hont, *Katalin Ilosvay,
Ferenc Horváth*

**A WOMAN MAKES A NEW
START (Egy asszony elindul)**
Imre Jeney, *Klári Tolnay, Ferenc
Ladányi, Teri Horváth*

JOHNNY (Janika)
Márton Keleti, *Sándor Szabó,
Ida Turay, Kálmán Latabár*

222

ANNA SZABÓ (Szabóné)
Félix Máriássy, *Kornélia Sallay,
Sándor Pécsi, Éva Ruttkai, Ádám
Szirtes*

MATTIE THE GOOSE BOY
(Lúdas Matyi)
Kálmán Nádasdy and László Ranódy,
*Imre Soós, Teri Horváth, György
Solti, Éva Ruttkai*

1950

LIBERATED LAND
(Felszabadult föld)
Frigyes Bán, *Ádám Szirtes, Ági
Mészáros*

SINGING MAKES LIFE
BEAUTIFUL (Dalolva szép az élet)
Márton Keleti, *Ferenc Ladányi,
Kálmán Latabár, Violetta Ferrari,
Imre Soós*

CATHERINE'S MARRIAGE
(Kis Katalin házassága)
Félix Máriássy, *Ádám Szirtes,
Ági Mészáros*

STARS (Csillagosok)
László Ranódy, *Márta Fónay,
József Bihari*

1951

BAPTISM BY FIRE (Tűzkeresztség)
Frigyes Bán, *József Bihari, Manyi
Kiss*

HONESTY AND GLORY
(Becsület és dicsőség)
Viktor Gertler, *János Görbe, Mária
Sulyok*

BATTLE IN PEACE
(Ütközet békében)
Viktor Gertler, *Ádám Szirtes,
Zsuzsa Gyurkovics*

UNDERGROUND COLONY
(Gyarmat a föld alatt)
Zoltán Fábri, *Ferenc Ladányi, Andor
Ajtay, Erzsi Orsolya*

MADAME DÉRY (Déryné)
László Kalmár, *Klári Tolnay,
János Sárdy*

TRY AND WIN (Civil a pályán)
Márton Keleti, *Imre Soós, Violetta
Ferrari, Kálmán Latabár*

A STRANGE MARRIAGE
(Különös házasság)
Márton Keleti, *Gyula Benkő, Miklós
Gábor, Hédi Temessy, Artúr Somlay*

FULL STEAM AHEAD (Teljes gőzzel!)
Félix Máriássy, *Imre Sinkovits, Ilona
Kiss, Ferenc Bessenyei*

WEST ZONE (Nyugati övezet)
Zoltán Várkonyi, *Artúr Somlay,
Ádám Szirtes, Gyula Benkő,
Éva Spányik*

1952

THE FIRST SWALLOWS
(Az első fecskék)
Frigyes Bán, *Nóra Kovács, Ferenc
Kállai, Margit Ladomerszky,
Kamill Feleki*

SEMMELWEIS
Frigyes Bán, *Imre Apáthi, Juci
Komlós, Tivadar Uray*

THE STORM (A vihar)
Zoltán Fábri, *József Bihari, Manyi
Kiss, Ferenc Bessenyei*

DEPARTMENT STORE
(Állami áruház)
Viktor Gertler, *Zsuzsa Petress,
Miklós Gábor, Kálmán Latabár*

ERKEL
Márton Keleti, *Sándor Pécsi,
Éva Szörényi*

1953

RÁKÓCZI'S LIEUTENANT
(Rákóczi hadnagya)
Frigyes Bán, *Éva Vass, Ferenc Zenthe,
Tibor Bitskey*

UNDER THE CITY (A város alatt)
János Herskó, *Elma Bulla, Ferenc
Bessenyei, László Kemény*

YOUNG AT HEART (Ifjú szívvel)
Márton Keleti, *Hédi Váradi, Gyula
Szabó, Sándor Pécsi, Imre Soós,
Kálmán Latabár*

PENNY (Kiskrajcár)
Márton Keleti, *Ági Mészáros,
Ferenc Bessenyei, Ádám Szirtes*

THE SEA HAS RISEN
(Feltámadott a tenger)
Kálmán Nádasdy, László Ranódy
and Mihály Szemes, *János Görbe,
Zoltán Makláry*

DAY OF WRATH (A harag napja)
Zoltán Várkonyi, *Ferenc Bessenyei,
Erzsi Somogyi, Andor Ajtay*

1954

FOURTEEN LIVES SAVED (Életjel)
Zoltán Fábri, *Béla Barsi, Iván Darvas*

ME AND MY GRANDFATHER
(Én és a nagyapám)
Viktor Gertler, *Éva Ruttkai,
Gyula Gózon*

CHIN UP! (Fel a fejjel!)
Márton Keleti, *Kálmán Latabár,
Violetta Ferrari, Gyula Benkő*

LILIOMFI
Károly Makk, *Mariann Krencsey,
Iván Darvas*

RELATIVES (Rokonok)
Félix Máriássy, *László Ungvári,
Klári Tolnay*

LOVE TRAVELS BY COACH
(Hintón járó szerelem)
László Ranódy, *Ádám Szirtes,
Mária Medgyesi*

TWICE TWO IS SOMETIMES FIVE
(Kétszer kettő néha öt)
György Révész, *Ferenc Zenthe,
Violetta Ferrari*

THE BIRTH OF MENYHÉRT
SIMON (Simon Menyhért születése)
Zoltán Várkonyi, *Ádám Szirtes,
Ági Mészáros, Sándor Pécsi*

1955

ACCIDENT (Gázolás)
Viktor Gertler, *Imre Apáthi, Iván
Darvas, Violetta Ferrari*

MERRY-GO-ROUND (Körhinta)
Zoltán Fábri, *Mari Törőcsik,
Imre Soós*

GALA EVENING (Díszelőadás)
Márton Keleti
A film-concert

THE BRIDGE OF LIFE
(Az élet hídja)
Márton Keleti, *János Görbe,
Ági Mészáros, József Bihari*

CLERK GABRIEL (Gábor diák)
László Kalmár, *Mariann Krencsey,
Ferenc Zenthe, Imre Sinkovits*

WARD NO. 9
(A 9-es számú kórterem)
Károly Makk, *Tibor Molnár, Iván
Darvas, Miklós Gábor, Mariann
Krencsey*

SPRING COMES TO BUDAPEST
(Budapesti tavasz)
Félix Máriássy, *Miklós Gábor,
Zsuzsa Gordon*

A GLASS OF BEER
(Egy pikoló világos)
Félix Máriássy, *Éva Ruttkai,
Tibor Bitskey*

GEORGES DANDIN
(Dandin György)
Zoltán Várkonyi, *Sándor Pécsi,
Ági Mészáros, Tivadar Uray*

STRANGE MARK
OF IDENTITY (Különös ismertetőjel)
Zoltán Várkonyi, *Ferenc Bessenyei,
Imre Sinkovits, Violetta Ferrari*

1956

THE EMPIRE GONE WITH A
SNEEZE (Az eltüsszentett birodalom)
Tamás Banovich, *Imre Soós, Mariann
Krencsey, József Tímár*

EXTINGUISHED FLAMES
(A császár parancsára)
Frigyes Bán, *Ferenc Bessenyei,
Éva Ruttkai*

PROFESSOR HANNIBAL
(Hannibál tanár úr)
Zoltán Fábri, *Ernő Szabó, Manyi Kiss,
Zoltán Greguss*

DOLLAR DADDY (Dollárpapa)
Viktor Gertler, *János Rajz,
Iván Darvas*

THE FOOTBALL STAR
(A csodacsatár)
Márton Keleti, *László Ungvári,
Manyi Kiss, Éva Schubert*

TALE OF THE TWELVE
POINTS (Mese a tizenkét találatról)
Károly Makk, *István Somló, Klári
Tolnay, Éva Ruttkai, Iván Darvas*

PLEASE SIR (Tanár úr kérem)
Frigyes Mamcserov, *Zoltán Makláry,
Imre Apáthi*

ABYSS (Szakadék)
László Ranódy, *Imre Sinkovits,
Margit Bara, Tibor Molnár*

GALA DINNER (Ünnepi vacsora)
György Révész, *Lajos Básti,
Klári Tolnay, Ferenc Ladányi*

THE BITTER TRUTH
(A keserű igazság)
Zoltán Várkonyi, *Ferenc Bessenyei,
Miklós Gábor, Éva Ruttkai*

1957

PLAYING WITH LOVE
(Játék a szerelemmel)
Imre Apáthi, *László Mensáros,
Margit Németh*

A QUIET HOME
(Csendes otthon)
Frigyes Bán, *Ferenc Zenthe,
Erzsi Galambos, László Ungvári*

SPIRAL STAIRCASE
(A csigalépcső)
Frigyes Bán, *Rudolf Somogyvári,
Éva Vass*

SUMMER CLOUDS (Bolond április)
Zoltán Fábri, *László Mensáros,
Mariann Krencsey*

AN ADVENTURE IN
GEROLSTEIN (Gerolsteini kaland)
Zoltán Farkas, *Erzsébet Házy,
Iván Darvas, Kamill Feleki*

SUNDAY ROMANCE (Bakaruhában)
Imre Fehér, *Margit Bara, Iván Darvas*

BIRD OF HEAVEN (Égi madár)
Imre Fehér, *Ádám Szirtes,
Ferenc Kiss, Ildikó Szabó*

FEVER (Láz)
Viktor Gertler, *Ferenc Bessenyei,
Zsuzsa Gordon, Margit Bara*

A REMARKABLE CASE
(A nagyrozsdási eset)
László Kalmár, *Antal Páger,
Ferenc Zenthe, Imre Sinkovits*

TWO CONFESSIONS
(Két vallomás)
Márton Keleti, *Mari Törőcsik,
Tibor Csőgör, Mariann Krencsey*

SUBURBAN LEGEND
(Külvárosi legenda)
Félix Máriássy, *Sándor Kőmíves,
Imre Sinkovits, Mari Törőcsik*

DANSE MACABRE
(A tettes ismeretlen)
László Ranódy, *Andor Ajtay,
Margit Bara*

AT MIDNIGHT (Éjfélkor)
György Révész, *Éva Ruttkai,
Miklós Gábor*

DAN (Dani)
Mihály Szemes, *Klári Tolnay,*
Ferenc Kállay

HEAVY GLOVES (Nehéz kesztyűk)
Dezső Varasdy, *László Papp,*
János Rajz

1958

ST PETER'S UMBRELLA
(Szent Péter esernyője)
Frigyes Bán, *Sándor Pécsi,*
Mari Törőcsik, Károly Machata

ANNA (Édes Anna)
Zoltán Fábri, *Mari Törőcsik,*
Mária Mezey, Zsigmond Fülöp

BOGÁNCS, THE DOG (Bogáncs)
Tamás Fejér, *Zoltán Makláry,*
Béla Barsi, Éva Vass

UP THE SLOPE
(Felfelé a lejtőn)
Viktor Gertler, *Erzsébet Házy,*
György Kálmán

THE IRON FLOWER
(PAPRIKA) (A vasvirág)
János Herskó, *Mari Törőcsik,*
István Avar, Zoltán Várkonyi

THE BELLS
HAVE GONE TO ROME
(A harangok Rómába mentek)
Miklós Jancsó, *Miklós Gábor,*
Ferenc Deák

THE LADY AND THE GIPSY
(Fekete szem éjszakája)
Márton Keleti, *Nicole Courcel,*
Gyula Buss

DON JUAN'S LAST ADVENTURE
(Don Juan legutolsó kalandja)
Márton Keleti, *Zoltán Várkonyi,*
Margit Bara, Antal Páger

THE HOUSE UNDER THE ROCKS
(Ház a sziklák alatt)
Károly Makk, *János Görbe,*
Irén Psota, Margit Bara

SMUGGLERS (Csempészek)
Félix Máriássy, *Margit Bara,*
Gábor Agárdi

RAID (Razzia)
László Nádasy, *Ádám Szirtes,*
János Görbe

WHAT A NIGHT (Micsoda éjszaka)
György Révész, *Kálmán Latabár,*
Klári Tolnay, Éva Ruttkai

PILLAR OF SALT (A sóbálvány)
Zoltán Várkonyi, *Antal Páger,*
Anna Tőkés, Éva Ruttkai

1959

FATIA NEGRA (Szegény gazdagok)
Frigyes Bán, *Gyula Benkő,*
Mariann Krencsey, Margit Bara

THE BRUTE (A dúvad)
Zoltán Fábri, *Ferenc Bessenyei,*
Tibor Bitskey, Mária Medgyesi

SWORD AND DICE
(Kard és kocka)
Imre Fehér, *Miklós Gábor,*
Éva Ruttkai, Samu Balázs

A WALK TO HEAVEN
(Gyalog a mennyországba)
Imre Fehér, *Mari Törőcsik, Zoltán*
Latinovits, István Avar,
Mariann Krencsey

A LOVE STORY IN NONSENSE-
VERSE (Szerelem-csütörtök)
Tamás Fejér, *Sándor Pécsi,*
Ferenc Zenthe, Mária Takács

RED INK (Vörös tinta)
Viktor Gertler, *Éva Vass,*
György Pálos, Myrtill Nádasi

A FEW STEPS TO THE
FRONTIER (Pár lépés a határ)
Márton Keleti, *Ádám Szirtes,*
Gyula Szabó, Zoltán Várkonyi

YESTERDAY (Tegnap)
Márton Keleti, *Zoltán Makláry,*
Ferenc Ladányi, Sándor Pécsi

A WINDOW ONTO HEAVEN
(Égre nyíló ablak)
József Kis, Margit Dayka, Lajos
Németh, István Sztankay

OUR LAND (A mi földünk)
József Magyar

BRIGADE NO. 39 (A 39-es dandár)
Károly Makk, József Bihari,
Ádám Szirtes

SLEEPLESS YEARS
(Álmatlan évek)
Félix Máriássy, Éva Ruttkai,
Géza Tordy, István Avar

A SIMPLE LOVE
(Fapados szerelem)
Félix Máriássy, Mariann Krencsey,
Ferenc Zenthe

FROM SATURDAY TO MONDAY
(Szombattól hétfőig)
Gyula Mészáros, Éva Vass,
József Láng, Manyi Kiss

FOR WHOM THE LARKS SING
(Akiket a pacsirta elkísér)
László Ranódy, Éva Papp,
Géza Tordy, Klári Tolnay

THE RIGHT MAN
(A megfelelő ember)
György Révész, Kamill Feleki,
Samu Balázs, Mária Mezey

OUR KID (Kölyök)
Mihály Szemes, Mari Törőcsik,
Gyula Szabó

CRIME AT DAWN (Merénylet)
Zoltán Várkonyi, Lajos Básti,
Antal Páger

1960

A HUSBAND FOR SUSY
(Rangon alul)
Frigyes Bán, Ildikó Sólyom,
Tibor Bitskey

A TOWN WITHOUT ASPECT
(Arc nélküli város)
Tamás Fejér, Ferenc Bessenyei,
Ferenc Ladányi, Sándor Pécsi

LOVE AND MONEY
(A Noszty fiú esete Tóth Marival)
Viktor Gertler, Károly Mécs,
Mariann Krencsey, Tivadar Uray

A HOUSEFUL OF HAPPINESS
(Két emelet boldogság)
János Herskó, Edit Domján,
Flórián Kaló, Mariann Krencsey,
Dezső Garas

DAY IS BREAKING (Virrad)
Márton Keleti, Klári Tolnay,
Ferenc Ladányi, József Bihari

SUMMER RAIN (Zápor)
András Kovács, Margit Bara,
Antal Páger, Ferenc Bessenyei

DON'T KEEP OFF THE GRASS
(Fűre lépni szabad)
Károly Makk, Györgyi Polonyi,
Géza Tordy, Klári Tolnay,
Antal Páger, Zoltán Makláry

IT IS A LONG WAY HOME
(Hosszú az út hazáig)
Félix Máriássy, Misi Sebők, Elma Bulla

TEST TRIP
(Próbaút)
Félix Máriássy, Imre Sinkovits,
Mariann Krencsey

CALVARY (Kálvária)
Gyula Mészáros, Antal Páger,
Gábor Agárdi, Mária Majcen

BE FAITHFUL UNTO DEATH
(Légy jó mindhalálig)
László Ranódy, Laci Tóth,
Ferenc Bessenyei, József Bihari

A CERTAIN MAJOR BENEDEK
(Alázatosan jelentem)
Mihály Szemes, Miklós Gábor,
Tivadar Uray, György Pálos

CSUTAK AND THE GREY HORSE
(Csutak és a szürke ló)
Zoltán Várkonyi, *Gábor Veres,*
Ferenc Kállay, Mari Szemes

THREE STARS (Három csillag)
Miklós Jancsó–Károly Wiedermann–
Zoltán Várkonyi, *Apostol Karamitev,*
Miklós Gábor, Mari Törőcsik,
Zoltán Várkonyi

1961

SUNSHINE ON THE ICE
(Napfény a jégen)
Frigyes Bán, *Ferenc Bessenyei,*
Manyi Kiss, Mária Mezey, Irén Psota

I'LL APPEAL
TO THE MINISTER
(Felmegyek a miniszterhez)
Frigyes Bán, *Antal Páger,*
János Rajz, László Bánhidy

TWO HALF-TIMES IN HELL
(THE LAST GOAL)
(Két félidő a pokolban)
Zoltán Fábri, *Imre Sinkovits, Dezső*
Garas, László Márkus, Tibor Molnár

BON VOYAGE, BUS
(Jó utat, autóbusz)
Tamás Fejér, *Zsuzsa Balogh,*
Tibor Benedek

JUST A JOKE (Nem ér a nevem)
Márton Keleti, *Klári Tolnay,*
Antal Páger

UNTIL THE DAY BREAKS
(Amíg holnap lesz)
Márton Keleti, *Imre Sinkovits,*
Ági Mészáros, Éva Ruttkai

GUNS AND DOVES
(Puskák és galambok)
Márton Keleti, *László Tóth, Gábor*
Agárdi, Béla Barsi

MAY FROST (Májusi fagy)
József Kis, *Mariann Moór,*
István Sztankay

ON THE ROOFS OF BUDAPEST
(Pesti háztetők)
András Kovács, *Lajos Cs. Németh,*
Ildikó Pécsi, Ilona Agárdi

THE FANATICS (Megszállottak)
Károly Makk, *György Pálos,*
Sándor Pécsi, Éva Papp

MILITARY BAND (Katonazene)
Endre Márton, *Ádám Szirtes, Ferenc*
Kállai, Tivadar Uray, Margit Bara

THE LAND OF PROMISE
(Az ígéret földje)
Gyula Mészáros, *Mari Törőcsik,*
István Sztankay, Mariann Krencsey

A GIRL HAS BEEN KILLED
(Megöltek egy leányt)
László Nádasy, *Éva Papp,*
Tamás Végvári

A BUS DOES NOT STOP
(Mindenki értetlen)
György Palásthy, *József Szendrő,*
Klári Tolnay, Imre Ráday

FOUR CHILDREN IN THE
FLOOD (Négyen az árban)
György Révész, *Juci Komlós,*
Imre Sinkovits

ALBA REGIA (Branded)
Mihály Szemes, *Miklós Gábor,*
Tatyana Samoilova, Hédi Váradi

FATA MORGANA
(Délibáb minden mennyiségben)
Miklós Szinetár, *Gábor Agárdi,*
Hédi Váradi, Vera Sennyei

FAILED IN MATRIMONY
(Házasságból elégséges)
Károly Wiedermann, *Mari Törőcsik,*
Gyula Bodrogi, Manyi Kiss

APRIL ALARM
(Áprilisi riadó)
Pál Zolnay, *Lajos Őze, Andor Ajtay,*
József Horváth

1962

WOMAN AT THE HELM
(Asszony a telepen)
Imre Fehér, *Éva Ruttkai, András
Swetz, Gyula Benkő*

**THE TRUTH CANNOT BE
HIDDEN** (Húsz évre egymástól)
Imre Fehér, *Ferenc B. Deák,
Ferenc Bessenyei, Antal Páger*

LOVE IN THE SUBURBS
(Kertes házak utcája)
Tamás Fejér, *Margit Bara,
Miklós Gábor, György Pálos*

**THE MAN WITH THE
GOLDEN TOUCH**
(Az aranyember)
Viktor Gertler, *Ilona Béres,
András Csorba*

A RAINY SUNDAY
(Esős vasárnap)
Márton Keleti, *Gyöngyi Polonyi,
Teri Torday, Judit Halász,
Károly Mécs*

ON THE WAY (Félúton)
József Kis, *Kati Gyöngyössy,
Ádám Szirtes*

AUTUMN STAR
(Isten őszi csillaga)
András Kovács, *István Avar
Mari Törőcsik*

PARADISE LOST
(Elveszett paradicsom)
Károly Makk, *Mari Törőcsik,
György Pálos*

**THE TWO LIVES OF AUNT
MICI** (Mici néni két élete)
Frigyes Mamcserov, *Manyi Kiss,
Antal Páger*

EVERY DAY SUNDAY
(Pirosbetűs hétköznapok)
Félix Máriássy, *Jana Breichová,
Miklós Gábor, Éva Ruttkai*

AN EGYPTIAN TALE
(Egyiptomi történet)
Gyula Mészáros, *Mariann Krencsey,
Laci Tóth, Jahaja Shahun*

STOLEN HAPPINESS
(Lopott boldogság)
László Nádasy, *Éva Vass, Tibor
Molnár*

THE NAKED DIPLOMAT
(A meztelen diplomata)
György Palásthy, *Mariann Krencsey,
László Márkus, József Szendrő,
Dezső Garas*

TALE OF A LONG JOURNEY
(Legenda a vonaton)
Tamás Rényi, *Imre Sinkovits,
István Sztankay*

TWO DAYS LIKE THE OTHERS
(Mindennap élünk)
Tamás Rényi, *Károly Sándor,
Ilona Agárdi, Gábor Koncz*

LAND OF ANGELS
(Angyalok földje)
György Révész, *Tamás Végvári,
Franciska Győry, Klári Tolnay*

HAIL DAYS
(Fagyosszentek)
György Révész, *Gábor Agárdi,
Klári Tolnay*

**MEMORIES OF A STRANGE
NIGHT** (Utolsó vacsora)
Zoltán Várkonyi, *Antal Páger,
Miklós Szakáts, Mária Sulyok,
Miklós Gábor*

CANTATA (Oldás és kötés)
Miklós Jancsó, *Zoltán Latinovits,
Edit Domján, Mária Medgyesi*

1963

THE LAST BUT ONE
(Az utolsó előtti ember)
Károly Makk, *Attila Nagy,
Erika Szegedi, Irén Psota*

DARKNESS IN DAYTIME
(Nappali sötétség)
Zoltán Fábri, *Lajos Básti,*
Erika Szegedi

SKYLARK (Pacsirta)
László Ranódy, *Antal Páger,*
Klári Tolnay, Anna Nagy

NO PROBLEMS IN SUMMER
(Nyáron egyszerű)
Péter Bacsó, *Benedek Tóth,*
Mária Laurentzy

WELL, YOUNG MAN?
(Hogy állunk, fiatalember?)
György Révész, *Ferenc Kállai,*
Klári Tolnay, Balázs Kosztolányi

THE DISASTER (Bálvány)
Frigyes Mamcserov, *Gábor Kiss,*
Mari Törőcsik, József Madaras

BUNNY (Tücsök)
Miklós Markos, *Ádám Szirtes,*
Cecília Esztergályos, Imre Sinkovits

DIALOGUE (Párbeszéd)
János Herskó, *Imre Sinkovits,*
Anita Semjén

MISS WINDBAG
(Szélhámosnő)
László Kalmár, *Ferenc Kállai,*
Annamária Szilvási, Attila Nagy

VILLA NEGRA (Hattyúdal)
Márton Keleti, *Antal Páger,*
István Sztankay, Gyula Bodrogi

THE MAN
WHO DOESN'T EXIST
(Egy ember, aki nincs)
Viktor Gertler, *Miklós Gábor, Éva*
Vass

PHOTO HABER (Foto Háber)
Zoltán Várkonyi, *Zoltán Latinovits,*
Éva Ruttkai

CURRENT (Sodrásban)
István Gaál, *András Kozák,*
Andrea Drahota

NEW GILGAMESH (Új Gilgames)
Mihály Szemes, *Iván Darvas,*
Edit Domján

1964

GOLIATH (Karambol)
Félix Máriássy, *István Bujtor,*
Zsuzsa Balogh

YES (Igen)
György Révész, *Iván Darvas,*
Ilona Béres

DIFFICULT PEOPLE
(Nehéz emberek)
András Kovács *(a film-interview)*

TWENTY HOURS (Húsz óra)
Zoltán Fábri, *Antal Páger,*
Ádám Szirtes

HIS MAJESTY'S DATES
(Mit csinált Felséged 3–5-ig?)
Károly Makk, *Iván Darvas, Irén Psota*

FOUR GIRLS IN A COURTYARD
(Négy lány egy udvarban)
Pál Zolnay, *Mari Törőcsik,*
Szilvia Dallos, Miklós Gábor

ONE AND A HALF MILLION
(Másfél millió)
György Palásthy, *Zoltán Makláry,*
Imre Sinkovits, Ferenc Bessenyei

FROM NOON TO DAWN
(Déltől hajnalig)
Tamás Rényi, *Erika Szegedi,*
István Bujtor

THE COUNTERFEITER
(Pénzhamisító)
Frigyes Bán, *Sándor Pécsi, Itala Békés*

LADY-KILLER IN TROUBLE
(Özvegy menyasszonyok)
Viktor Gertler, *Dezső Garas,*
Irén Psota

EVIDENCE
(Ha egyszer húsz év múlva)
Márton Keleti, *István Bujtor,*
Margit Bara

THE AGE OF DAYDREAMING
(Álmodozások kora)
István Szabó, *András Bálint,*
Ilona Béres

A STRICTLY PRIVATE AFFAIR
(Már nem olyan időket élünk)
Endre Marton, *Miklós Gábor,*
Hédi Váradi

UNDISTURBED HAPPINESS
(Miért rosszak a magyar filmek?)
Tamás Fejér, *Miklós Gábor,*
Margit Bara

ETERNAL DANCE
(Az életbe táncoltatott lány)
Tamás Banovich, *Levente Sipeki,*
Adél Orosz

MY WAY HOME
(Így jöttem)
Miklós Jancsó, *András Kozák,*
Sergei Nikonenko

THE GOLDEN HEAD (Aranyfej)
Richard Thorpe, *George Sanders,*
Buddy Hackett, Jess Conrad,
Cecília Esztergályos, Lorraine Power

1965

NO (Nem)
György Révész, *Gyula Bodrogi,*
Mari Törőcsik

CYCLISTS IN LOVE
(Szerelmes biciklisták)
Péter Bacsó, *Tibor Orbán, Nóra Káldi*

THE MARTYRDOM OF ST JOHN
(Szent János fejevétele)
Márk Novák, *István Sztankay,*
Ilona Béres

FIG-LEAF (Fügefalevél)
Félix Máriássy, *László Sinkó,*
Jutka Halász

ALL BEGINNINGS ARE HARD
(Minden kezdet nehéz)
György Révész, *Tamás Major*

NO LOVE, PLEASE
(Tilos a szerelem)
Tamás Rényi, *István Avar,*
Mari Törőcsik, Iván Darvas

DIVERSION AT THE
MUSEUM (Játék a múzeumban)
Róbert Bán, *Miklós Gábor,*
Mária Dallos

THE DOCTOR'S DEATH
(Az orvos halála)
Frigyes Mamcserov, *Antal Páger,*
Elma Bulla

TWO HAVE DIED
(Ketten haltak meg)
György Palásthy, *Teri Torday,*
Géza Tordy

CAR CRAZY (Kár a benzinért)
Frigyes Bán, *Sándor Pécsi,*
Dezső Garas, Éva Vass

THE CORPORAL AND
THE OTHERS
(A tizedes meg a többiek)
Márton Keleti, *Imre Sinkovits,*
Tamás Major, Iván Darvas

GRIMACE (Gyermekbetegségek)
Ferenc Kardos, János Rózsa,
Jutka Halász, István Avar

THE STORY OF MY
STUPIDITY (Butaságom története)
Márton Keleti, *Lajos Básti,*
Éva Ruttkai

LIGHT BEHIND THE
SHUTTERS (Fény a redőny mögött)
László Nádasy, *Zoltán Latinovits,*
Ildikó Pécsi, Attila Nagy

MEN AND BANNERS
(A kőszívű ember fiai)
Zoltán Várkonyi, *Zoltán Latinovits,*
Károly Mécs, Géza Tordy, Ilona Béres

JÁNOS HÁRY (Háry János)
Miklós Szinetár, *Ádám Szirtes,*
Mária Medgyesi

OPERATION "CLEAN LINEN"
(Patyolatakció)
Tamás Fejér, *Lajos Cs.*
Németh,
Annamária Szilvási

GREEN YEARS (Zöldár)
István Gaál, *Benedek Tóth, Virág Dőri*

ABHORRENCE (Iszony)
György Hintsch, *Andrea Drahota,*
Ferenc Kállai

THE ROUND-UP
(THE HOPELESS ONES)
(Szegénylegények)
Miklós Jancsó, *Zoltán Latinovits,*
János Görbe, Gábor Agárdi

1966

COLD DAYS (Hideg napok)
András Kovács, *Zoltán Latinovits,*
Margit Bara

THE GOLDEN KITE
(Aranysárkány)
László Ranódy, *László Mensáros,*
Ilona Béres, Bence Tóth

LATE SEASON (Utószezon)
Zoltán Fábri, *Antal Páger, Lajos*
Básti, Noémi Apor

THE FIRST YEAR (Az első esztendő)
Gyula Mészáros, *Ágnes Voith,*
Lajos Cs. Németh

FAITHFUL FOR NOTHING
(Sok hűség semmiért)
György Palásthy, *Teri Torday,*
Andor Ajtay

BACK-STREET (Sikátor)
Tamás Rényi, *Mari Törőcsik,*
Gábor Koncz

THE TREES PASS BY
(Hogy szaladnak a fák)
Pál Zolnay, *István Iglódi, Manyi Kiss*

AND THEN THE GUY
(És akkor a pasas)
Viktor Gertler, *Imre Sinkovits,*
Irén Psota

I DON'T TELL LIES
(Nem szoktam hazudni)
György Kárpáti, *Ágnes Voith,*
Zsigmond Fülöp

FATHER (Apa)
István Szabó, *András Bálint, Miklós*
Gábor, Klári Tolnay, Katalin Sólyom

THE HEALING WATER (Büdösvíz)
Frigyes Bán, *Attila Nagy, János*
Körmendi, Mari Szemes

HELLO, VERA (Szevasz, Vera)
János Herskó, *Mária Neményi,*
Tamás Bálint

MEN ARE DIFFERENT
(A férfi egészen más)
Tamás Fejér, *Ferenc Kállai,*
Mariann Krencsey

THE LAST NABOB
(Egy magyar nábob)
Zoltán Várkonyi, *Ferenc Bessenyei,*
Éva Papp, Iván Darvas

ZOLTÁN KÁRPÁTHY
(Kárpáthy Zoltán)
Zoltán Várkonyi, *István Kovács,*
Zoltán Latinovits, Éva Ruttkai

SWEET AND BITTER
(Édes és keserű)
Mihály Szemes, *Margit Bara,*
Tibor Szécsényi, Attila Nagy

HARLEQUIN AND HIS
SWEETHEART
(Harlekin és szerelmese)
Imre Fehér, *István Bujtor, Ildikó Sáfár*

1967

CHANGING CLOUDS
(Változó felhőzet)
Márton Keleti, *Imre Sinkovits,*
Judit Halász, Péter Huszti

TEN THOUSAND SUNS
(Tízezer nap)
Ferenc Kósa, *János Koltai,*
Gyöngyi Bürös, András Kozák

THE MUMMY INTERFERES
(A múmia közbeszól)
Gábor Oláh, *István Avar, Éva Ruttkai*

OH, THESE YOUNG PEOPLE
(Ezek a fiatalok...)
Tamás Banovich, *Ferenc Kállai,
Zsuzsa Koncz, the "Illés Ensemble"*

THREE NIGHTS OF A LOVE
(Egy szerelem három éjszakája)
György Révész, *Vera Venczel,
Benedek Tóth, Ilona Béres*

RED-LETTER DAYS (Ünnepnapok)
Ferenc Kardos, *Gábor Koncz,
Teri Horváth, János Görbe*

THE WIDOW AND THE POLICE
OFFICER (Az özvegy és a százados)
György Palásthy, *Klári Tolnay,
Imre Sinkovits*

THE RED AND THE WHITE
(Csillagosok, katonák)
Miklós Jancsó, *András Kozák,
Krystina Mikolayewska*

SUMMER ON THE HILL
(Nyár a hegyen)
Péter Bacsó, *László Mensáros,
Katalin Gyöngyössy*

I WON'T WAIT TILL
TOMORROW (Nem várok holnapig)
Gyula Kormos, *Teréz Várhegyi,
István Iglódi*

SIGNAL (Lássátok feleim)
Lajos Fazekas, *Éva Almási,
Péter Huszti*

A STUDY ABOUT WOMEN
(Tanulmány a nőkről)
Márton Keleti, *Éva Ruttkai,
Zoltán Latinovits*

THE VALLEY (A völgy)
Tamás Rényi, *Gábor Koncz,
Magda Kohut, Mária Sulyok,
Irén Psota*

A HOUSE OF CARDS
(Kártyavár)
György Hintsch, *Mari Törőcsik,
Éva Ruttkai, György Kálmán,
Zoltán Latinovits*

BOYS FROM THE SQUARE
(Fiúk a térről)
Péter Szász, *Iván Darvas,
István Kovács, Ági Margittay*

BONDAGE (Kötelék)
Félix Máriássy, *Hédi Váradi,
Viktor Róna*

BAPTISM (Keresztelő)
István Gaál, *Éva Ruttkai,
Zoltán Latinovits, János Koltai*

CLOWNS ON THE WALL
(Bohóc a falon)
Pál Sándor, *Vera Venczel,
Gábor Ferenczi*

THE FAKE "ISABELLA"
(A hamis Izabella)
István Lauró Bácskai, *István Iglódi,
Éva Ruttkai*

WALLS (Falak)
András Kovács, *Miklós Gábor,
Zoltán Latinovits, Bernadette Lafont,
Philippe March*

1968

THE GIRL (Eltávozott nap)
Márta Mészáros, *Kati Kovács,
Teri Horváth*

SILENCE AND CRY
(Csend és kiáltás)
Miklós Jancsó, *Mari Törőcsik,
István Bujtor*

HASTY MARRIAGE
(Elsietett házasság)
Márton Keleti, *Klári Tolnay,
Lajos Básti*

THE FATAL SHOT (Fejlövés)
Péter Bacsó, *Kati Kovács,
Károly Horváth*

YOU WERE A PROPHET,
MY DEAR (Próféta voltál, szívem)
Pál Zolnay, *Iván Darvas, Kati Berek*

ESTHER AND THE MEN
(Mi lesz veled, Eszterke?)
Róbert Bán, *Judit Halász,*
László Tahi Tóth

BEFORE GOD AND MEN
(Isten és ember előtt)
Károly Makk, *Irén Psota,*
János Görbe, Lajos Balázsovits

THE LAST CIRCLE (Az utolsó kör)
Viktor Gertler, *Ferenc Bessenyei,*
Piroska Molnár

THE LOST TALISMAN
(Egri csillagok)
Zoltán Várkonyi, *István Kovács,*
Vera Venczel

BINDING SENTIMENTS
(Holdudvar)
Márta Mészáros, *Mari Törőcsik,*
Lajos Balázsovits

ON HOME GROUNDS
(Hazai pálya)
György Palásthy, *Zoltán Latinovits,*
Sándor Pécsi, Józsa Hacser

CONFRONTATION
(Fényes szelek)
Miklós Jancsó, *András Kozák,*
Andrea Drahota

SPARROWS ARE BIRDS TOO
(A veréb is madár)
György Hintsch, *László Kabos,*
Ildikó Piros

DEVIL'S FERRY (Pokolrév)
Miklós Markos, *András Kozák,*
Anna Széles

THE BOYS OF PAUL STREET
(A Pál utcai fiúk)
Zoltán Fábri, *Anthony Kemp,*
William Burleigh, John Moulder-Brown
Sándor Pécsi, Mari Törőcsik

THE THROWN-UP STONE
(Feldobott kő)
Sándor Sára, *Lajos Balázsovits*

THE HEIR (Az örökös)
György Palásthy, *Zoltán Latinovits,*
Éva Almási

FORBIDDEN GROUND
(Tiltott terület)
Pál Gábor, *György Bánffy,*
István Avar, Gyöngyi Bürös

ISLE OF THE LION
(Az oroszlán ugrani készül)
György Révész, *Andor Ajtay,*
Irén Psota, István Bujtor

ALFA ROMEO AND JULIET
(Alfa Romeo és Júlia)
Frigyes Mamcserov, *Zoltán*
Latinovits, Éva Ruttkai

THE TALKING CAFTAN
(A beszélő köntös)
Tamás Fejér, *István Iglódi,*
Annamária Detre

1969

DO YOU KNOW
"SUNDAY–MONDAY"?
(Ismeri a Szandi-Mandit?)
Lívia Gyarmathy, *Ila Schütz,*
István Sztankay, László Szabó

A CLOUDLESS VACATION
(Bolondos vakáció)
Károly Makk, *Béla Ernyei,*
Ilinka Tomoroveanu

A LADY FROM
CONSTANTINOPLE
(Sziget a szárazföldön)
Judit Elek, *Manyi Kiss*

THE MASTER CRIMINAL
(Az alvilág professzora)
Mihály Szemes, *Zoltán Latinovits,*
Edit Domján

IMPOSTORS (Imposztorok)
Félix Máriássy, *Nándor Tomanek,*
Edit Domján, Margit Bara

THE WINDOWS OF TIME
(Az idő ablakai)
Tamás Fejér, *Ivan Andorov, Miklós
Gábor, Beata Tyskiewiz,
Krystyna Mikolayewska*

THE BESPECTACLED
(Szemüvegesek)
Sándor Simó, *István Bujtor,
Mária Ronyecz*

THE TÓTH FAMILY
(Isten hozta, őrnagy úr)
Zoltán Fábri, *Zoltán Latinovits,
Imre Sinkovits, Vera Venczel*

SIROCCO (Sirokkó)
Miklós Jancsó, *Jacques Charrier,
Marina Vlady*

PALM SUNDAY (Virágvasárnap)
Imre Gyöngyössy, *Frantisek Velecky,
Benedek Tóth, Gábor Koncz,
Mária Medgyesi*

CHILI-CHALA, THE MAGICIAN
(A varázsló)
György Palásthy, *Gábor Agárdi,
Judit Tóth, Krisztián Kovács*

A MAD NIGHT (Egy őrült éjszaka)
Ferenc Kardos, *Ferenc Kállai,
László Mensáros, Beata Tyskiewiz*

LOVE EMILIA!
(Szeressétek Odor Emíliát)
Pál Sándor, *Gabriella Szabó,
Elma Bulla, Mária Ronyecz*

KREBS, THE GOD
(Krebsz, az isten)
Tamás Rényi, *Ferenc Kállai,
Dezső Garas*

CHARMERS (Bűbájosok)
János Rózsa, *Éva Vodicková,
Judit Halász, István Bujtor*

A JOURNEY
AROUND MY SKULL
(Utazás a koponyám körül)
György Révész, *Zoltán Latinovits,
Éva Ruttkai*

FACE TO FACE (Szemtől szembe)
Zoltán Várkonyi, *Lajos Básti,
Imre Sinkovits, Gyula Szabó*

THE FACE (Arc)
Pál Zolnay, *Márk Zala,
Andrea Drahota*

JUDGEMENT (Ítélet)
Ferenc Kósa, *Ferenc Bessenyei,
Tamás Major*

N. N., ANGEL OF DEATH
(N. N., a halál angyala)
János Herskó, *Miklós Gábor,
Iván Darvas, Éva Ruttkai*

1970

HISTORICAL PRIVATE AFFAIRS
(Történelmi magánügyek)
Márton Keleti, *Lajos Básti,
Éva Ruttkai*

THE BIG BLUE SIGNAL
(A nagy kék jelzés)
László Nádasy, *Nóra Káldi,
László Tahi Tóth*

TEMPERATE ZONE
(Mérsékelt égöv)
Zsolt Kézdi Kovács, *Rudolf
Somogyvári, András Kozák,
Mari Törőcsik*

JUST A PHONE CALL
(Csak egy telefon)
Frigyes Mamcserov, *Miklós Gábor,
Éva Ruttkai*

A GALLANT STORY
(Szép magyar komédia)
Tamás Banovich, *István Sztankay,
Beata Tyskiewiz, Katalin Gyöngyössy*

THE FALCONS (Magasiskola)
István Gaál, *Ivan Andorov,
György Bánffy, Judit Meszléry*

LOVE FILM (Szerelmesfilm)
István Szabó, *Judit Halász,
András Bálint*

DREAMS OF LOVE (Liszt)
(Szerelmi álmok)
Márton Keleti, *Imre Sinkovits,*
Ariadna Sengelaja, Klara Lutcho

CONSTRUCTORS (Érik a fény)
Mihály Szemes, *András Csiky,*
Ádám Szirtes, Katalin Gyöngyössy

DON'T CRY, PRETTY GIRLS
(Szép lányok, ne sírjatok)
Márta Mészáros, *Márk Zala,*
Jaroslava Schallerova

KNIGHT OF THE TV-SCREEN
(Gyula vitéz télen-nyáron)
István Bácskai Lauró, *Gábor Koncz,*
Éva Almási

THE MURDERER IS IN THE
HOUSE (A gyilkos a házban van)
Róbert Bán, *Stanislaw Mikulski,*
Péter Huszti, Éva Vass

LOVE (Szerelem)
Károly Makk, *Lili Darvas,*
Mari Törőcsik, Iván Darvas

IT'S ME, JEROME
(Én vagyok Jeromos)
István Timár, *József Markos*
(Alfonso), Gábor Harsányi,
Irén Psota

OUTBREAK (Kitörés)
Péter Bacsó, *Sándor Oszter,*
Katalin Lendvai

RELAY RACE (Staféta)
András Kovács, *Ilona Bencze,*
András Bálint

SARAH, MY DEAR!
(Sárika, drágám)
Pál Sándor, *Irma Patkós, András Kern,*
Erika Bodnár

HORIZON (Horizont)
Pál Gábor, *Péter Fried, Szilvia*
Marosi, Lujza Orosz, Zoltán Vadász

AGNUS DEI (Égi bárány)
Miklós Jancsó, *Daniel Olbrichsky,*
Anna Széles

1971

A CHARMING FAMILY
(Reménykedők)
Tamás Rényi, *Klári Tolnay,*
Ferenc Kállai, Erzsi Pásztor

THE IMMORTAL LEGIONARY
(A halhatatlan légiós)
Tamás Somló, *Lajos Őze, Virág Dőri,*
János Rajz

HI, JUNIOR! (Hahó, Öcsi)
György Palásthy, *Manyi Kiss,*
Gábor Koncz, Krisztián Kovács

IT'S MONDAY, AT LAST
(Végre hétfő)
Gábor Kenyeres, *Márk Zala,*
Gabriella Szabó

ANTS' NEST (Hangyaboly)
Zoltán Fábri, *Éva Vass, Éva Papp,*
Margit Makai

BIRDIES (Madárkák)
Géza Böszörményi, *Ildikó Bánsági,*
Ila Schütz, György Cserhalmi

SINDBAD (Szindbád)
Zoltán Huszárik, *Zoltán Latinovits,*
Margit Dayka, Anna Nagy,
Éva Ruttkai

THE GIPSY PRINCESS
(Csárdáskirálynő)
Miklós Szinetár, *Anna Moffo,*
René Kollo, Dagmar Koller, Karl
Schönböck, Sándor Németh,
Irén Psota, Zoltán Latinovits

PRESENT INDICATIVE (Jelenidő)
Péter Bacsó, *Ágoston Simon*

THE WHISTLING COBBLE STONE
(A sípoló macskakő)
Gyula Gazdag, *played by secondary-*
school pupils

IN THE PRIME OF LIFE
(A legszebb férfikor)
Sándor Simó, *Éva Tímár,*
István Bujtor, Zoltán Latinovits

RED PSALM (Még kér a nép)
Miklós Jancsó, *József Madaras,*
Andrea Drahota

JUNIOR COMES (Hahó, a tenger)
György Palásthy, *Lajos Balázsovits,*
Anna Muszte, Krisztián Kovács

DEAD LANDSCAPE (Holt vidék)
István Gaál, *István Ferenczy,*
Mari Töröcsik

RESURRECTION
OF TWO YOUNG MEN
(Meztelen vagy)
Imre Gyöngyössy, *Sándor Oszter,*
István Szeghő

CATCH ON TO THE CLOUDS
(Kapaszkodj a fellegekbe)
Péter Szász, *László Mensáros,*
Svetlana Svetlicnaya, Gunnar Cilinsky

1972

ROMANTICISM (Romantika)
Zsolt Kézdi Kovács, *István Szeghő,*
Ádám Szirtes, Ilona Bencze

I'VE BECOME A COP (Hekus lettem)
Tamás Fejér, *Gábor Harsányi,*
Gábor Koncz, Ilona Bencze,
Zsuzsa Balogh

RUN TO BE CAUGHT
(Fuss, hogy utolérjenek)
Márton Keleti, *Sándor Pécsi,*
Gyula Bodrogi, Sarolta Zalatnay

BALD HEAD FOR BALD HEAD
(Forró vizet a kopaszra)
Péter Bacsó, *István Gyarmati,*
Lajos Szabó, Erzsi Pásztor

JOURNEY WITH JACOB
(Utazás Jakabbal)
Pál Gábor, *Péter Huszti, Ion Bog,*
Erika Bodnár

I LIVED UNDER THIRTY-TWO
NAMES (Harminckét nevem volt)
Márton Keleti, *Péter Huszti,*
Erika Bodnár

KIDNAPPING—HUNGARIAN
STYLE (Emberrablás magyar módra)
Zoltán Várkonyi, *Ferenc Kállai, Lajos*
Őze, László Tahi Tóth, Ildikó Piros

PETŐFI '73 (Petőfi '73)
Ferenc Kardos, *played by secondary-*
school pupils

TO SEE NAPLES AND...
(Nápolyt látni és...)
István Bácskai Lauró, *Hédi Váradi,*
István Bujtor, Béla Ernyei, Judit Halász

THE GIRL WHO LIKED PURPLE
FLOWERS (Lila ákác)
István Székely (Steve Sekely),
Judit Halász, András Bálint,
Marianne Moór, Imre Rádai

PARALLEL FACES
(Lányarcok tükörben)
Róbert Bán, *Erika Bodnár,*
Márta Egri, László Márkus,
Gábor Maros

MAKRA (Makra)
Tamás Rényi, *Jácint Juhász,*
Mari Csomós, Piroska Molnár

RABBITS IN THE CLOAK-ROOM
(Nyulak a ruhatárban)
István Bácskai Lauró, *Antal Páger,*
István Iglódi, Ila Schütz

THERE WAS ONCE A FAMILY
(Volt egyszer egy család)
György Révész, *Zoltán Latinovits,*
Éva Ruttkai, Béla Ernyei

THE BRIDEGROOM ARRIVES
AT EIGHT
(A vőlegény nyolckor érkezik)
József Magyar, *Imre Pongrácz, Éva*
Schubert, Györgyi Andai, Péter Kőszegi

PHOTOGRAPHY (Fotográfia)
Pál Zolnay, *István Iglódi, Márk Zala*

FALLOW LAND (A magyar ugaron)
András Kovács, *Zoltán Latinovits,*
Andrea Drahota, Sándor Horváth

ONE DAY MORE OR LESS
(Plusz–mínusz egy nap)
Zoltán Fábri, *Ferenc Bencze,*
Márton Andrássi, Ildikó Pécsi

THE MAGIC JACKET
(A kincskereső kisködmön)
Mihály Szemes, *Ádám Szirtes,*
Péter Haumann, Mária Medgyesi

BEYOND TIME (Nincs idő)
Ferenc Kósa, *Lóránt Lohinszky,*
Péter Haumann

1973

THE LAST CHANCE
(A harmadik nekifutás)
Péter Bacsó, *István Avar,*
Alice Matza, Ilona Kassai

MARTIN CUCKOO (Kakuk Marci)
György Révész, *Gábor Harsányi,*
Péter Haumann, Éva Szerencsi

25, FIRE BRIGADE STREET
(Tűzoltó utca 25)
István Szabó, *Luczina Winniczka,*
Rita Békés, András Bálint

INNOCENT ASSASINS
(Ártatlan gyilkosok)
Zoltán Várkonyi, *Péter Huszti,*
László Tahi Tóth, László Mensáros

A LAD ON A WHITE HORSE
(Egy srác fehér lovon)
György Palásthy, *Sándor Oszter,*
Mária Goór Nagy, Gábor Koncz

WAIT A SEC! (Álljon meg a menet)
Lívia Gyarmathy, *Sándor Horváth,*
Éva Rass, István Rajts

SEVEN TONS OF DOLLARS
(Hét tonna dollár)
György Hintsch, *László Kabos,*
György Bárdi, Iván Darvas

THE LIMITS OF LOVE
(A szerelem határai)
János Szüts, *Andrea Drahota,*
Tibor Bitskey

THE ORANGE COLOURED
WATERING TRUCK
(A locsolókocsi)
Zsolt Kézdi Kovács

RIDDANCE
(Szabad lélegzet)
Márta Mészáros, *Gábor Nagy,*
Erzsébet Kútvölgyi

FOOTBALL OF THE GOOD
OLD DAYS
(Régi idők focija)
Pál Sándor, *Dezső Garas*

A PLACE UNDER THE SUN
(Egy kis hely a nap alatt)
Péter Szász

PALKO CSINOM (Csinom Palkó)
Márton Keleti, *Gábor Nagy,*
Péter Benkő

COBWEB (Pókháló)
Imre Mihályfi, *István Avar*

THE TURKISH SPEAR
(A törökfejes kopja)
Éva Zsurzs

A FRAGRANT WAY TO PASS
AWAY (Illatos út a semmibe)
József Magyar, *György Bárdi,*
Imre Sinkovits, Ferenc Kállai

WHO IS IN THE EGG?
(Ki van a tojásban?)
Sándor Szalkay, *László Mensáros,*
Ferenc Kállai, Nándor Tomanek

AT THE END OF THE ROAD
(Végül)
Gyula Maár, *László Szacsvay,*
Jozef Kroner

1974

DASHING GIRLS
(Szikrázó lányok)
Péter Bacsó, *Erika Bodnár,*
Ildikó Bánsági

DREAMING YOUTH
(Álmodó ifjúság)
János Rózsa, Zoltán Csoma, Csaba
Daminia, Éva Rass, Loránd Lohinszky

THE GIANT STAGS
(A szarvassá vált fiúk)
Imre Gyöngyössy, Mari Törőcsik,
Sándor Lukács, András Kozák

THE PENDRAGON LEGEND
(A pendragon-legenda)
György Révész, Zoltán Latinovits,
Iván Darvas, Teri Torday

141 MINUTES FROM THE
UNFINISHED SENTENCE
(141 perc a Befejezetlen Mondatból)
Zoltán Fábri, András Bálint,
Mari Csomós, László Mensáros

HEYDUCKS (Hajdúk)
Ferenc Kardos, Dzsoko Roszics, József
Madaras, Sándor Oszter, Dragomir
Felba

WITH BOUND EYES
(Bekötött szemmel)
András Kovács, József Madaras,
András Kozák

BE RESPONSIBLE FOR
YOURSELF — working title
(Vállald önmagadat)
Frigyes Mamcserov

REWARD JOURNEY — working
title (Jutalomutazás)
István Dárday

CAT'S PLAY (Macskajáték)
Károly Makk, Margit Dayka,
Elma Bulla

STRANGE FACES
(Idegen arcok)
Rezső Szörény, Erzsébet Kútvölgyi,
László Szacsvay, Tibor Boroska

SNOW-STORM (Hószakadás)
Ferenc Kósa, Imre Szabó,
Péter Haumann, Pola Raksa

SIGN LANGUAGE
(Jelbeszéd)
Mara Luttor, Jana Breichová,
Ildikó Jani, András Nyiri

ELECTRA, MY LOVE
(Szerelmem Elektra)
Miklós Jancsó, Mari Törőcsik,
György Cserhalmi, Lajos Balázsovits

RUNNING AMOK (Ámokfutás)
Lajos Fazekas, Péter Huszti,
Kati Gyöngyössy

MOTOR VEHICLE — working title
(Autó)
Géza Böszörményi, Éva Rass,
Jácint Juhász, Giles Legris

THE BOATMAN ON THE DANUBE
— working title
(A dunai hajós)
Miklós Markos, Gábor Koncz,
Gábor Agárdi, István Bujtor

NO. 74 BASTION PROMENADE
— working title
(Bástyasétány hetvennégy)
Gyula Gazdag

TOMORROW WE'LL HAVE A
PHEASANT — working title
(Holnap lesz fácán)
Sándor Sára

List of Films Mentioned in the Text

Merry-Go-Round (Körhinta)
173, 174, 175, 176, 177, 189
Mickey Magnate (Mágnás Miska)
155, 156
The Militiaman (A népfölkelő) *24*
The Milliner (A masamód) *57*
Miss Julie (Júlia kisasszony) *47*
Monna Vanna *32*
The Mother *35, 51, 58*
My Daughter Is Not That Sort *106*
My Way Home (Így jöttem) *199, 200*

N

Nantas *46*
A Nest of Nobles (Gentryfészek) *119*
Never Ask about the Past
(Ne kérdezd, ki voltam) *124*
The Newborn Father (Az újszülött apa)
32
The New Gilgamesh (Új Gilgames) *197*
The New Relation (Az új rokon) *94*
Night and Morning (Éj és virradat) *47*
Night in the Pharmacy
(Éjjel a patikában) *80*
A Night in Venice
(Egy éj Velencében) *79*
The Nightmare (A gólyakalifa) *30*
Nine Days of a Year *198*
Ninety-nine (Kilencvenkilenc) *32*
No Answer from Europe
(Európa nem válaszol) *119, 128*
No Kissing (Tilos a csók) *46*
No. 111 *55, 57*
The Notary of Peleske
(Peleskei nótárius) *34*
No Thoroughfare (Behajtani tilos) *115*

O

Obžalovany *193*
Officer's Honour (A tiszti kardbojt) *29*
Old and New *165*
The Old Rogue (Vén gazember) *91, 145*
Oliver Twist *46*
One Fool Makes a Hundred
(Egy bolond százat csinál) *118*
One Kiss and Nothing More
(Egy csók és más semmi) *118*
One More Day (Egy nap a világ) *118*

On the Roofs of Budapest
(Pesti háztetők) *204*
Opium Waltz (Ópiumkeringő) *124*
Ordeal of the Bier (Tetemrehívás) *32, 33*
Our Kid (Kölyök) *197*
Outbreak (Kitörés) *215*
The Outlaw (Betyár) *127*
Opportunity (Alkalom) *124*

P

Paisà *161*
Paradise Lost
(Az elveszett paradicsom) *194, 195*
La Passion de Jeanne d'Arc *35, 58*
Penny (Kiskrajcár) *168*
People on the Alps
(Emberek a havason) *119, 126, 132,
133, 134, 137, 144, 145, 151, 162*
Petőfi '73 *215*
Piri Knows Everything
(Piri mindent tud) *79, 103*
Pista Dankó (Dankó Pista) *112, 114*
Please Sir (Tanár úr kérem) *182*
Present Indicative (Jelenidő) *215*
Prince Bob (Bob herceg) *34*
The Prodigal Son (A tékozló fiú) *48*
Prodigy (A csodagyerek) *58*
Professor Hannibal
(Hannibál tanár úr) *173, 176, 177*
Prophet of the Fields (Mezei próféta)
144, 151
Pufi Buys Boots (Pufi cipőt vesz)
23, 24, 25
Purple Acacia *83, 85*

Q

Queen Elizabeth (Erzsébet királyné) *119*
A Quiet Home (Csendes otthon) *184*

R

Rákóczi's Lieutenant
(Rákóczi hadnagya) *169, 170*
The Rákóczi March (Rákóczi-induló)
80, 81, 82, 85, 91, 112, 114
The Red and the White
(Csillagosok, katonák) *201, 202, 203*
Red-letter Days (Ünnepnapok) *215*
Red Psalm (Még kér a nép) *204*

IN THE BEGINNING

1. This price-list advertisement of Projectograph was published in the review *Mozgófénykép Híradó* and its photograph reprinted in my monograph, where all details of this chapter and of the Hungarian silent film are elaborated in greater detail. István Nemeskürty: *A mozgóképtől a filmművészetig*. Budapest, 1961.
2. *Mozgófénykép Híradó*, 1908. No. 7.
3. In the book: *Az ezredéves kiállítás eredménye* (Results of the Millennial Exhibition of 1896). Budapest, 1897. p. 108. Ignác Alpár was the best Hungarian architect at that time.
4. Viktor Lányi–István Radó–Albert Held: *A 25 éves mozi* (The 25-year-old Cinema). Budapest, 1920. p. 37.
5. Lajos Körmendy-Ékes: *A mozi* (The cinema). Budapest, 1915. pp. 102–104.
6. Lajos Körmendy-Ékes: *op. cit.* pp. 102 and 74.
7. *Mozgófénykép Híradó*, 1909. No. 11.
8. *Mozgófénykép Híradó*, 1911. Nos. 4 and 13.

THE INDUSTRY TAKES SHAPE

1. *Mozgófénykép Híradó*, 1912. p. 1068.
2. *Világ* (a daily paper), September 1, 1912.
3. *Nyugat* (review), 1915. vol. I. p. 504.
4. *Mozgófénykép Híradó*, 1913. No. 34.
5. *Mozgófénykép Híradó*, 1913. p. 153.
6. *Mozihét* (review), 1917. No. 51.
7. *Mozgófénykép Híradó*, 1914. No. 16.

THE ART TAKES SHAPE

1. *A complete list of Korda's films made in Hungary:*

1.	A becsapott újságíró	1914	The Duped Journalist
2.	Tutyu és Totyó	1915	Tutyu and Totyó
3.	Lyon Lea	1915	Lea Lyon
4.	A tiszti kardbojt	1915	Officer's Honour
5.	Fehér éjszakák (Fedora)	1916	White Nights (Fedora)
6.	A nagymama	1916	The Grandmother
7.	Mesék az írógépről	1916	Tales of the Typewriter
8.	A kétszívű férfi	1916	The Man with Two Hearts
9.	Az egymillió dolláros bankó	1916	The Thousand Pound Note
10.	Ciklámen	1916	Cyclamen
11.	Vergődő szívek	1916	Struggling Hearts
12.	A nevető Szaszkia	1916	The Laughing Saskia
13.	Szent Péter esernyője	1917	St Peter's Umbrella
14.	A gólyakalifa	1917	The Nightmare
15.	Mágia	1917	Magic
16.	Harrison és Barrison	1917	Harrison and Barrison

17. Faun	1917	Faun
18. Az aranyember	1918	The Man with the Golden Touch
19. Marian	1918	Marianne
20. Ave Caesar!	1919	Ave Caesar!
21. Fehér rózsa	1919	The White Rose
22. Yamata	1919	Yamata
23. Se ki, se be	1919	Neither in Nor out
24. A 111-es	1919	No. 111

2. *The German title of Babits's novel "Der Storchkalif" is a literal translation of the Hungarian, alluding to the oriental tale of Hauff.*

3. *A complete list of Kertész's (Michael Curtiz's) films made in Hungary:*

1. Ma és holnap	1912	Today and Tomorrow
2. Rablélek	1913	Captive Soul
3. Az éjszaka rabjai	1914	Slaves of the Night
4. A tolonc	1914	The Vagrant
5. Bánk bán	1914	Bánk bán
6. A kölcsönkért csecsemők	1914	Borrowed Babies
7. Akit ketten szeretnek	1915	Loved by Two
8. A karthauzi	1916	The Carthusian
9. Makkhetes	1916	Seven of Clubs
10. A fekete szivárvány	1916	The Black Rainbow
11. Az ezüst kecske	1916	The Silver Goat
12. A farkas	1916	The Wolf
13. Doktor úr	1916	The Doctor
14. A magyar föld ereje	1916	The Force of the Hungarian Soil
15. Zoárd mester	1917	Master Zoard
16. A vörös Sámson	1917	The Red Samson
17. Az utolsó hajnal	1917	The Last Dawn
18. Tavasz a télben	1917	Spring in Wintertime
19. Senki fia	1917	Nobody's Son
20. A szentjóbi erdő titka	1917	The Secret of Saint-Job Forest
21. A kuruzsló	1917	The Charlatan
22. A halálcsengő	1917	The Death Bell
23. A föld embere	1917	The Man of the Soil
24. Az ezredes	1917	The Colonel
25. Egy krajcár története	1917	The Story of a Penny
26. A béke útja	1917	The Road to Peace
27. Az árendás zsidó	1917	Lessee the Jew
28. Tatárjárás	1917	Invasion
29. Az ördög	1918	The Devil
30. A napraforgós hölgy	1918	The Lady with Sunflowers
31. Lulu	1918	Lulu
32. Kilencvenkilenc	1918	Ninety-nine
33. Júdás	1918	Judas
34. A csúnya fiú	1918	The Ugly Boy
35. Alraune	1918	Alraune
36. A víg özvegy	1918	The Merry Widow

37. Varázskeringő	1918	Magic Waltz
38. Lu, a kokott	1918	Lu the Cocotte
39. Liliom	1919	Liliom (unfinished)

4. Mozihét, 1917. No. 21.
5. *This is one of the classic scenarios that are constantly re-made. During the last war Billy Wilder based on it his* Five Graves to Cairo. *The first version was directed by Jenő Janovics in 1918.*
6. *All the articles of Jenő Török in Korda's review* Mozihét: *1916–1918.*

THE FILM,S ROLE IN THE REPUBLIC OF COUNCILS
1. *Mozihét,* 1918. No. 51.
2. *Színházi élet,* April 13. Account by Andor Lajta.
3. Viktor Lányi–István Radó–Albert Held: *op. cit.,* p. 113.
4. *Vörös Film* (daily paper), 1919. No. 17.
5. *Vörös Film,* 1919. No. 12.

DEAD SILENCE
1. *Mozgófénykép Híradó,* 1921. See the whole volume.
2. S. Ginzburg: *Kinematografiya Dorevolyutsionnoi Rossii.* Moscow, 1963. Supplement No. 66. The original title of the story was *The Hostess* (Hozyayka). The title of the Russian version is *Ilya Murin.*
3. István Békés: "Dostoievsky on the Hungarian Silent Screen." In *Filmvilág* (review), 1960. No. 10.
4. A complete list of Fejős's silent films made in Hungary:

1. A fekete kapitány	1920	The Black Captain
2. Jóslat	1920	Prophecy
3. Lidércnyomás	1920	Nightmare
4. Pán	1920	Pan
5. Újraélők	1920	Revived
6. Egri csillagok	1923	The Stars of Eger

5. *Jahrbuch der Filmindustrie.* Berlin, 1923. p. 54.

THE DREAM CAR DECADE
1. Róbert Kálmán–Gyula Peregi: *A film és a mozi Magyarországon* (Films and Cinemas in Hungary). Budapest, 1959. p. 17. For more details of this chapter and of the Hungarian sound-film, see my monograph: István Nemeskürty: *A meseautó utasai.* (The Passengers of the Dream Car.) Budapest, 1965.
2. Kálmán–Peregi: *op. cit.* p. 99.
3. János Smolka: *Mesegép a valóságban* (The Phantasy-Machine in Reality). Budapest, 1933.
4. Ilya Ehrenburg: *Die Traumfabrik,* Berlin, 1931. pp. 71, 181, 186.
5. István Szőts: *Röpirat a magyar filmművészet ügyében* (A Pamphlet on the Hungarian Film). Budapest, 1945. p. 65.
6. *Filmkultúra* (review), 1932. No. 3.
7. Andor Lajta: *A tízéves magyar hangosfilm* (The Hungarian Talkie is Ten Years Old). Budapest, 1942. p. 34.
8. *Filmkultúra,* 1934. No. 3.
9. *Filmújság* (weekly), 1935. No. 9.

10. István Mihály: "Témák az aszfalton" (Themes on the Pavement), *Filmkultúra,* 1932. No. 5.
11. *Filmújság,* 1933. No. 9.
12. János Smolka: *op. cit.* p. 75.
13. 1934: 10 films; 1935: 16; 1936: 20; 1937: 36; 1938: 32 films. Thus the average over five years is 23.
14. Smolka: *op. cit.* p. 62.
15. *Filmújság,* 1934. No. 25.
16. *Magyar Film* (weekly), 1943. No. 12.
17. Andor Lajta: *op. cit.* p. 56.
18. *Filmlexikon.* Budapest, 1941. p. 367.
19. *Filmújság,* 1934. No. 9.
20. Lewis Jacobs: *The Rise of the American Films.* New York, 1939. p. 453.: "Direction today... is so hampered by commercial demands and economic incumbrances—to say nothing of pressure on special interests regarding movie content—that artistically the director is sadly fettered."
21. A complete list of Ladislas Vajda's films made in Hungary:

1. Halló, Budapest!	1935	Hallo, Budapest!
2. Ember a híd alatt	1936	Man under the Bridge
3. Szenzáció, 2. epizód	1936	–
4. A három sárkány	1936	The Three Dragons
5. Az én lányom nem olyan	1937	My Daughter Is Not That Sort
6. A kölcsönkért kastély	1937	The Borrowed Residence
7. Magdát kicsapják	1938	Magdalena Expelled from School
8. A döntő pillanat	1938	Decisive Moment
9. Fekete gyémántok	1938	Black Diamonds
10. Péntek Rézi	1938	Theresa Friday

Ladislas Vajda's Hungarian-made films were sold by the producer to Italy as well. Vittorio de Sica saw them and decided to remake two of them. These became Sica's second and third films; *Maddalena Zero in Condotta* (1940), based on Vajda's *Magdalena Expelled from School,* and *Teresa Venerdi* (1941), after the film *Theresa Friday.*

GUNS DIRECT THE MUSE
1. *Filmlexikon* (1941). p. 367.
2. *Filmlexikon* (1941). pp. 368–369.
3. *Filmlexikon* (1941). p. 369.
4. *Magyar Film,* 1942. No. 48.
5. *Magyar Film,* 1941. No. 21.
6. János Dáloky: *Így készül a magyar film* (The Way Hungarian Films Are Made), Budapest, 1942. p. 13.
7. *Magyar Film,* 1941. No. 12. and 1943. No. 16.
8. *Filmújság,* 1937. Nos. 45–46; and 1938. No. 41.
9. *Magyar Film,* 1942. No. 8.; 1943. Nos. 13. and 25.
10. *Moziújság,* 1943. No. 30.
11. *Híd* (review), 1941. No. 9.
12. Andor Lajta: *op. cit.* p. 119.
13. *Moziújság,* 1943. No. 33.

SOMEWHERE IN EUROPE

1. *Moziélet*, 1946. No. 1.
2. *Fényszóró*, 1945. Nos. 17 and 21.
3. Guido Aristarco: *Storia delle teoriche del film*. Torino, 1951. p. 57.

CINEMA OF THE HUNGARIAN PEOPLE

1. First a National Film Office was founded to act as the highest guiding organization, headed by György Angyal. The Film Industry Directorate was appointed to deal with economic affairs, under the leadership of Dezső Révai. Films were made by the National Enterprise for Film Production; every film studio, literary department, and all directors as well as dramaturges belonged to this firm. Later the Film Industry Directorate merged with the National Enterprise for Film Production. The manager of this firm was Ferenc Hont, the director was Béla Both, the chief reader Gyula Háy. The institution established to produce scripts was located at 9–11, Lenin Boulevard. In 1951 Dezső Révai became manager of this institution, with Zsuzsa Simon acting as chief reader. Zoltán Fábri, head of the Pioneer Theatre, left his post to become the leading authority on art among directors at all film studios. In the mid-fifties, when Fábri was directing films regularly, it was András Kovács who shared the work of chief reader and director with Zsuzsa Simon. The readers were Imre Fehér, Gábor Thurzó, Péter Bacsó, Péter Halász, Péter Szász, Lajos Bartha, Péter Bogáti, István Kormos, János Czibor, György Somlyó, Magda Apró. The ministerial department was headed by István Kende, Miklós Szántó, János Tárnok and Szilárd Újhelyi.
2. In January 1948, the daily press still reported that *The Soil Under Your Feet* —known under the provisional title of *Red Góz* (Piros Góz) or *One Has to Live* (Élni kell)—was to be directed by István Szőts, with Éva Bartók, János Görbe, István Egri, József Bihari, and Lajos Gárday in the lead. "However, an unforeseen serious obstacle has arisen: there is no snow. Part of the film is to be shot in the snowy regions of Bihar County. As long as there is no snow, the shooting of the film cannot be started."
3. *Szabad Nép*, August 7, 1951, p. 6.
4. *Szabad Nép*, May 27, 1956.
5. *Ocherki istorii sovetskogo kino*, III. Moscow, 1961, pp. 615–619.
6. Béla Balázs: *A Film* (The Film), Budapest, 1961. pp. 228–229.
7. *Op. cit.* p. 226.
8. "On September 4, 1946, the Bolshevik Party published a statement concerning the film entitled *Great Life*. Besides this film, the first version of Pudovkin's *Admiral Nakhimov*, the second part of Eisenstein's *Ivan the Terrible*, and Kozintsev's and Trauberg's *Simple People* were also criticized." Pudovkin–Smirnova: *The Soviet Film Looks Back on Thirty Years* (in Hungarian). Budapest, 1949. p. 16.
9. *Op. cit.* p. 16.
10. *Pudovkin a magyar filmről* (Pudovkin on Hungarian Films). Budapest, 1952; *A szovjet filmművészet mesterségbeli kérdései* (Technical Aspects of Soviet Film Art). Budapest, 1953; Nóra Somogyi: *Miért a film a legfontosabb művészet?* (Why Is the Film the Most Important Art?) Budapest, 1951.

11. "Underground Colony: a new Hungarian film" (Gyarmat a föld alatt: új magyar film). *Szabad Nép,* September 16, 1951.
12. These dates are to be found in the book of Róbert Kálmán and Gyula Peregi: *Op. cit.* pp. 16, 104, 150, 168, 169.
13. Louis Chauvet–Jean Fayard–Pierre Mazars: *Le cinéma à travers le monde.* Paris, 1961. p. 229.
14. Ulrich Gregor–Enno Patalas: *Geschichte des Films.* Gütersloh, 1962, pp. 257, 288.
15. Ulrich Gregor–Enno Patalas: *Op. cit.* p. 399.